ANTHROPOLOGY FOR ARCHAEOLOGISTS
AN INTRODUCTION

ANTHROPOLOGY FOR ARCHAEOLOGISTS:

An Introduction

Bryony Orme

Cornell University Press

Ithaca, New York

First published 1981 by Cornell University Press

International Standard Book Number 0-8014-1398-2

Library of Congress Catalog Card Number 80-69817

Printed in Great Britain

Contents

For Jean & John Orme

Illustrations

Preface

My purpose in writing *Anthropology for Archaeologists* has been to lure colleagues from the pitfalls of ethnographic parallels, as much as to tempt those who retreat from an historical interpretation of the past to the fastnesses of artefact description. For too long, archaeologists have picked an example here and an example there from ethnographers' accounts of other peoples, to reinforce an interpretation of the evidence. And for too long, other archaeologists have plucked other examples from the literature to undermine that interpretation. The resultant pessimism in some quarters, regarding the value of ethnography to archaeologists, is understandable, and justified in so far as parallels are random. But there is a value to the student of the past in anthropology, if structured comparative studies can be set in the place of random parallels. This *Introduction* is written in the hope of demonstrating that value, and to encourage more archaeologists of whatever period or specialisation to look beyond the horizons of their own culture when they seek to understand the raw material of their discipline.

It is perhaps also worth noting here what this book is not, in case any reader should be misled. It is not, obviously, a compendium of handy parallels. Nor is it in any sense an introductory textbook of anthropology. There are others far better qualified than myself who have written or will write such books. Moreover the use of anthropological material here is undoubtedly biased and selective, and probably naive and out-of-date, as so often happens when specialists venture into other disciplines. But I am no specialist, being part-historian, part-archaeologist and part-anthropologist by training, and I would argue that my poaching is in fact legitimate, as the territories of all three subjects overlap to a greater degree than is commonly accepted.

Thirdly, this book is not a comprehensive survey of Anthropology and Archaeology and their diverse relationships and common ground. That field is too complex and developing too rapidly, to be

given such a treatment, and it is principally just one aspect that we
are concerned with here, the contribution of anthropology to the
archaeologists' interpretation of the past.

If this Preface should read less fluently than the pages that follow,
that will only serve to underline all that I owe to my father, John
Orme, for his patient and thorough work on the text. My thanks go
also to John Alexander and John Coles, for their comments and
advice after reading early versions of several chapters, to Mike
Rowlands who first introduced me to anthropology, and especially to
Peter Ucko who supervised my research at UCL (though he may wish
to deny all responsibility for later developments). The librarians of
Exeter University and those of The Royal Anthropological Institute
and The Society of Antiquaries of London have between them made
good the deficiencies of local collections, and I am grateful for the
many books and articles which they secured for me, often at short
notice. Many individuals and institutions have helped in the
provision of photographs, and they are acknowledged in the
captions. Exeter City Museum through the kind offices of Susan
Pearce, provided an extensive range of artefacts for study, a few of
which are included here in the photographs taken by Seàn Goddard.
John Saunders and the Photographic Department of the University
produced all the Curtis photographs, and a number of others. All
typing of the manuscript was done by the secretaries of the History
and Archaeology Department, and my thanks go to them for
deciphering so many unfamiliar names of places and people, neither
historical nor archaeological, and to the colleagues who allowed me to
take up so much office time. Even more drawing-office time was
taken, and for their co-operation here and in so many other respects
while this book was in the writing, I thank Bob Higham, Valerie
Maxfield and Malcolm Todd. Finally, my thanks to Seàn Goddard
for the results of that drawing-office time, the line illustrations which
provide the essential complement to the text.

Exeter 1980   Bryony Orme

Introduction

Archaeologists have made use of anthropology from the first stirrings of their discipline, and yet many of them at work today have only a hazy idea of what anthropology is, and the full potential of its contribution to archaeology is largely ignored. Anthropologists themselves are not of one mind concerning the exact definition of their subject, but they are in broad agreement that it includes the description and analysis of primitive societies which are both non-literate and non-industrial and which are organised on a small scale compared to the complexities of the modern industrialised world. Anthropologists also work among literate and urbanised peoples and in societies which are far from small-scale in their organisation, their field of study impinging on those of the geographer and the sociologist. But the focus, or core, of the discipline remains the small-scale society.

Anthropology in the archaeological literature is usually referred to as 'ethnography', a term which is becoming old-fashioned but which originally served to distinguish descriptive fieldwork carried out in another culture from the subsequent analyses and interpretation that constituted social anthropology. A study of the Australian Aborigines would be ethnography, whereas a study of kinship systems, which might well include much information from the Australian work, would be social anthropology. Today, the distinction is beginning to fall out of use, openly discarded because field studies inevitably involve analysis and interpretation, and discreetly dropped because 'ethnography' is redolent of nineteenth-century fieldwork and dry and dusty museums. But it was not for these reasons that the title chosen for this book is 'Anthropology for Archaeologists' rather than 'Ethnography for Archaeologists'; the choice was made to emphasise that the archaeologist can use not simply ethnographic parallels, but the whole field of anthropological studies.

It is hoped that this book will go some way to introduce students of archaeology to the field of descriptive ethnography and also to anthropology˙ at its analytical and interpretive levels. It is not intended to be an encyclopaedia of useful parallels, but a step towards the anthropological education of archaeologists and towards a rapprochement of the two disciplines in their study of human culture.

History

Both archaeologists and anthropologists have seriously questioned whether either discipline has much to offer the other, and particularly whether archaeology can profit from ethnographic borrowings. The different arguments will be examined more fully below, for they have had considerable influence on recent developments, but the whole subject rests on the key question of whether or not archaeology and anthropology have enough common ground to establish a sound bridge between the two disciplines. Doubts stem from differences in the raw material of study, differences in field methods and differences in aims and methods at all levels of analysis and interpretation. It is feared that the lack of common ground makes it impossible to create a scientific link between the two subjects, and that the only link can be an intuitive one which will do little to further serious academic study.

But most of these doubts are unnecessary. Archaeological interpretation has depended on ethnography from its infancy in the sixteenth century, through the great growth spurt of the nineteenth century, to the present day. There would be no archaeological interpretation as we know it without ethnography, both at the level of the recognition and interpretation of artefacts, and at the level of discerning and explaining the processes of human cultural development. These admittedly crude categories will be useful for tracing developments over the centuries, as they emphasise that the ethnographic contribution to archaeology has been at both practical and theoretical levels, and throughout archaeologists have viewed their subject matter through ethnographic spectacles: they have seen prehistoric man as primitive.

The developments will be traced as they occurred in Britain, but a similar pattern could be found in other European countries, notably in France and in Scandinavia (e.g. Klindt-Jensen 1976).

Among English-speaking antiquaries, the identification of

prehistoric and primitive man was first made in the late Tudor period. Man's interest in his own past lay dormant for much of the Middle Ages, or perhaps it was expressed through myth and legend rather than in historical studies. But with a change in both political and intellectual spheres in the early sixteenth century, with the establishment on the English throne of the Tudor dynasty and the influence of Renaissance scholarship, the antiquary appeared on the scene.

The first generation of antiquaries, men such as John Leland, were interested in the past history of their own country, including that dimly recorded period which preceded the Roman Conquest, the age of the Ancient Briton. Despite their classical learning, these men do not appear to have been interested in the ideas of primitive and early man expressed by the Greeks, and the picture of Ancient Britain which emerges from their writings is of an island peopled with characters from Caesar and Tacitus, living in a world curiously akin to the sixteenth century. The manners and customs of the Ancient Britons were not questioned, and probably assumed to be similar to those of the contemporary world; the heated arguments of the day dwelt on topics such as which of Noah's descendants first reached the shores of Albion once the floodwaters receded from Mount Arrarat. The occasional antiquary such as John Twynne envisaged a rather different and perhaps more uncouth situation, based on Greek accounts of the savage and primitive life of early man. But such views met with little success in a prosperous society newly aware of its own past, and desirous of a respectable ancestry.

By the end of the sixteenth century, however, a change in attitude towards Britain's remote past can be discerned, a change due to the Elizabethans' direct contact with primitive man, in Ireland and in North America. It is worth looking at this in some detail, for its influence is felt throughout the subsequent development of archaeology, and it is one of the most important instances of the use of ethnography in helping to understand the past.

Among the Elizabethan seafarers who reached North America were two gentlemen possessed of considerable powers of observation, and the ability to make relatively objective records, the one in words and the other visually.

Thomas Harriot, the writer, published *A brief and true account of the new found land of Virginia* in 1588. This described, in admirable detail, both the country and the inhabitants encountered in the New World. The Indians were treated as human beings, dignified and worthy of respect although they were not Christians: Harriot felt that their manners and customs were no doubt strange, but in some respects their simple and noble life could well serve as an example to the Elizabethans, tainted by the luxuries of London. A couple of short extracts will serve to illustrate both Harriot's own reaction to the Indians, and the nature of the information which he provided for his readers. The first describes the Virginians' use of raw materials:

> *Rakiok*, a kind of trees that are so called that are sweet wood of which the inhabitants that were neere unto us doe commonly make their boats or *Canoes* of the form of *Trowes*; only with the help of fire, hatchets of stone, and shels; we have known some so great being made in that sort of one tree that they have carried well **XX** men at once, beside much baggage ... (there is) a kind of grey stone, like unto marble, of which the inhabitants make their hatchets to cleeve wood ... For if everie household have one or two to cracke nuttes, grinde shelles, whet copper, and sometimes other stones for hatchets, they have enough. (Harriot 1588, 27-9)

The second extract compares the Virginians with the English, and finds them poor in material terms, but

> notwithstanding, in their proper manner considering the want of such meanes as we have they seem very ingenious. For although they have no such tooles, nor any such craftes, sciences and artes as wee; yet in those things they doe, they shew excellence of wit. (Harriot 1588, 32)

John White, the artist, was later to become a Governor of Virginia (and his granddaughter was the first European to be born in that territory). White's first reactions to the land he later came to administer may be seen in Figs. 1 and 2. His work is the visual complement of Harriot's verbal description. It is worth noting here that neither Harriot nor White showed anything but respect for the Indians; their accounts depict people living in a viable alternative to European culture, and they introduced their audience to a view of primitive man far removed from Shakespeare's Caliban.

It is the next move which makes this material relevant in the present context. In 1592, the Virginian work of Harriot and White was published in *America* (part 1) by Johannes de Bry, who added an appendix, entitled

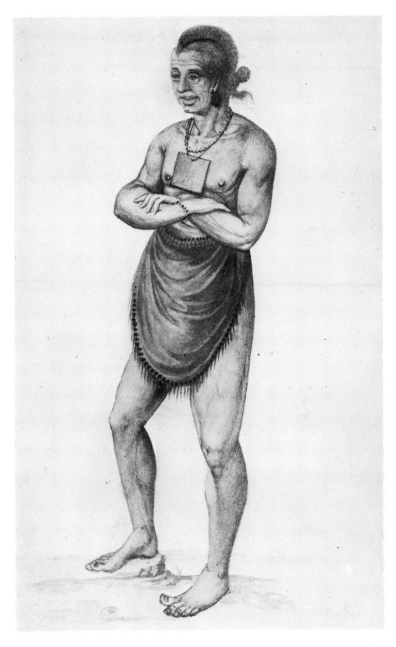

Figure 1. A Virginian Indian chief, drawn by John White during the Virginian expedition of *c.* 1586 (British Museum)

Figure 2. The Virginian Indians fishing, as recorded by John White, *c.* 1586 (British Museum)

Som picture
OF THE PICTES
which in the olde
tyme dyd habite one part of the
great Britainne

It was 'to showe how that the Inhabitants of the Britainne have been in times past as sauvage as those of Virginea'. There followed five superb drawings by John White, some of which are reproduced here (Figs 3-5).

These Ancient Britons, so carefully drawn, are modelled on the Chief Lorde of Roanoke, and those other Indians sketched by White in Virginia. They are indeed naked savages, out of this world, beyond the Elizabethan experience. For the first time, man's forebears had been visualised as primitive. The contrast with earlier drawings could be discussed at length, but one has only to look at the Ancient Britons in Holinshed's *Chronicles* to appreciate the change in outlook (Fig. 6) and both artists drew on the same classical sources for information.

It would be wrong to suggest that Harriot and White revolutionised antiquarian studies as a result of their American reportage. There was no sudden realisation of the savagery of prehistoric Albion, no imaginative leap into a past that was different, totally different from contemporary life. But, almost unnoticed, John White's comparisons came to the attention of many people for de Bry's edition of the *Brief and True Report* was popular and widely read. One or two antiquaries began to refer to the American material here and there in their works, as one can see, for example, in Daniel's *The first part of the History of England* (1612) and Speed's *The History of Great Britaine* (1611). Speed reproduced White's Ancient Britons, though rather more decently clad, and he christened the civilised female from Kent 'Boadicea' (Fig. 7). So the savage American made his way into the body of ideas that men held about their remote past, and the idea of a past different from the present, a keystone of archaeology, was established through the use of ethnography.

Before a century had passed, one finds antiquaries deliberately turning to ethnographic material, sometimes to stimulate their imagination, as when Dr Plot discussed the hafting of stone tools (Plot 1686), and sometimes to control that of others, as when Edward Lhuyd wrote of certain Scottish finds:

Figure 3. John White's view of an Ancient Briton as savage as a Virginian Indian, late 1580s (British Museum)

Figure 4. A female Ancient Briton, by John White, late 1580s (British Museum)

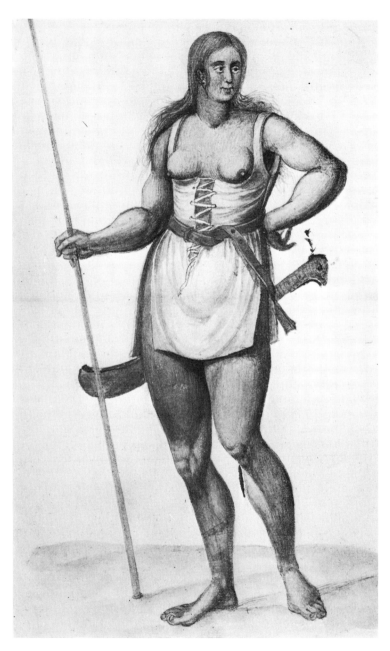

Figure 5. An ancestor, from Kent, whose more civilised appearance John White based on classical sources, late 1580s (British Museum)

Figure 6. Holinshed's Boadicea, as modern as Queen Elizabeth I, 1577 (Society of Antiquaries)

Figure 7. Speed's Ancient Britons based on John White's original view of the more civilised, and now more decorous, inhabitants of Kent, 1611

These elf arrowheads have not been used as amulets above thirty or forty years ... whence I gather they were not invented for charms, but were once used in shooting here as they are still in America. The most curious, as well as the Vulgar thro'out this country, are satisfied they often drop out of the air, being shot by Fairies, and relate many instances of it; but for my part I must crave leave to suspend my faith, until I see one of them descend. (Lhuyd 1713, 93ff.)

Plot and Lhuyd being Keepers of the Ashmolean Museum, as well as antiquaries, were likely to come across both ethnographic and archaeological material in the course of their studies, and perhaps the most important way in which ethnography influenced antiquarian studies at this time was in the interpretation of stone tools. Plot and Lhuyd lived in a world unattuned to Stone Age man, as Lhuyd's letter shows with its amulets and elf arrows, and yet they contributed to the slow realisation that stone tools existed, as well as metal ones, that such tools could be found in the British Isles, and that they were probably made by men as savage as the Indians, in the days before the Roman Conquest. It was undoubtedly the Keepers' familiarity with their ethnographic collections that prompted this new understanding. Already in these early centuries we can determine the use of ethnography at two levels: for the understanding of artefacts such as the stone tools, and for the comprehension of development in human culture.

Throughout the eighteenth century new ethnographic reports were becoming available in the western world, the most popular being those from the South Seas. Both Piggott and Burrow have shown how these were used in many aspects of cultural life, from prints to poetry (Piggott 1968, Burrow 1966), and antiquarian studies were no exception. But it was probably the American material which continued to be most significant for archaeological studies; it was not necessarily the most popular among antiquaries, but the way in which it was used affected the subsequent development of the subject more than any of the Polynesian allusions. The work of Pownall in the later eighteenth century, and that of Daniel Wilson in the mid-nineteenth century both reveal how primitive man, and his tools and weapons and his social organisation, were interwoven in the fabric of archaeology so that, without question, one *knew* that prehistoric man was primitive, one *knew* what a stone axe was and how it was hafted, one *knew* the logical progression of human culture from savage, stone-using hunters to barbarian farmers with bronze tools, to urbanised, literate, iron-using civilised man.

Pownall had relatively little influence on his contemporaries, but his work is of interest to us today as an illustration of the intellectual climate of his times. He lived and worked in North America for several years in the mid-eighteenth century, and on his return home he studied the antiquities of the British Isles, comparing the past cultures which they represented with the present primitive cultures of America and elsewhere. His frequently stated belief was that 'Man is, in the natural course of his being, always the same thing, under the same circumstances' (Pownall 1795, 31). Hence the comparisons between prehistoric and primitive peoples; Pownall represents those late-eighteenth-century scholars who saw the remote past of the western world in the same primitive light, and who gradually built up a case for the development of mankind through successive technological, economic and political stages. Theoretically, he left most antiquaries far behind him, some of them still struggling in the wake of Noah's sons, but the ideas he absorbed in America and applied to archaeology on his return home did eventually prompt the critical developments of the mid-nineteenth century, as can be illustrated through the work of Daniel Wilson (Orme 1974).

The works of Daniel Wilson were undoubtedly influential in his own time, and they are also representative of the best of mid-nineteenth century publications. This was perhaps the most important formative period in the development of archaeology, the decades when it adopted the principles, the methods and the character which are the foundations of today's discipline. Therefore, if one can trace a significant contribution from ethnography at this time, it will help to substantiate the claim made above, that ethnography and archaeology can be used together in the study of man's past.

In the introduction to his first major publication, *Archaeology and the Prehistoric Annals of Scotland* (1851), Wilson stressed the value of ethnographic studies to the antiquary. In the next, written after his move from Edinburgh to Toronto, it is evident that direct contact with the American Indians had fulfilled all his expectations. Their life was that of early man, and ethnography could shed such light on the past, that to ignore it and confine oneself to mere antiquities would be like 'reading by candlelight at noonday' (Wilson 1862, vii).

It is surely significant that Wilson was expecting the American Indians to be like his interpretation of prehistoric man in Britain. Their way of life did not come as a shock to him, rather it brought to life his preconceived ideas. This would suggest that Wilson, as an archaeologist, had consistently interpreted his material on the understanding that man in the remote past was, in most respects, like contemporary primitive man. And it was in this light that he presented his archaeological work to the public.

Other nineteenth-century scholars reveal a similar equation of prehistoric and primitive man. It is present, for example, in works such as Tylor's *Researches into the Early History of Mankind* (1865) and Lubbock's *Prehistoric Times* (1865). Subsequently, Tylor's work has been taken as part of the foundations of anthropology, whereas Lubbock, better known perhaps as Lord Avebury, is seen as a pioneer of archaeology. With hindsight, this is a fair assessment, but during the 1860s it is doubtful that the distinction would have been made, either by Tylor and Lubbock themselves or by their public.

There was but one subject in these years, man in his pre-civilised state, and archaeology and anthropology converged to a greater degree than ever before or since (Orme 1972).

In the later nineteenth century, both archaeological and anthropological data were accumulated at a great rate, and as field techniques developed and knowledge increased and had to be classified, so specialist fields of study began to emerge, and those who knew about primitive man ceased to be familiar with the prehistoric evidence, and vice versa. At the same time, the vast influx of data, and the need to reduce it to order, whether by creating kinship systems or pottery typologies, caused both the anthropologists and the archaeologists to lose their historical perspective to a certain extent, thereby diminishing the common ground between them.

Over the first decades of the twentieth century archaeologists continued to make piecemeal use of ethnography, and never quite lost touch with the notion that man in the past was not unlike primitive man studied by the anthropologists. But there were no significant developments until the mid-1960s, when a rapprochement between the two disciplines began to seem possible once more. This is not to imply that there were no developments in the intervening years, but to note that ethnography contributed to little that was new. By the 1960s, however, archaeologists were becoming much more conscious of the theoretical basis of their subject, and more concerned with interpretation than they had been previously, and, aided by the use of radiocarbon dates, interest was renewed in historical interpretation, in the study of the development of cultures and not merely their reconstruction in a static state. A similar shift among some schools of social anthropology, from the study of the structure of societies at one moment in time towards a study of change and development, has made it easier for the two disciplines to find matters of common interest in each other's work, as they did a century ago.

These developments can be traced in the archaeological literature through the increased use of ethnographic parallels, and one publication can be used to illustrate the turning point. This is Grahame Clark's study of the stone axe trade, a paper which brought together the archaeological and the anthropological evidence for the production and redistribution of stone axes and which was published (perhaps significantly?) in neither an archaeological nor an anthropological journal, but in the *Economic*

History Review (Clark 1966). Clark had used, and discussed the use of, ethnography on several occasions previously, but this paper marks a new departure in presenting a coherent view of the traffic in stone axes in the primitive world to balance the archaeological evidence, instead of the till-then more usual collection of piecemeal parallels.

The next stage in the developing use of ethnography is marked by two conferences, one held in Chicago and one in London and both exploring the common interests of anthropologists and archaeologists in relation to specific fields of study. The American conference, published in 1968 as *Man the Hunter* (Lee and De Vore 1968), has been particularly influential in the field of Palaeolithic and Mesolithic studies and there are few archaeologists working on these periods today who do not use the ethnographic contributions to *Man the Hunter*, or the subsequent literature (e.g. Sahlins 1974). Lee's work on the !Kung Bushmen has proved especially popular, and it has served to introduce many archaeologists of the Old Stone Age to a wider use of ethnography, at least for economic interpretations – and it will appear in later chapters of this book (Lee 1968). Another indication of the very wide influence of *Man the Hunter* is the frequency of its appearance in the bibliographies of subsequent publications.

The London conference, published as *The Domestication and Exploitation of Plants and Animals* (Ucko and Dimbleby 1969) was held to promote an interdisciplinary approach to the problems of how and why and where and when man turned from hunting to farming. The focus of the problem was therefore prehistoric, but contributions included anthropologists, geographers, botanists and all who might be interested in the central theme. Like *Man the Hunter*, the conference has had far-flung effects, perhaps not so much in the direct influence of the papers as in the subsequent work of the participants, and the subsequent conferences that brought together a similar range of scholars to discuss first *Man, Settlement and Urbanism* (Ucko, Tringham and Dimbleby 1972) and then *The Explanation of Culture Change* (Renfrew 1973). From here, the developments are legion – and in many ways this book is one of them.

The debate

Before examining the recent developments in the use of

ethnography, a useful perspective will be obtained by looking briefly at what archaeologists have said and are saying about the use of ethnography.

Before the 1960s, most of the discussion was along lines very similar to those of the nineteenth century. When Crawford wrote in the first issue of *Antiquity* that 'to see the past in the light of the present is to give it life and substance' (Crawford 1927, 3), he was echoing Wilson's reaction to the North American Indian: '... realising in the living present nearly all that I had conceived of in studying the chronicles of Britain's prehistoric centuries' (Wilson 1863, xv). And when Grahame Clark argued that 'just as the student of the Pleistocene Ice Age turns to areas where glacial conditions still obtain, or the palaeontologist considers fossil bones in relation to living animals, so must the archaeologist strive to reconstruct the vanished world of antiquity by reference to existing societies' (Clark 1951, 50), he was thinking in the same vein as Nilsson, the Scandinavian antiquary who declared in his influential work *The Primitive Inhabitants of the Scandinavian North*, that '... If natural philosophy [the natural sciences] has been able to seek out in the earth and to discover the fragments of an animal Kingdom which perished long before man's appearance in the world, and by comparing the same with existing organisms, to place them before us almost in a living state, then also ought this science archaeology to be able, by availing itself of the same comparative method, to collect the remains of human races long since passed away, and of the works which they left behind, to draw a parallel between them and similar ones, which still exist on earth, and thus cut a way to knowledge of circumstances which *have been*, by comparing them with those which still exist' (Nilsson 1863, lviiff).

There was a certain amount of opposition or antipathy to the use of ethnography, although in Britain little of it found its way into print, except for an article by M.A. Smith which dwelt on the lack of a logical link between 'the human activities we should like to know about and their visible results' (Smith, M.A. 1955, 6). Without the bridge of material culture, one could not infer past behaviour from that of the present. Prehistorians on the continent were more vocal in their distrust of ethnography (Orme 1974) – Leroi-Gourhan, for example, attacked the wholesale and intuitive adoption of analogies, which could only 'paralyse the scientific imagination' (Leroi-Gourhan 1964, 4).

Most archaeologists appear to have steered a careful course

between these various arguments, taking note of Clark and Childe's cautious advocacy of the use of parallels, but avoiding the excesses so deplored by Leroi-Gourhan. Few of them made sufficient use of ethnography to need the general rules formulated by Clark and Childe, in favour of analogies drawn between societies with similar environmental, technological, economic, and if possible historical, backgrounds (Clark 1951 and 1952; Childe 1956).

With the conferences of the late 1960s, and the arrival of vociferous American archaeologists on the European stage, a new round of arguments began. A few still felt that ethnography was a dangerous and probably stultifying aid to archaeological interpretation. Freeman's views, expressed in *Man the Hunter*, illustrate this attitude well: '... the use of assumed similarities with modern behaviour in the explanation of the behaviour of extinct groups is not only fallacious, it is also deleterious to research since it prevents the discovery that the postulated similarities do not exist' (Freeman 1968, 265). This is a dubious argument, for one can learn as much from the differences as from the similarities that emerge when a comparison is examined in detail. But Freeman did make further points which remain relevant, namely that we must remember the existence of biological differences between modern *Homo sapiens sapiens* and his Pleistocene ancestors, and that it would be wrong to ignore the possibility of past behaviour patterns that no longer exist in the modern world. To anticipate the arguments of the final chapter, these points, and especially the latter, need not prohibit the use of ethnography, but they can help to determine how it is used and may act as positive stimuli to interpretation.

Recent arguments in favour of the use of ethnography, and of anthropology in the broader sense, have been couched as much in terms of how it should be used as why. Ucko, who initiated much of the renewed interest in ethnography in Britain, says in several different ways that 'the primary use of ethnographic parallels ... is to widen the horizons of the interpreter' (Ucko 1969, 262; cf. Ucko 1967, 151 and 153). To achieve this, the more ethnography the better: 'The more varied and the more numerous the analogies that can be advanced, the more likely one is to find a convincing interpretation for an archaeological fact. The more numerous and the more detailed the parallels, the more likely one is to be able to assess the likelihood of a particular parallel being a significant one, and the greater the possibility of checking against the content and the context of the archaeological material' (Ucko 1967, 157).

Ucko's belief in the value of ethnography for archaeological interpretation found expression in the conferences referred to above, and at the second of these Flannery contributed a paper, 'The village as settlement types in Mesoamerica and the Near East: a comparative study', in which he described his working methods, which one can now see were to be those of a number of archaeologists but which he was one of the first to formulate clearly. 'In the course of preparing this paper, I detected in the archaeological record what appeared to be two types of early sedentary communities: one, a compound or homestead of small circular houses, and the other, a true village of somewhat larger rectangular houses. My next move was to search the ethnographic literature on Mesoamerica, the Near East, and adjacent areas for example of societies with similar communities. Examples were so many, and so varied, that I was forced to set up a series of *ideal types* against which the archaeological data could be tested. Each ideal type was an abstraction from various ethnographic examples, defined on the basis of structural features which I felt should be preserved archaeologically. I evaluated the ideal types on the basis of shared structural features with actual prehistoric communities ... I did not expect any one archaeological site to resemble precisely any one ethnographically documented community; all I asked was that both appear to be examples of the same "ideal type"' (Flannery 1972, 29). Flannery's paper will reappear in later contexts. What is most relevant here is his formulation of the idea of an 'ideal type' (i.e. model) which by avoiding specific analogies between past and present societies avoids both the difficulties and the dangers which these involve. In effect, Flannery systematised Ucko's advocacy of as many parallels as possible. A number of prehistorians have since done likewise, though usually describing their efforts as 'models' rather than 'ideal types', and a good example of one of the more detailed attempts to set up an ethnographic model for the interpretation of past situations is Jochim's *Hunter-Gatherer Subsistence and Settlement: A Predictive Model* (Jochim 1976).

To end this survey of other people's views concerning ethnography, or anthropology, and archaeology, there is a rich source in the contributions to *Archaeology and Anthropology* (Spriggs 1977). Among these, the papers by Groube, Leach, and Rowlands and Gledhill express divergent if positive attitudes to the use of anthropological scholarship in archaeological interpretation, and they are on common ground in moving towards a comparative historical approach to the study of human culture. Groube's main concern is the development of ethnohistorical studies, where archaeology has much to contribute, but he also states the archaeologist's need for a 'general anthropological education' and plenty of ethnographic bedtime reading. He suggests that the general conclusions of anthropology are unlikely to help the archaeologist much, as they are apt to change as research proceeds (Groube 1977) – but then, so do the general conclusions of all disciplines, archaeology included.

Leach takes the opposite view to Groube in suggesting that it is above all the general theory of anthropology which is relevant to archaeology: 'If archaeology and anthropology are to come together, as I think they might, it will not be under the banner of either ecological or economic determinism. What is common to the two disciplines is that they are concerned with men, and the unique peculiarity of men is that they have language and that they have ideas' (Leach 1977, 169). He suggests some ways in which the anthropologists' studies of how men think could be applied to archaeological interpretation, for example in attitudes towards burial, and he concludes that the categories of thought of prehistoric man might not be as far from our grasp as archaeologists so readily assume.

Rowlands and Gledhill explore the developments of archaeology and anthropology that have helped towards establishing common ground, concentrating more on the anthropological trends than the present account has done. They agree with Leach rather than with Groube that it is 'the general conclusions and concepts that anthropologists have reached ... that can most usefully be employed by archaeologists for the analysis of their material' (Rowlands and Gledhill 1977, 149). In their concluding sentence, they express an opinion that is implicit in much of the recent renewal of interest in ethnography and in an interdisciplinary approach to the past: 'For all its faults, the commonality of views and aims that characterised early evolutionism recognised the essential complementarity of archaeology and anthropology as a single field of study – a perception of the science of man which, in our opinion, could be restored to the benefit of both' (157).

How far is this 'essential complementarity' exploited in practice, and to what ends? The answers to these questions will provide a useful framework for the various uses of ethnography and anthropology that will emerge in the course of successive chapters, and so they are now briefly described and classified, no doubt more rigidly than the situation really allows, but then one of the main values of typologies lies in their simplification.

Recent trends in the use of ethnography and anthropology

In practice, most uses of ethnography and anthropology can be fitted into one of the following five categories: the piecemeal use of parallels, ethnohistorical studies, ethnoarchaeology, ethnographic background and models, and comparative studies focussed on the past.

Piecemeal parallels

Certainly in the decades leading up to the recent revival of interest in ethnography this was the most common way in which ethnography was used, and it still remains so for the many archaeologists who appreciate that ethnography can be useful but have no great familiarity with anthropology in general. Normally the use of piecemeal parallels stems from the discovery of archaeological data that cannot be satisfactorily interpreted in the light of past work. It could be the discovery of a previously unknown type of artefact, or a pattern of postholes, or a type of site, and it prompts a search of the ethnographic literature for references to things which might be similar in shape and function.

The identification of artefacts in this manner was more common in previous centuries than today, when few new types appear, and a classic example of the method is the nineteenth-century search for parallels to the objects generally known as *bâtons de commandement* (Orme 1972). It is still a useful aid to interpretation when new objects are discovered – as in the Somerset Levels when curved wooden pins made from yew-wood were found in a neolithic context. These pins, about 20cm long, had been deliberately bent, and commonsense indicated that they were therefore not wooden arrowheads. A brief search through the ethnographic literature (and illustrations) soon revealed similar objects made of wood or bone in use to hold clothes together or as a hairpin or as a nose-pin, and these three possible functions were then suggested for the neolithic yew pins (Coles and Orme 1976).

Other examples of the recent use of piecemeal parallels are the comparison of features of Iron Age hillforts with Maori *pa*, with an eye to finding fighting platforms or raised storehouses (Ellison and Drewett 1971), the frequent recourse to Lee's !Kung work in recent Mesolithic studies (e.g. Woodman 1976), and two instances that we shall return to in the context of Ritual and Religion, namely the comparison of structures within henges to Cherokee council houses (Wainwright and Longworth 1971) and the search for a better understanding of causewayed enclosures (Drewett 1977).

Ethnohistory

Ethnohistorical studies have developed largely outside Europe, naturally enough as they seek to combine the information available in the earliest ethnographic reports from a region with the results of archaeological fieldwork in the same area. North American archaeologists have combined ethnohistory and excavation for some while now, as, for example, in the studies of Pueblo Indian culture or, at artefact level, in Binford's essay on the interpretation of smudge pits (Hill 1966, Binford 1967). Recently, ethnohistorical studies have burgeoned in New Zealand, fostered by Groube's belief in the potential of this approach for providing better anthropological as well as better archaeological results (Groube 1977). Groube supports his claims by showing how archaeological fieldwork, aided by recourse to the very earliest records of Maori society made before Europeans had had any great impact on the country, have together shown that much of 'traditional' Maori society as portrayed by Best, Firth and others, in fact developed in response to European colonisation. (N.B. This does not necessarily invalidate the use of Best and Firth's observations, as we shall find later.) Groube's fieldwork has since been amplified by that of Fox (e.g. Fox 1976 and 1978), and the understanding of the development of New Zealand from the time of first settlement to that of European colonisation is rapidly increasing.

Ethnoarchaeology

Ethnoarchaeology is another field of recent and rapid development, sometimes known as 'living archaeology' and occasionally associated with experimental archaeology. Ethnoarchaeology is the study of living communities from the point of view of the archaeological evidence that they will leave and the behaviour that it represented in the living group – an attempt, in fact, to establish the link between behaviour and its material results that Smith and others thought did not exist. Ethnoarchaeology can be directed at settlement structures or patterns, at artefact distribution, at pottery making, at hunting practices, or any other facet of culture that interests the observer. There is no restriction on the subject matter so long as the human activities leave a material residue. Stiles has made a survey of the aims and methods of ethnoarchaeology (Stiles 1977), and published fieldwork includes Hodder's work on boundaries between tribes in Kenya (Hodder 1977 and 1978), Birmingham's analysis of pottery manufacture, sale and use in Kathmandu (Birmingham 1975), Bonnichsen's excavation of a recently abandoned Indian camp in the Canadian Rockies (Bonnichsen 1973), and further work on the !Kung Bushmen of the Kalahari desert (Yellen 1977).

Practitioners of ethnoarchaeology tend to be vociferous in their advocacy of its virtues, and sometimes imply that it is the only avenue to the use of ethnography in archaeology. However, it is often closely related to ethnohistorical studies, and both are somewhat specialised approaches to the archaeologist's use of ethnography, and to the combined use of ethnography and archaeology, for both depend on the existence of living or recent primitive communities in the region of archaeological fieldwork. They are for obvious reasons more popular and more practicable among North American archaeologists than among those who are European-based. As techniques, therefore, their application is limited – but the results of ethnohistory and ethnoarchaeology are as useful a source of comparative material as any other we shall encounter.

Ethnographic background and models

Jochim's study of hunter-gatherer subsistence and settlement referred to above depends on a carefully constructed and very detailed ethnographic model, which indicates how hunter-gatherers ought to act for optimum survival, given certain conditions. It might be thought quite different in its approach to the use of ethnography to something like Ucko's 'Ethnography and archaeological interpretation of funerary remains' (Ucko 1969), which ranges over a wide spectrum of ethnographic examples in order to provide, not a specific predictive model for interpretation but a background to the sort of things that people do, in this instance with the dead. But both

Jochim and Ucko are taking the use of ethnography further than piecemeal parallels, and perhaps represent extremes of a range that includes Flannery's concept of ideal types, Renfrew's use of anthropological theory to interpret Western European megaliths (Renfrew 1976) and Rowlands' application of ethnography to the interpretation of Bronze Age metalworking (Rowlands 1971). Flannery uses models based on tangible settlement evidence, whereas Renfrew draws primarily on the anthropological theory of social organisation and only secondarily on ethnographic illustration, and Rowlands' survey of the ethnographic literature provides a background to the interpretation of prehistoric bronze-working rather than a specific model to be tested. These examples, which vary in the nature of their anthropological borrowings as well as in the method of its use, have common ground in the systematic application of a coherent body of comparative material to the elucidation of particular archaeological phenomena. The use of the results of ethnohistorical and of historical studies is basically similar, and could be included here – recent examples are Alexander's application of the results of the historians' frontier studies and Coles' survey of historically-documented pioneer farming in European Russia and in North America, both used in relation to the events of European prehistory (Alexander 1977 and 1978, Coles 1976).

Comparative studies and synthesis

The dividing line between background and models on the one hand and comparative studies on the other is not always clear, but the former tend to start from an archaeological base which directs the ethnographic search, whereas the latter are as likely to start from an anthropological base or from the cumulative results of the use of ethnography, as from a specific archaeological problem. The distinction made here between ethnography and anthropology is deliberate, to distinguish between the primary data of ethnography which is generally (though not invariably) used for background studies and models, and the analytical nature of anthropological studies which can also be used to create models (e.g. Renfrew and chiefdoms, 1973), but which are pre-eminently suited to comparative studies and synthesis.

Bender's recent paper 'From gatherer-hunter to farmer' stems from the accumulation of ideas gleaned from the ethnographic studies relating to the inception of farming, which suggest that it in fact had very little to do with domestication as such, and a lot more to do with social developments and trends towards a sedentary life, which Bender then explores further via the anthropological literature (Bender 1978). The study of urbanisation, of trade patterns, and of the development of socio-political systems are other obvious candidates for comparative studies along similar lines, and the many papers on these topics suggest that, as with the development of farming, results will accumulate to the point where new insights are achieved.

But the anthropological contribution to such syntheses should not be overstressed, for archaeology and history alike can generate ideas about man's past which are then tested against the evidence from all three disciplines. And it is always essential to remember that all three are only as good as their basic groundwork, whether excavation, participant observation or the study of documents.

The potential of comparative studies, or the synthesis of accumulated interpretations, indicated in the 'essential complementarity of archaeology and anthropology as a single field of study – a perception of the science of man' (Rowlands and Gledhill), is further explored in the final chapter of this book.

Some problems

All these applications of ethnography and anthropology in archaeological contexts have proved of value in advancing our understanding of the past. But the circumstances appropriate to their use and the kind of results that can be achieved vary, and it is important to recognise this, and to acknowledge, for example, that whereas piecemeal parallels intended to elucidate the function of a tool may require technological similarity between the ethnographic and archaeological societies in question, and models of hunter-gatherer subsistence obviously depend primarily on examples drawn from societies with this sort of subsistence base, comparative studies are unlikely to be bound by any such restrictions, and indeed may progress as much via contrasts as resemblances.

It was mentioned above that ethnohistory and ethnoarchaeology are in a sense techniques for the recovery of information, and in this sense they are not included in this book, any more than we are concerned in detail with the field techniques of ethnographers. As techniques, their use is limited to the few people who have the necessary training in both ethnographic and archaeological field methods and access to the regions where they may be applied. Only a small percentage of archaeologists will in practice be able to work in New Guinea or New Zealand, but all archaeologists, whatever their home base and their specialisations, can use the results of ethnohistory and ethnoarchaeology, just as they can use the results of 'straight' ethnography and anthropology.

The chapters that follow therefore deal mainly with the use of ethnography to provide background information and for setting up models or 'ideal types', and for comparative studies. In the main, the emphasis is on background information in the first chapters, followed by an attempt to set up an 'ideal type' for Pastoralism, and a final chapter devoted to the synthesis of previous results.

A brief word is necessary concerning the divisions of the subject matter into food, settlement, etc. This has been done for the purpose of easier description, but it should not be allowed to distract the reader from the close interaction of the categories. They do not function independently of each other. The choice of categories has been influenced more by ethnographic than by archaeological conventions, in order to further the archaeologist's introduction to the general spheres of anthropological interest. Nevertheless, there are omissions from both fields: no detailed study of kinship which one would expect in an ethnography, nor of technology which is so often the archaeologist's concern. Nor is there any treatment of art or of music, despite the considerable literature available on both topics. But these, and many other subjects, can be studied once a common core of archaeological and anthropological interests has been established, and it is hoped that the topics chosen here provide a reasonably balanced foundation.

With regard to the ethnography, there are one or two conventions to note, and problems that the reader should be aware of. Much of the ethnographic literature is written in the present tense, whether or not the people studied still live in the manner described. This use of the *ethnographic present*, as it is known, means that the Maori or the Australian Aborigines, for example, are described in their pre-contact state as if it still existed, but it is only a convention of the discipline – and a convenient one at times. Another convention that can give rise to misunderstandings is the use of the word *primitive*. Outside the anthropological literature, 'primitive' has acquired a perjorative meaning, but as an anthropological term it is used to indicate a small-scale society, pre-literate, non-urbanised and pre-industrial. It is a useful shorthand, and is used as such here.

The problems relate chiefly to the bias of the observer. First there is the bias of the ethnographer in the field, who cannot hope to comprehend all the ins and outs of another culture, and who will probably focus on one or two aspects which he finds most rewarding to study, and who will bring to bear, unconsciously or otherwise, all his own prejudices and attitudes. No ethnographer can be entirely objective, and it is as well to remember this.

Secondly, there is the bias of the archaeologist in selecting material from the ethnographic literature. Why is it, asked Groube, that archaeologists searching to interpret burial customs avoid the references to cannibalism, head-hunting and infanticide but swoop on those concerning the ritual killing of adulterers and murderers? Why, to take a less dramatic example, in the interpretation of the neolithic wooden pins discussed above, do most audiences give serious consideration to the possibility that they were clothes-pins or hairpins, but none at all to a vision of neolithic man wearing a nose-ornament? In both cases, I think the archaeologists select the ethnographic instances that come closest to their own cultural experience which they project, probably unconsciously, into the past. Adultery and murder have a place in our own society, whether we like it or not, but most of us probably sincerely hope that head-hunting, infanticide and cannibalism do not.

Then there is the danger of the single parallel. Much of the misuse of ethnography by archaeologists can be attributed to this trap, which is all too easy to fall into. When there is archaeological evidence to be explained, and the ethnographic literature provides a single neat example that appears to have all the answers, it is tempting to adopt this one example wholesale, and to forget about the many other parallels that might exist. Single parallels have been used in the past at all levels of interpretation, from the equation of weapons to the equation of whole cultures, and it is these uses that have stultified and restricted archaeological interpretation, by providing an answer that discourages full investigation both of the ethnographic background and of the archaeological evidence. The drawbacks are perhaps best realised by contrast with Flannery's description of his search through the ethnographic literature for examples similar to his archaeological settlement types, followed by the isolation of several 'ideal types' from the mass of ethnographic information, and the comparison of these abstracts with the archaeological data. A single parallel can never give the same thorough understanding of the data, and it would often be better to use no ethnography at all than to be hoodwinked by the mere appearance of similarity.

Most of what follows concentrates initially on the anthropological rather than the archaeological field. It is, after all, intended to introduce archaeologists to the former subject and to the ways in which it can serve the advancement of their own studies. However, some specific archaeological applications are suggested, and these are worked out in more detail as the book progresses. The examples chosen are taken mainly from western European prehistory, and often concentrate on the British Isles. This has been done partly through the author's greater familiarity with these regions, and also (and more important) because the examples of each chapter are designed to have a cumulative effect and to contribute to the final discussion of the interpretation of western European prehistory. However, there is no intention of suggesting that anthropology is only of value in the interpretation of western European evidence, or even restricted to prehistory. Its application is relevant to all studies of man in the past throughout the world.

Anthropology for archaeologists is an exercise in translation, and the good interpreter is he who knows both sides well enough to go beyond the limitations of a literal rendering, in order to transpose the essence of meaning from one culture to another.

1.   Food and Raw Materials

In modern complex societies, subsistence requirements are met by extensive trade networks; essential foods and raw materials, as well as luxuries, are obtained from afar. In small-scale societies, both food and raw materials may be traded, but the bulk of subsistence requirements is met from within a group's territory, whether culled by the hunter or cultivated by the farmer. This chapter will examine how such locally-based subsistence is achieved and consider what potential it offers and what restraints it imposes on a community. Later (Chapter 4) it will become apparent that few, if any, societies are totally self-sufficient, but it is likely that for the greater part of his existence man has lived in small communities that survived by exploiting their immediate environment.

Hunting, fishing and gathering

It has become fashionable to point out that a hunting way of life represents man's longest and most stable adaptation to his environment, and that man evolved as a hunter-gatherer over several million years. It could be argued that he is still physically and psychologically adapted to such an existence rather than farming, let alone life in the urban jungle (Reynolds 1972). Whatever the truth of this, prehistoric man subsisted by hunting and fishing and gathering throughout the Palaeolithic and Mesolithic, and moreover he did not abandon these techniques as farming developed.

In the late 1960s, at much the same time as it became fashionable to claim that man was by nature a hunter-gatherer, having evolved as such, it was suggested that this way of life was not one of Hobbesian nastiness and hardship. In the words of Marshall Sahlins, chief advocate of the new outlook, the hunter belonged to 'the original affluent society' (Sahlins 1968). Before investigating this claim, however, it is necessary to look at earlier attitudes to hunting and gathering, for it is these which have coloured most interpretations of prehistory to date.

Popular accounts of primitive tribes written in the earlier part of this century noted that people such as the Australian aborigines, the Bushmen, the Pygmies and the Esquimo were all scattered thinly over their territories, living in small nomadic groups, doing little but search for food, and accumulating few possessions. Apparently they could not support the elderly or infirm, or too many infants. Sometimes, under extreme conditions, they starved to death. Where they survived, they were increasingly coming under the influence of local farmers, or white colonists (e.g. Sollas 1911). All this demonstrated that their life was not easy, and that a farming economy was probably both more successful and more attractive. If the hunting life was so hard and harsh, then the Neolithic was indeed a Revolution, a first step towards civilisation that left the hunter irrevocably doomed to a life of savagery.

Some exceptions were recognised, and treated as indeed exceptional. The most obvious were the Indian tribes of the North West Coast of North America, hunter-fishers who lived in permanent villages for much of the year, and devoted much time and energy to accumulating more personal possessions than their neighbours. Their existence showed that some hunters had the leisure and the resources to develop their culture, especially in its artistic and social aspects. The abundance and regularity of the salmon runs were thought to make this possible, in that these particular hunters had as assured a food supply as any farmers. Parallels were sometimes drawn with the artistic peoples of the Upper Palaeolithic, who were equally exceptional hunters judging by the archaeological record and they probably had an equally exceptional steady food supply, maybe salmon from the Dordogne, maybe reindeer and buffalo from the plains.

However, some ethnographers have always recognised hunting and gathering as an acceptable alternative to farming (e.g. Radcliffe Brown 1922), and now the idea that hunters are affluent, having food and leisure in ample quantities, has rapidly become very popular due largely to the 1966 Man The Hunter conference and its subsequent publication (Lee and De Vore 1968), and Sahlins' resulting essay 'The original affluent society' (Sahlins 1972). The factual basis that spurred the development of this new outlook was provided by several work studies carried out among the Australian Aborigines and the Kalahari Bushmen. The most striking Australian evidence was provided by the research of McCarthy and

McArthur, who studied two groups of aborigines from Arnhem Land: they found that both men and women spent only 3-5 hours a day collecting food, and that not all adults worked to get food, and yet there was sufficient food for all (McCarthy and McArthur 1960).

The next, and perhaps more startling, evidence came from the work of R.B. Lee whose aim was 'to outline the subsistence strategy that enables the !Kung Bushmen, with only the simplest of technologies, to live well in the harsh environment of the Kalahari Desert' (Lee 1969, 47). Lee showed that even in a bad year the Bushmen could live relatively well with little effort, ignoring a number of edible plants because they did not like the taste, letting Mongongo nuts (a staple food) rot because they had no need for them, and spending 4-5 days a week on activities other than food-collecting (Lee 1968 and 1969).

Other reports were available to corroborate the emerging picture of a good life. North of the Kalahari, in the vicinity of Lake Rudolf, Woodburn reported that the Hadza were inefficient hunters in the first place and secondly spent most of their time gambling, yet they did not go hungry (Woodburn 1968, 53). Turnbull described a similar lack of concern among the Mbuti pygmies of the Ituri, living a pleasant and generally easy life, and treating their forest environment as a permanently stocked larder to be raided at will (Turnbull 1965). Both Hadza and Mbuti looked on farmers as slaves to their crops. In their eyes, and increasingly in the eyes of ethnographers, only the hunter was free.

This was the background to Sahlins' advocacy of the 'original affluent society' (Sahlins 1972). In an extensive and persuasive essay, Sahlins argued that Man the Hunter was neither possessive nor materialistic, that his way of life was therefore based on the satisfaction of minimal needs, and that his environment easily satisfied those needs, as witnessed by countless ethnographic reports. Judged independently of Western values subsistence based on hunting, fishing and gathering was far from deprivatory. Sahlins' work had an immediate impact on both the anthropological and the archaeological world, and much effort was put in to replacing the earlier popular visions of hardship and starvation with one of relative ease and affluence (e.g. Clarke, D.L. 1976).

Thus our image of the hunter has swung over to a primeval Golden Age, where the Noble Savage lives a pure and simple life uncorrupted by the materialistic wants that bedevil modern man. One begins to wonder how farming evolved, and why. Why did prehistoric man break away from the ease and abundance of a hunting economy? Perhaps because the Original Affluent Society is as distorted an interpretation as that which sees the life of the primitive hunter as 'solitary, poor, nasty, brutish and short'. The swing of the pendulum from one extreme view to the other has a long history (Piggott 1968, Smith, B. 1960). Both have survived because they contain an element of truth, while neither reflects the whole of reality. For if one thing is clear in surveying the literature on existing and recent hunting peoples, it is that an enormous variety of hunting adaptations have evolved over the four million years or so of *Homo sapiens'* existence. There is no universal hunting economy. Both culture and environment contribute to the present diversity, and both have varied through time as well as geographically from one region of the world to another. Even within a region there need not be uniformity: one Esquimo group may flourish, while another starves because of local failure in the caribou migrations, and yet another group may avoid starvation by practising infanticide, thereby surviving in relative affluence but at a very reduced population density.

Granted that interpretation of the ethnographer's data at a popular level is likely to be swayed by fashion, this does not mean that there is no division of opinion among the ethnographers themselves and it would be well to recognise that even in the first stages of interpretation different cases can be argued from the same evidence. It has been suggested, for example, that the Potlatch system of the North West Coast Indians, whereby huge quantities of foods and goods are wasted, is a means of coping with super-abundance (Suttles 1968). It has also been argued that the Potlatch serves basically as a mechanism for redistribution in an environment where one group lives in plenty while their neighbours may starve, due to the fickle nature of salmon runs (Piddocke 1965). Such multiplicity of interpretation is true of so many disciplines that one would expect all academics to realise it, but it is a curious fact that once outside their own field, scholars tend to accept generalisations far too readily, and the archaeologist borrowing from anthropology is undoubtedly vulnerable in this respect.

Therefore, the archaeologist should be wary of adopting any easy generalisations, although this has been done in the past. In much the same way as the ethnographic vision of primitive man has varied, so the hunter of the Stone Age has popularly been described as anything from greatly impoverished (usually Mesolithic) to living off the fat of the land (usually Upper Palaeolithic). Both views are possibly correct, though not necessarily for the times and places they are traditionally ascribed to. It is possible that prehistoric hunting groups encountered the same diversity of circumstances as do modern groups, though this does not imply that they lived in exactly the same conditions. Probably the variety of environments was even greater than today, since the range of hunter-gatherers was then wider, encompassing virtually the whole world over many millennia, and through several major climatic and environmental changes.

Hunting and fishing

Whether the hunter's life is easy or not, how does he get his food? This is the archaeologist's first problem, to investigate what people ate; only afterwards can he speculate about riches and poverty.

Primitive peoples, both hunters and farmers, obtain a wide range of animal foods from the wild. From large game such as elephants and whales, to tadpoles, grubs and insects, the animals used for food depend on what is available locally and also to a considerable extent on the cultural preferences of the hunter. The Alaskan Esquimo, for example, prefer to eat caribou and if there are no caribou they hunt wild sheep instead, and if these fail they resort to birds and eggs. Some Brazilian Indians appear to rely quite heavily on fish; the Congo pygmies, living in a not dissimilar tropical forest environment, never exploit this source of protein: for them, fish do not exist as food (Turnbull 1965). The Bushmen, despite living in a desert environment, regard only ten of the fifty-four mammal species available as edible (Lee 1968). In the New Guinea highlands, where there are few animals of any size, people exploit a wide range of mascroscopic fauna such as tadpoles and insects, although here again they are selective (Pospisil 1972).

The many ways in which culture can affect the choice of animal eaten is well illustrated in Spencer and Gillen's account of the food restrictions practised in Central Australia. Here, men did not in general eat their totemic animal, though some would do so on special occasions. People did not eat animals if they had been killed by certain of their relatives. Young men faced a number of temporary restrictions at the time of initiation and women did not eat meat during the early months of pregnancy. Children were forbidden a wide range of foods, from kangaroo tails to emu fat, thereby 'reserving the best things for the use of the elders' (Spencer and Gillen 1899, 467-73).

The prehistorian cannot hope to disentangle such complex eating patterns, but he should realise that they exist. People in any society very rarely make use of all the animal protein available to them, and edible species are consistently ignored because, in the eyes of the hunter, they are not suitable as food. Therefore the food-animal remains from an archaeological site will very probably not represent the total fauna of the area. Moreover, eating patterns can change for cultural reasons, and a change in bone remains may reflect this. Such circumstances, as much as any environmental or economic change due to farming, could lie behind the fluctuating percentages of red-deer bones from European Neolithic sites (Tringham 1971, Jarman 1971). If one can generalise at all, the ethnographic literature suggests that more animals are potentially available for food than any one culture exploits.

The next aspect to consider is the technology of hunting, the artefacts and techniques used by the hunter, and the traces that these might leave in an archaeological context.

Sometimes there is no trace at all. A man can hunt and catch other animals with no equipment other than his own hands. Birds can be lifted off branches as they roost, fish tickled from streams, mammals pulled from their burrows. Even quite large animals can be run down by an energetic hunter. Much equipment is ephemeral: a branch used as a digging-stick, a stone as a missile, gum on a bird's perch, poison in a stream. Even the more durable artefacts will not necessarily have an archaeological lifespan. Bone fishhooks, bamboo spears, birdbeak arrowheads and grass snares will all disintegrate under normal conditions. Of course, some things do survive, such as the stone barbs of a bone harpoon, or a bone point lost in a limestone cave, or a flint arrowhead and a slate knifeblade dropped in the snow. But except in very rare instances it is only *part* of the artefact which survives.

It is this differential decay whereby the whole range of artefacts is selectively reduced to the archaeological record that makes the ethnographic evidence useful to the archaeologist. He should not expect to find exact replicas of prehistoric stone tools in use, complete with their hafts and bindings, but he may come to appreciate how essential the organic parts are to the complete artefact and how much equipment may have decayed beyond all archaeological recognition. This is evident if one compares an archaeological toolkit, with an ethnographic collection, as is done in Figs 8 and 9 where the scant tools of a European Mesolithic culture

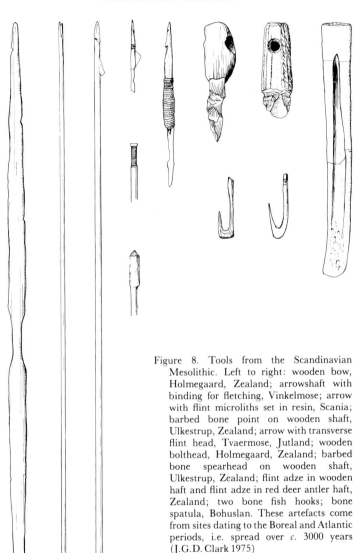

Figure 8. Tools from the Scandinavian Mesolithic. Left to right: wooden bow, Holmegaard, Zealand; arrowshaft with binding for fletching, Vinkelmose; arrow with flint microliths set in resin, Scania; barbed bone point on wooden shaft, Ulkestrup, Zealand; arrow with transverse flint head, Tvaermose, Jutland; wooden bolthead, Holmegaard, Zealand; barbed bone spearhead on wooden shaft, Ulkestrup, Zealand; flint adze in wooden haft and flint adze in red deer antler haft, Zealand; two bone fish hooks; bone spatula, Bohuslan. These artefacts come from sites dating to the Boreal and Atlantic periods, i.e. spread over *c.* 3000 years (J.G.D. Clark 1975)

S.G.

contrast with the abundance of a recent North American subsistence toolkit.

It would be impossible fully to describe here the great variety of hunting equipment still in use, or recently consigned to museums. Rather than attempting a rapid world survey, the equipment of a single group of peoples will be considered, namely that of the Athapaskans illustrated in Figs. 9 and 10.

The Athapaskans consist of several tribes who lived and still live by hunting and gathering, in the northern latitudes of North America, immediately to the south of Esquimo territory. Their pre-contact winter hunting tools included wooden bows with a twisted rawhide string, wooden-shafted arrows fletched with feathers lashed on with sinew, and various arrow heads including blunt bone heads, barbed bone points and copper and iron points. Quivers to carry the arrows were made of goat skin, decorated with dyed porcupine quills. Fish nets were made of twisted sinew thread. Clubs were made of moose legbones, with a moose-skin carrying strap; knocking sticks were made of caribou antler, with an inset stone blade. Skinning knives were made of long flat pieces of bone with a serrated end and maybe a hole for a carrying thong, and split roots might be bound round the knife as a handle. Many sinew snares with wooden toggles were used for catching both small rabbits and the much larger caribou. Skin bags were used for carrying equipment and catch, and snowshoes and sleds were essential to winter mobility.

In the summer the Athapaskan hunter turned fisherman. Nets were made of willow bast, as well as rawhide. Floats could be made from bark or wood, sinkers from stone or antler (caribou or moose). Fishhooks were likely to be composite artefacts, having a bone barb lashed with spruce roots or rawhide to a wooden shank, with a rawhide line attached. Sometimes the hooks were carved out of a

Figure 9. Athapaskan hunting equipment. Wooden caribou spear with iron point attached with strip of skin, 1.68m; wooden bow with babiche string, 1.35m; arrow with wooden shaft partly stained with red pigment, barbed iron point and triple-fletched feather flight lashed to shaft with sinew, 0.76m; quiver of mountain-goat skin sewn with sinew and ornamented with white, brown and ochre woven porcupine-quill work and quill-wrapped thongs, 0.816m; caribou antler knocking stick with incised and reddened decoration (original inset stone blade missing), 0.57m; moose leg-bone club, one end wrapped with skin sewn with sinew and a tanned moose-skin carrying strap, 0.32m; skinning knife, polished bone with serrated working end, handle wrapped with cloth and bound with split roots, 0.225m; hunting bag of tanned caribou skin and netted babiche decorated with pigments, wool, beads, goose quills and cotton, 0.535m (McFadyen Clark 1974)

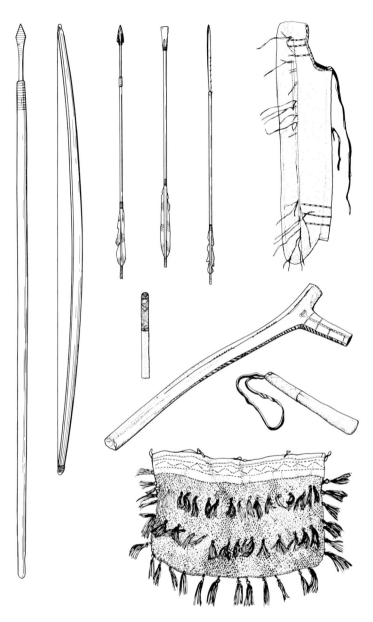

SG

single piece of bone. Fish spears or leisters were also used: two barbed wooden prongs with a bone point between them, lashed with sinew to a wooden haft. Canoes were made from birch bark sewn over a wooden frame, using spruce roots for thread. In Fig. 10 some of these items are illustrated. In Fig. 11 the non-perishable elements of Figs. 9 and 10 are shown.

The Athapaskans also made use of traps and weirs in their hunting. Wooden fish traps might be used in conjunction with stone weirs, or the weirs could be used alone and then the fish would be speared or netted. Caribou were caught by building fences, perhaps several miles long, which consisted of pairs of posts about six foot high with a noose hanging from a horizontal pole set across the top. Two fences might serve to funnel the caribou into a compound, where they could easily be killed (McFadyen Clark 1974, Van Stone 1974).

Fishweirs and fences on this scale demand considerable manpower for their construction, although exactly how much does not seem to have been recorded for any community. They represent an investment in the land, something which is unusual for hunters, something to remember when considering why and how hunting peoples became tied to their territories. Perhaps, as Lewis Binford has suggested (Binford 1968), this type of investment was a necessary cultural development in the evolution of farming, in that it encouraged regular visits to a particular spot and demonstrated that the environment could profitably be altered to provide more food for less energy expended.

The dangers of concentrating on a single ethnographic example have been discussed in the Introduction, and the Athapaskan material should therefore be compared with other descriptions of hunting equipment and techniques. Useful accounts may be found in Asen Balikci's *Netsilik Esquimo*, which describes subsistence in a colder and more barren North American environment. Spencer and Gillen's *Native-Tribes* and Jane Goodale's *Tiwi Wives* provide contrasting views of hunting in Australia, Turnbull's description of

Figure 10. Athapaskan fishing equipment. Spear for trout, wooden shaft, 2 wooden prongs and central moose-bone point, lashed with sinew and babiche, 1.10m; fishing net made from willow bast, 27.4m; net shuttle, bone, 0.245m; net gauge, wood 0.065m; net sinker, moose antler, 0.115m; net float, balsam poplar bark, 0.145m; club for killing fish, birch with babiche wrist strap 0.255m; fish hook made from moose nose-bone, 0.135m; fish hook with bone barb lashed with sinew to wooden shank, and babiche line, 0.075m (McFadyen Clark 1974)

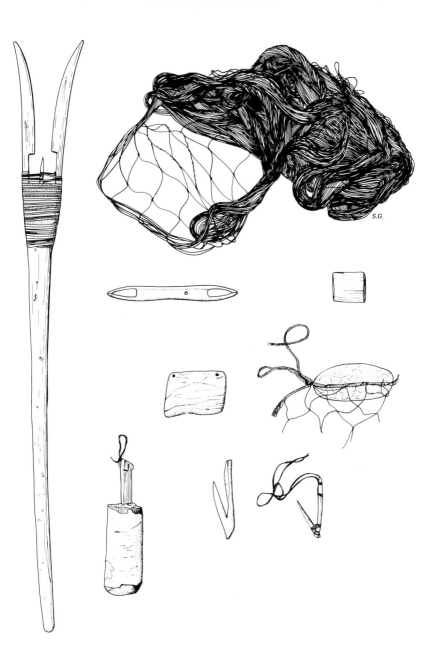

S.G.

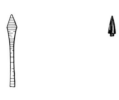

Figure 11. The inorganic elements
    of figures 9 and 10. Unless
    unusual conditions favoured the
    preservation of bone or wood,
    only three of the 19 objects
    might be represented on an
    archaeological site: the iron tips
    of the hunting spear and arrow
    (above) and the decorative
    beads on the hunting bag
    (below). Iron, however, has a
    poor survival rate, and it could
    well be that all that remained of
    this hunting and fishing
    equipment was a few decorative
    beads.

the hunters of the Ituri forest, *Wayward Servants*, dwells on communal hunting drives, and, to show that farmers also hunt, there is Pospisil's detailed analysis of New Guinea methods, in *Kapauku Papuan Economy* (Balikci 1970, Spencer and Gillen 1899, Goodale 1971, Turnbull 1965, Pospisil 1972). This is by no means an exhaustive list.

Just as people generalise about the ease or hardship of subsistence based on hunting and fishing, so it is often taken for granted that in any society it is the men who hunt, while women gather vegetable foods and look after their children. Broadly speaking this is true but once again there are sufficient exceptions to the generalisation to be noteworthy. Athapaskan women both hunt and fish. Kapauku women go fishing. Tiwi women hunt rather more than the men, and Jane Goodale describes how the Tiwi classify animals according to whether they may be hunted by men or women or both. She concludes that women mostly hunt land animals, while men hunt birds and water-animals (Goodale 1971, 151-4). However, apart from the Tiwi, it is rare for women to be *referred to* as hunters, whether by the ethnographer or by their own menfolk. One suspects that male prestige is involved here, for a man can gain great honour through being a mighty hunter, and it is true that the larger and fiercer animals are usually killed by men, not women. It should be noted, though, that whatever men say, women do catch quite a lot of animals.

Perhaps connected with the way in which hunting, as opposed to the mere catching of animals, is a male prerogative, particularly when an element of danger is involved, some hunting expeditions are surrounded by ritual, and obviously provide the participants with rather more than food. The Lapps treated bears as semi-sacred, and had elaborate rules for hunting them, which involved the use of a special vocabulary, consulting shamans for favourable omens, and killing the animal with special bear-pikes. The rituals did not stop with the animal's death: the hunters would sing to the corpse, and beat it, and take it home still singing. There they would be greeted by their women according to further special rules, and still more rules governed the way in which the bear was cooked and eaten, and its skeleton buried. Various sexual prohibitions would be enforced for several days, following which a final cleansing ceremony was then held, for the spirit of the bear was very powerful. In terms of Lapp culture as a whole, the food value of the bear was almost a residual factor, compared with the sacred aspects of the bear hunt. The Naskapi *mokoshon*, which exhibits a similar entanglement of subsistence and ritual in a caribou marrow feast, is examined more fully in the context of ritual and religion (Chapter 5).

The Lapp bear-feast involved sharing the meat with the whole community. This sharing of food is another recurring feature of hunting societies, which might affect archaeological interpretations. Lee, for example, stresses the way in which Bushmen always share food, and Spencer and Gillen describe very elaborate sharing rules for the Aborigines, so elaborate as to be irksome at times. Ethnographers have pointed out that this sharing ensures enough food for everybody, and that it also served to bind people together in what is often otherwise a very loose-knit community. As usual, there are exceptions, such as the Hadza who mostly fend for themselves. But it may be useful for archaeologists to note that because of food-sharing, the bone débris at a campsite does not necessarily correlate with the number of inhabitants. This is particularly true when a large animal has been killed, and there may be an influx of people from neighbouring areas to help eat it, as when the Mbuti kill an elephant. Or parts of the animal may be sent away to adjacent camps. In either case, food-sharing habits can play havoc with calculations of meat-weight, minimum animal numbers and population densities, particularly if they are based on evidence from a single site. Area studies may perhaps be less affected since sharing will tend to be confined within tribal territory.

Gathering

Most plants are perishable, and many when used as food leave little or no débris, unlike animals with their bones and teeth and horns and antlers. Therefore, archaeologists have tended to ignore plant foods, because they find little or no evidence for their use in the past. But even the most unlikely environments can be harvested: in an article written expressly for archaeologists, Thomson described the wide range of vegetable foods collected by the Wik Monkan of Arnhem Land in Australia. The foods came to a surprising amount for a bare environment, and they included roots, stems, leaves, buds, seeds and berries (Thomson 1939).

Other ethnographers, describing more lush environments, have been able to concentrate their studies on just this one aspect of a culture, the collection and use of plant foods and raw materials (e.g. Yarnell 1964), and gathered plant foods should be assumed as an element in all diets – even of those Esquimo whose only vegetable intake may be the stomach contents of hunted caribou.

Gathering is not particularly exciting, challenging or dangerous. Indeed, it is probably rather boring. It is normally the acknowledged duty of women and children, although men in practice collect vegetable foods, just as women in practice go hunting. It is normally the women, however, who collect sufficient supplies for the whole family or band; this work assumes considerable significance where people rely heavily on vegetable foods, whether it be all year round or seasonally to see them through an otherwise lean period.

In some environments, enough plant food must be gathered in summer and autumn to last through the winter. Whether acorns in California or berries on the North West Coast, the examples of such large-scale gathering that we know of are provided mostly from North America. In such situations, the food must be stored, perhaps by drying or smoking. There is ample evidence, also from North America, that hunter-gatherers do store plant foods, and that there is nothing intrinisic in their way of life to prevent this happening when the need arises. In tropical and sub-tropical areas, plants do not lend themselves to long term preservation: they rot. At the same time, there is no need to store food in these areas, since fresh supplies are available all year. In temperate and sub-arctic regions on the other hand, the plants themselves are adapted for foodstoring since they, like humans, must survive the winter. Therefore in these regions it is not so difficult to keep plant-food supplies edible for several months, and it may be vital to survival to do so. Both storage pits and granaries are made by hunters as well as by farmers: the Athapaskans bury some of their supplies, the Ainu of Japan build raised storage huts (Starr 1904).

Gathering can be accomplished with little equipment beyond a stick for digging, a knife and a container. The stick is perhaps the most essential, and universal, of gathering tools. It is little different from many a farmer's digging stick, or hunter's spear for that matter. Knives vary in morphology from one culture to another (Fig. 12), and are not always used, for teeth and hands will do instead or, alternatively, a heavier axe may be required. Containers are also very varied, except in the general absence of pottery which is too heavy and fragile to carry around. Materials commonly used to make containers include wood, bark, basketry and netting, and skins, all of which are fairly light and robust. Fig. 13 illustrates containers from Central Australia, from North American (Athapaskan) and from New

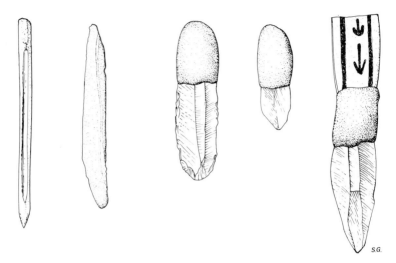

Figure 12. Knives. Left to right: Kapauku bamboo knife, 0.15m long; Kapauku stone knife; three Australian knives with flint blades and resin handles, the decorated example being used for fighting as well as other purposes (Pospisil 1972 and Cranstone 1973)

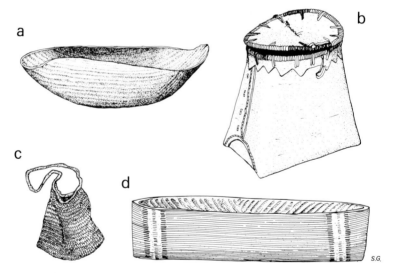

Figure 13. Containers. (a) and (d) two Australian wooden dishes, for collecting, carrying and storing food (Spencer & Gillen 1968); (b) Athapaskan berry basket, birch bark sewn with spruce root, rim reinforced with wood splints, lid tied with babiche, decorated with spruce-root lashing, some dyed black and red, 0.335cm (McFadyen Clark 1974); (c) Kapauku net bag used by men for carrying tools and tobacco as well as food (Pospisil 1972)

Guinea (Kapauku). It shows incidentally that the Australians who have to travel long distances and the New Guinea farmers who are sedentary, both have quite simple containers, whereas the semi-nomadic American Indians have more, and more elaborate containers than either of the other groups. Once again, there seems to be no regular correlation between different aspects of culture.

Gathering has neither the prestige nor the paraphernalia of hunting but it has already been suggested that it can be important, indeed vital, to survival. It demands a certain skill, and an intimate knowledge of the environment, and many ethnographers have paid tribute to the importance of a good gatherer, by recording how a family, or maybe a whole community, starved for lack of plant foods, or how a man prospered because his wives were skilled and conscientious foragers (e.g. Hart and Pilling 1960).

It seems that although meat is often much more highly prized as a food, vegetables provide the bulk of man's food outside the Arctic regions. They may even provide more protein than meat. Lee's analysis of Bushman diet demonstrates this so well that it is fast becoming a classic ethnographic example. His world-wide material is summarised in Table 1:

Table 1: Primary Subsistence Source by Latitude

Degrees from the Equator	Primary Subsistence Source			
	Gathering	*Hunting*	*Fishing*	*Total*
More than 60°	—	6	2	8
50°–59°	—	1	9	10
40°–49°	4	3	5	12
30°–39°	9	—	—	9
20°–29°	7	—	1	8
10°–19°	5	—	1	6
0°–9°	4	1	—	5
World	29	11	18	58

Broadly speaking, the amount of vegetable food eaten by hunters increases steadily as one moves towards the Tropics. The Esquimo live almost entirely off animals. Sub-arctic people eat up to about 60 per cent meat, but in temperate zones at least half the food supply is from plants and in tropical regions generally very much more.

However, there do not seem to be any non-farming peoples who are entirely vegetarian.

It has already been noted that diet may vary seasonally, and that reliance on plant foods may be crucial to survival through a particular season. In many cultures, the relative importance of hunting, fishing and gathering changes from one season of the year to the next, and the actual foods eaten may be quite different at different points in the annual cycle. As a result, the equipment used to get that food and the debris resulting from its consumption may also vary from season to season, perhaps so much so as to appear like different cultures in the archaeological record. This point was made strongly by Thomson in his study of the Wik Monkan, indeed his main purpose was to convince archaeologists of its validity, but it is only now slowly being accepted and applied (e.g. Jochim 1976, and see below, p. 117ff).

In spite of many cultures' acknowledged reliance on plant foods, few hunters tell stories of great vegetable feasts, or describe legendary gluts of roots and berries. It is animal-hunts which are remembered, meat-feasts which are celebrated in song, meat which is culturally important. Plant food is basic and dull, and probably the staff of life. Meat is real food, possibly exciting and dangerous to catch, certainly good to eat and full of prestige. Now archaeologists probably grossly over-emphasise the contribution of meat to subsistence in the past, because bones survive so much better than leaves and stems and berries, and even nuts. But it is unlikely that they exaggerate the *cultural* importance of meat which almost always far exceeds that of plant foods; witness the Hadza who claim hunger when meatless, though replete with nuts or berries. Paradoxically, for once it is probably easier to deduce past ideology than subsistence.

Raw materials

The raw materials for the hunter's artefacts, for his shelter and for his clothing are collected from the wild, and farmers may also depend quite heavily on such resources. Relatively little information is available on this subject, for the study of technology has suffered even more than that of food at the expense of the social aspects of culture. However, the Esquimo literature provides good evidence from the very specialised Arctic situation where raw materials other than ice and snow are scarce. It could be man's ingenuity in coping with this situation that excited the ethnographer's interest.

Traditionally the Netsilik Esquimo used snow blocks to build winter houses, and the beds and tables inside. Windbreaks for sealing and fishing could also be built from snow. Slabs of ice were occasionally used as a building material. Special tools were used, snowknives of caribou antler, snow shovels made of antler and sealskin, and ice chisels with a hard bear-bone point (Fig. 14).

Most clothing was made out of caribou skins, prepared with a variety of bone scrapers and sewn with bone needles. Sinew and rawhide was used for thread. Caribou skins were also used for bedding. Sealskins, which were more waterproof, were used for covering kayaks, for tents, and for boots. Sometimes bird and fish skins would be used; a fish-skin, for example, could be turned into a container. Animals might therefore be hunted as much for their skins as their meat.

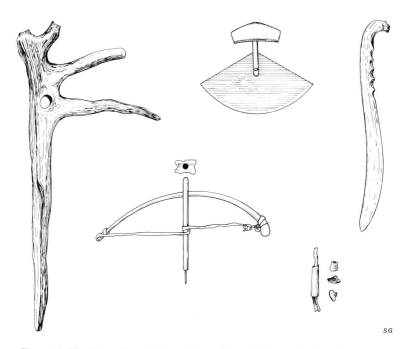

S.G.

Figure 14. Netsilik artefacts. Left to right: antler straightener, itself made of antler; bow drill for making holes through bone and wood, made from caribou or bear rib-bone with sealskin thong; caribou ankle-bone mouth piece and wooden shaft with iron drill point; woman's knife, bone and iron; snow-knife, caribou antler; needle case and thimbles, antler case with skin needle-holder, sealskin thimbles. The snow-knife is *c.* 0.30m long (Balikci 1970)

Bone and antler were particularly valuable, due to the scarcity of wood. They were worked using a bow-drill with a flint point, an adze, a whittling knife and a saw. Large objects such as bows and harpoons were made by rivetting pieces of bone together. Almost everything made by the Netsilik depended on bone and antler in some way, from sleds and tents to children's toys. Kayak frames, however, were made of wood, and lamps and pots were carved out of soapstone (Balikci 1970, 5-22).

True to Sahlins' dictum, most hunters are indeed essentially non-acquisitive, and yet they make use of a surprising number of different raw materials, given a less restricting environment than that of the Esquimo. The Hadza's inventory includes shelters made from branches with grass covering, clothing and sleeping mats made from the skins of various animals, ornaments made from fur and animal hair, and plant seeds and pods and ostrich eggshell and amulets of anteater scales and baboon tailbones. Bows are made of wood, with leather bindings and a string made from chewed sinews, preferably from zebra, eland or buffalo. If a gourd is attached to a bow, it can be used as a musical instrument. Arrows are made of several sorts of wood, with feathers and points tied on with sinew, or glued on with a sticky substance made from bulbs. Arrowheads are made of wood, or traded iron. Some are poisoned, the poison being obtained from one of two plants. Digging sticks are made of wood, and so are knife and axe handles, fire-drills and gambling discs. Skins are used to make bags. Stone is used for pipes. And yet Woodburn stresses the comparative poverty of the Hadza's material culture. Some of these objects are illustrated in Fig. 15, and in Fig. 16 an attempt has been made to single out the very small proportion which might find its way in to the archaeological record.

Farmers also use raw materials from the wild: Cranstone's account of the technology of the agriculturalists of Melanesia describes axes and adzes with wooden hafts and stone or shell blades bound with rattan. Obsidian, bamboo and shell are used for knife-blades. Woodworking tools include wooden drills with a stone point, rasps, with a shark-skin cover, and sharks' teeth and boars' tusks for carving. String and netting, which have innumerable uses, are made from a variety of plant fibres. Barkcloth is made mostly from the paper Mulberry tree; it is beaten out and may be dyed or painted, and several pieces can be glued together. Some pottery is made. Weapons include a wide range of bows and arrows, spears, clubs and daggers made from expected materials such as wood, and more

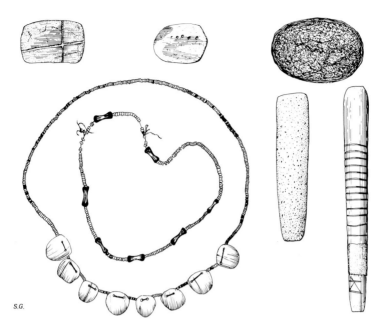

S.G.

Figure 15. Hadza artefacts. Left to right: three gambling discs, wood or bark, right hand master-disc of baobab bark; necklace with pangolin scales worn as treatment for chest pains; baboon tail bone belt worn as treatment for back and hip pains; stone pipe; wooden pipe strengthened with hide, c. 0.30m long (Woodburn 1970)

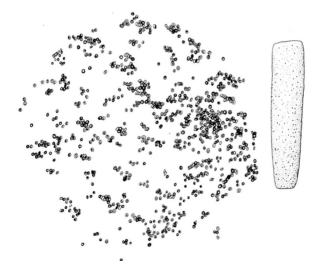

Figure 16. Hadza artefacts minus organic parts. A collection of beads and a single stone pipe

unusual items such as cassowary leg-bones and claws, and sting-ray spines. Shell is much used for ornaments and decoration, as well as for blades. Various colouring materials are made from minerals and plants. Large-scale constructions, whether houses, fences or boats, are made of wood bound with rope and string made from plant fibres. The raw materials for almost all these diverse artefacts are culled from the wild, and most are as perishable as those of the Athapaskan or the Hazda.

No account of hunting and gathering subsistence would be complete without reference to fire, water and salt, however brief. Fires are necessary for warmth, for protection from beasts and mosquitoes, for cooking, for making tools, for producing charcoal, for preparing skins, for firing pots, and for many other such practical ends as well as a wide range of ritual and magical purposes, from the small fire an Ituri pygmy lights for the forest when he goes hunting, to the elaborate fire-rituals of Bemba chiefs. Fuel is therefore essential. Wood may be collected during the daily round, or picked up around the campsite as it is needed. But if people stay in one place for any length of time, they will have to range quite far and wide for firewood. Fig. 17 shows a Sioux woman returning from an expedition to collect wood. It looks, and ethnographers say it is, an awkward and arduous task. In some instances, a local scarcity of firewood may prompt people to move. Binford reports that the Alaskan Esquimo may do so, and Campbell notes a similar restraint on Tuluaqmiut settlement (Campbell 1968). Fuel, it should be remembered, is but one aspect of man's need for wood, which forms the major part of most material cultures outside the extremes of arctic and desert – and wood is as perishable relative to stone as plant food is to animal, and it has been similarly neglected by archaeologists ever since the invention of the Stone Age (Coles, Heal and Orme 1978).

The necessity of water needs no demonstration and, given that man will die without it, he has developed a number of ways for coping with shortages. For instance, Bushmen lay trails of ostrich eggshells filled with water, which they bury in the ground against future need. Australians make use of a number of water-storing plants, and have a phenomenal knowledge of water-holes and other sources over a much larger territory than that they normally exploit. However, most peoples do not suffer from shortage of water, and their main problem is likely to be how to carry it from source to home. The water-containers of hunting societies are rarely made

Figure 17. Sioux Indian woman bringing home fuel (Curtis)

from pottery. Instead natural containers, such as gourds and bladders are used, or skins are sewn up, or wooden vessels hollowed out. Even basketry can be made waterproof. Therefore, one should never assume that people who lacked pottery had any difficulty in carrying or storing water, or in using water for cooking.

Salt is as vital as water. It may be found naturally in the things people eat, such as limpets and sea-weed; it may come from the ashes which stick to food cooked in an open fire; or it may be deliberately prepared. Heider gives a detailed account of how the Dugum Dani prepare salt, by soaking leaves in a salty spring, and then drying and burning them and carefully collecting the ash (Gardner and Heider 1968). Some other ethnographic data is available in the collection of papers *Salt: The Study of an Ancient Industry* (de Brisay and Evans 1975), and here also some of the archaeological implications of man's need for salt are explored.

One cannot summarise hunting and gathering subsistence in a few words, nor can one safely generalise on any aspect, except to point out that no two groups live in exactly the same way. Archaeologists should remember this: hunting and gathering is likely to have been at least as varied in the past as it is now. There do not seem to be any universal laws governing the life of the hunter-gatherer, and even if there were some feature common to all living groups it would not necessarily have occurred as consistently in the past. But there is no need to be as despondent as some prehistorians and reject all ethnography for this reason. What one can, and should, do is to search for those features which are typical of hunting societies (which is not at all the same thing as universal), to find out why they occur, what effect they have, and what archaeological evidence they might be expected to provide.

The variety itself is significant. Man has been able to live in the most diverse circumstances by hunting and gathering. As a farmer, he could not have colonised so great a part of the world, but by adapting hunting and gathering techniques to cope with different environments, almost every region has been settled. Even today there is no other means of subsistence as versatile. Only the Esquimo can lead an independent life in the Arctic, only the Aborigine in the Australian desert: cut off from their supply lines, oilmen and nuclear physicists would die.

This adaptability of the hunter-gatherer must have been crucial to man's initial spread across the world, and to his survival of the probably slow but certainly drastic environmental changes of the Pleistocene. In view of the great success of hunting in this respect as a means of subsistence for pioneering and for colonisation as well as for ordinary survival, it is unlikely that developments towards farming were triggered off by famine.

The adaptability of hunters is based on two things: mobility and a relatively low population density. Both these points will be examined more fully in the context of settlement. For the present, it can be suggested that it is the need for mobility which influences hunters to keep their possessions to a minimum. This in turn can lead to habits which affect the evidence later to be studied by the archaeologist. For example, many of the Australians' tools are multi-purpose: a spear-thrower is a dish is a fire drill is a digging and scratching tool (Fig. 18). Things are abandoned, not carried on every move: thus an Aborigine may leave a small collection of stone tools and lumps behind him when he moves on, and months or years or generations later these tools may be used again. Shelters, though still serviceable, are abandoned by most hunter-gatherers, except perhaps when they have dogs or horses to help with transport. Plenty of exceptions could be mentioned, but it remains true nevertheless that most hunters carry around as little as possible.

And this need or desire to travel light may contribute to the second factor, low population density. No woman wants more than one child that has to be carried if she lives a nomadic life. The population will also be kept low where people practice female infanticide: the reason may be to have a good ratio of hunters to dependents in the community; the result will be to curtail the breeding population. It has also been suggested from time to time that women in hunter-gatherer societies have low fertility rates in the first place, but not everyone would accept this. Whatever the reasons, hunter-gatherer communities *are* thinly scattered over their territories (Table 3) and the resulting small population has a good chance of surviving harsh times and living in places where the food supply is limited at the best of times.

Few people and few possessions: the success of the hunter-gatherer depends on these factors, and they are the very ones which limit his culture in its material aspects. Except in a few rare instances, material and social culture can only develop and alter within the restraint of these minimal levels, and they may also have operated in the past. The classic exception, which helps to show up these limitations by breaking away from them, is that of the Indian tribes of the North West Coast of America. Here, the Tlingit, the Haida and others lived for part of the year in large, permanent villages; they evolved elaborate class structures including hereditary chiefs, and they spent much time making and accumulating material goods which were highly valued. They were able to do this

Figure 18. Australian multi-purpose wooden dish (S. Goddard, Exeter City Museum)

partly because of the abundant and regular food supply that came to them every year: the salmon of the Pacific (Drucker 1963).

Occasionally one reads of other groups of hunters achieving semi-permanent large gatherings, and in many cases one finds that they are able to do so because they are living off fish and sea-foods. Radcliffe-Brown described the coastal Andaman Islanders as relatively settled, compared with inland groups. Eyre, in the mid 1840s, reported the following from Australia: 'At Lake Victoria ... I have seen 600 natives camped together, all of whom were living at the time upon fish procured from the lake, with the addition, perhaps, of the leaves of Mesembryanthemum ...' (quoted in Sahlins 1974, 25). Perhaps the salmon of the Dordogne and the carp of Lepenski Vir provided a similar stable food supply, and perhaps the Mesolithic shell-middens are all that remains of a like material abundance.

The impact on archaeology of recent developments in the ethnographic study of hunter-gatherer subsistence has already been felt to a certain extent, particularly on studies of the Mesolithic period in Europe. One of David Clarke's last papers dealt with the probable dependence of North West European groups on vegetable foods, and discussed the possible affluence of such a subsistence means (Clarke, D.L. 1976). Mellars has drawn extensively on ethnographic reports of forest-burning as a hunting technique, to reconstruct the possible effect of Mesolithic man on forest cover, and he has further suggested that by altering the environment hunters could begin to manage the herds of deer that were their prey (Mellars 1976). At somewhat greater length, Jochim has drawn up a complex predictive model of hunter-gatherer subsistence and settlement, based 'on explicit generalisations derived from numerous ethnographic studies' (Jochim 1976, xiii), which he has then applied to the later Mesolithic of the German Danube. All three prehistorians have to some extent rescued the Postglacial hunters from the view of the Mesolithic as a period of scarcity and 'poverty-gap' scavenging sandwiched between Upper Palaeolithic affluence and Neolithic security. And Jochim, in particular, has attempted to discover the constraints and potential that operated for one particular phase of the era, in one small region; his work is based on a very thorough exploration of certain aspects of hunter-gatherer subsistence and settlement, more detailed than anything attempted here and particularly useful for its analysis of seasonal variation in subsistence. What one hopes for are further studies that will provide not only a generalised picture of viable hunter-gatherer subsistence, but also some inkling, however slight, of the differences among the prehistoric situations. Some allowance will also have to be made for the short falls of a solely economic approach. Although scholars such as Higgs and Jarman have argued forcefully for the long term dominance of economic factors in human cultural development (Higgs 1975), the more one reads of other cultures' subsistence strategies the less this seems likely. Subsistence is determined not only by environment and level of technology, but by the whole gamut of culture, just as it in turn affects all other aspects. Jochim touches on this problem (Jochim 1976, 77-9), but his predictive model remains predominantly governed by environmental factors with some input from technology, and he quantifies the resources available to hunter-gatherers as if all cultures placed equal value on them, which is unlikely. There is one study that illustrates the difficulties involved here particularly well, namely Burch's work on the non-empirical factors that operate in northern Alaska to *prevent* the exploitation of considerable resources (Burch 1971). He shows how the presence of giant shrews and giant pike, wild babies and other malign or evil spirits deterred the Esquimo from hunting in the valleys or fishing in the lakes where these non-empirical beings dwelt. The relevance of this is *not* that wild babies should have been built into Jochim's model, nor that one should allow for giant shrews in the environment of Dolni Vestonice; it is to emphasise the need to view cultures as a whole as well as in their constituent elements of subsistence, settlement, religion, etc.

Farming: shifting agriculture

Despite lengthy discussion about the essential features of shifting agriculture, little has been agreed beyond Conklin's minimal definition of it as 'any continuing agricultural system in which impermanent clearings are cropped for shorter periods than they are fallowed' (Conklin 1957). Fortunately the essence of this definition, impermanent clearings, is an aspect that the archaeologist is familiar with, and able to study in many contexts. Interest has principally focussed on the early development and spread of farming, and it is here that studies of modern shifting agriculture seem most relevant. For while elements of the system do appear to have continued in use well into historic times in complex societies, there is now considerable evidence for more settled agriculture, in the form of permanent fields, from a range of prehistoric contexts (e.g. Bowen and Fowler 1978). In the following pages an attempt will be made to describe the farming techniques practised by several small-scale societies, most of which conform broadly to Conklin's definition. Certain recurring features emerge from this survey which, although not universal, are typical of the system, and their relevance to archaeological interpretation will therefore be considered.

Shifting agriculture, which is also termed slash-and-burn or shifting cultivation, is found from tropical to temperate latitudes, wherever there is sufficient land and water. The crops grown vary from one place to another, the most obvious difference being between roots or tubers and cereals. The other main difference is between those farmers who live through clearly defined seasonal changes in climate, and those who live in areas with little or no variation. The former must plant and harvest at set times of year. The latter may both plant and harvest at almost any time of year. However, in all places there is a sequence of events related to the growing cycle of the main crops, which starts with the choice of a suitable plot and ends with the harvest.

A farmer's first move must be to select a plot for cultivation, either from primary forest, or from an area once cultivated but since left fallow, perhaps for long enough for the tree-cover to have regenerated. Many factors will affect the choice of land: local rules of ownership and inheritance, or land use where there is no ownership; distance from home; safety from raiders (human and otherwise); omens and auguries, and so forth.

Sometimes agricultural considerations are important, as when the Bomagai-Angoiang of New Guinea look for a south-facing slope with a particular species of casuarina tree growing, for here both sunshine and soil will be good (Clarke, W.C. 1971). Farmers who are in a position to choose between virgin and secondary forest may, like the Iban, choose the former because it produces crops with less weeds, or, like the Kapauku, the latter to avoid felling heavy trees (Freeman 1970, Pospisil 1972). Yet the Yanomamo (Venezuela and Brazil) find primary forest easier to clear, so there is no consistency here (Chagnon 1968a). Obviously cultural factors affect people's choice quite strongly, and one cannot predict, from ecological considerations alone, what land will be farmed in a given area. But one can assume a sound knowledge of local soils and conditions, and the deliberate choice of land most suited to the crops, techniques and ideals of the farmer's culture (cf. Coles 1976, 60-1).

Having chosen a site, it must be cleared. No two groups set about this in exactly the same way, but there are some common features. Normally, undergrowth is cleared first, although in many cases the forest will have been exploited for its raw materials for some time before cultivation proper starts, and some large trees may have been removed to make canoes, houses etc. This is certainly true of Kapauku practices, and probably also for the Maori and the availability of raw materials may have affected the initial choice of plot. The undergrowth can usually be cleared using a knife, rather than an axe, and women and children work as well as men; much forestry work on undergrowth and saplings is in fact carried out with knives, not axes. Next the remaining large trees are felled, usually by the men alone, using stone or metal axes. This can be a dangerous task, and one that is often assigned considerable prestige value in contrast to the generally mundane range of agricultural operations. Hefty trees can also be felled by ringing or by fire, and a plot can be cleared in primary forest without the use of *any* stone or metal tools. Chagnon reports that the Yanomamo apparently achieved this in the days before traded metal reached them, unless they happened to find a stone axe-blade in the ground, abandoned centuries earlier – which amounts to a very confusing situation for the archaeologist (Chagnon 1968a). The likelihood of *no* tools being used is slight, but those that are in common use are not noticeably specialised nor obviously recognisable as farmer's tools.

The length of time taken over clearing operations is hard to record precisely: people stop to rest, to chat, to smoke, because it rains. However, Freeman reports that the Iban spend from one to two months on clearing each year. The Kapauku, who clear throughout the year as the need for more land arises, take 51 hours to clear about 1/10th hectare (1/4 acre) of its undergrowth, and a further 40 hours to fell the large trees. The Bomagai-Angoiang, fell a single large tree in 40 minutes, which includes the time taken to set up the felling platform. These figures are all taken from groups using metal axes. Some of them previously used stone blades, but the Kapauku at least say that although the new axes are more efficient, this does not mean they clear more land, simply that they have more time off. Several other felling operations have been recorded by ethnographers, and a range of experiments carried out (see Coles 1973 for examples) which so far only indicate that comparisons of felling times are notoriously difficult. So much depends on local variables such as the size, age and species of tree, the strength, sharpness and durability of the axe-blade and the skill and persistence of the axe-man. But even a cursory ethnographic survey shows that primitive farmers are capable of clearing all types of cover, from the dense, tough undergrowth of secondary forest to the massive trees of virgin land, in temperate and in tropical regions and hard as well as soft woods.

Cleared plots are far from neat and tidy. Fig. 19 shows a Bomagai-Angoiang clearing on a slope. One can see, amid the tangled mass of vegetation, that the tree-stumps stand quite high. This is common with shifting agriculture and all systems with impermanent fields, and it helps rapid regeneration as the tall stumps often survive firing, and sprout again as if coppiced. Regeneration is also fostered by incomplete clearing, some trees being left in full growth for economic, personal or religious reasons. The Bomagai leave pandanus trees because their leaves are useful, they leave one wild fern because its leaves provide shade and another because it is edible, and another tree, the Maoutia, is left because it provides fibre for string-making. The Kapauku never fell one particular species of cycad nor the banyan tree, for religious reasons; other trees may be consecrated by a shaman to evil spirits to keep them away from the village, and these trees must naturally be left alive. Wild bananas, lemons and limes are left for their fruit.

Once felled, the trees and undergrowth may be burnt, or some may first be used to provide timber for fencing the plot. Fencing is a hard but necessary task for many farmers. It takes a Kapauku up to 76 hours to fence the plot he cleared in 91 hours. The Bomagai-Angoiang, who build particularly solid-looking fences (Fig. 20), manage 50-60 feet a day. The main purpose of this fencing is to keep animals out, away from the growing crops. In New Guinea, both domestic and wild pigs are a menace, and in New Zealand, interestingly, plots were not commonly fenced before the introduction of pigs (Best 1925). Deer are partial to crops, especially cereals, and substantial fences are necessary to keep them out. Since deer and pigs, or their equivalents, are likely to have been at least as common in prehistoric times in North America and Eurasia, the necessity for fencing doubtless existed as it did for historically recorded clearances. For the archaeologist, fences could be one of the first signs of cultivation.

Fenced or not, the next task confronting the farmer is to burn his plot. Some farmers make quite careful preparation, spreading the

Figure 19. Bomagai-Angoiang fenced clearing, full of high tree stumps and living trees with potential for rapid regeneration after cultivation (W.C. Clarke)

Figure 20. Bomagai-Angoiang fence for field, built to protect crops from wild animals (W.C. Clark)

debris evenly over the whole plot, as do the Kapauku, or piling it up for bonfires. Others appear not to bother. It seems that those who do take steps to ensure a good, even burn, are aware of the advantages in terms of weed-killing and ash to fertilise the ground. The effects of burning have been discussed by Allan in *The African Husbandman* (Allan 1965) and it is clear from this, and from various experiments (e.g. Reynolds 1976), that burning helps greatly to reduce weeds, but whether or not the ash contributes much is debatable. However, given a well-cleared and evenly burned plot, shifting agriculture can give better yields for the amount of labour expended than other pre-industrial methods of farming.

Little other preparation is required before planting. There is no need to plough the ground, because there is no turf to break up with a forest-cleared plot. None of the farmers mentioned above use ploughs, nor do they dig over their whole plots by hand. The reason for this is that the ground under tree cover is usually quite soft, especially if it is in good condition, and a digging stick is the only tool necessary to make a hole for planting both cereals and other crops. The digging stick (Fig. 21) is in fact the farmers' chief tool. It

Figure 21. Polynesian digging-stick with carved footrest; contrast with the simple Kapauku stick illustrated in figure 24 (S. Goddard, Exeter City Museum)

is usually quite simple, no different from those of hunter-gatherers. In Polynesia, one finds some sticks with footrests, and with the end turned into rather more of a spade. The Maori examples are perhaps the most elaborate. In all cases, digging sticks are made of wood.

Planting is often carried out by women, and in a fairly haphazard fashion in among the stumps and unburnt logs. In most cases, the main crop is planted along with a variety of other types, even where people concentrate on cereals. Thus the Iban grow mustard, cucumbers, pumpkins, gourds, cassava, maize and pineapples alongside their rice. And in temperate North America, the Virginian Indians of the sixteenth century are reported to have grown an almost equal abundance of species, including maize, tobacco, beans, melons, and sunflowers (Harriot 1588).

But nothing can equal Clarke's description of a Bomagai-Angoiang garden, quoted here in a very much abbreviated form: 'To enter the garden is to wade into a green sea. To walk is to push through irregular waves of taro and *xanthosoma* (fern) and to step calf-deep in the cover of sweet potato vines. Overhead, manioc, bananas, sugar cane and *Saccharum edule* provide scattered shade ... In the next segment the *tu kaya* sweet potato is mixed with the *alepun* variety ... Next a 5-foot *wunum* variety of banana dominates the ground cover of *daier* sweet potato ... Then comes a *nunong* banana plant, followed by stumps of two trees felled to clear the plot. Beyond the stumps a spreading, vaselike cluster of sugar cane has yet to be tied together ... Beyond the pumpkin were several waist-high taro ... And so the garden continued with successive variation to its furthest edge' (Clarke 1971, 76-8).

Such lushness might not be found in temperate conditions, but the crops of shifting agriculturalists do tend to mirror in their variety the natural composition of the woodland they grow in. Moreover, not all the crops are for food. Many farmers, like the Virginians, grow tobacco for smoking or chewing; the Kapauku grow gourds for penis-sheaths; the Yanomamo grow cane for arrow shafts, cotton for hammocks and a variety of drugs and magical plants, including one which is said to cause women in enemy villages to suffer miscarriages.

If one thought only in terms of food-production, some of these plants would be termed weeds, which would be to mistake the whole character of primitive farming which by growing a range of commodities achieves a considerable degree of self-sufficiency. No group is entirely self-sufficient, but as suggested above, both hunters and primitive farmers are rather more so than members of more complex societies, and the farmers, being more sedentary than the hunters, have less opportunity to find all their non-food resources in the wild.

The next important stage in the sequence of cultivation is one which, like fencing, is not often referred to in the archaeological literature. It is weeding. Weeding is a slow, dull and tiresome process. It may have to be done again and again, and more often than not, it is delegated to the women (cf. gathering). For example, both the Iban and the Kapauku consider that weeding is women's work, and a man will do his utmost to persuade some female to carry out the task for him, if he has no wife. Iban women sometimes lessen the chore by joining forces, so they can talk as they weed each other's crops.

However dull, weeding is vital for a good harvest, especially where land has been cultivated for more than one year, or was cleared from secondary forest. The importance of weeding becomes clear when one finds that farmers may limit the amount of land according to the weeding forces available to them, and not to the difficulty of clearing the land, nor the number of people to feed, nor some other apparently obvious reason. Freeman first drew attention to this, in his study of Iban agriculture (Freeman 1955) and since then several anthropologists have noted the same phenomenon. One consequence, if for cultural reasons weeding is done by women only, is that a man can only increase the land he farms according to the number of women who will work for him – an argument for polygamy? Pospisil has argued that weeding can even affect a man's political career: to be successful he must have many pigs, pigs require food, and to produce this surplus food the man will need more wives to carry out the extra weeding involved.

Perhaps the other factors that influence the amount of land cultivated should be mentioned here. It seems that farmers are not limited to what they can clear so much as to what they can, or want, to look after. Maximum production is not always the desired goal. It is likely that the number of people and animals to be fed will be considered, although some doubt has been cast on this (Sahlins 1974). A surplus may be desired: the Iban grow extra rice for trade and the Kapauku extra sweet potatoes to raise pigs, and for feasts. Elsewhere, grain may be grown for brewing as well as for eating. Given these variations, and variations in crops and soils and climate, it is not possible to produce any realistic figures for the average amount of land required per person.

To go back to the problem of weeds, it has a further consequence. Each successive year of cropping sees more and more weeds in a plot, perhaps so many that the land is abandoned. There is no question of soil exhaustion, it is just that the weeds have become so bad that it is less troublesome to clear a new plot.

In due course, the crops will be ready for harvesting. Here the nature of both crop and climate will affect procedure. Cereal crops are normally harvested during a well-defined and quite short season, whereas roots and tubers grown in an even climate may be harvested all year round as they are needed, and even in temperate regions with marked seasons they can have an extended harvesting period. Not surprisingly, one finds rather more ceremony and ritual accompanying the short and clear-cut harvest than the extended or continual seasons. Rather than attempting to describe the many variations in harvesting, two contrasting situations will be outlined: the daily routine of the Kapauku and the seasonal event of the Iban.

A Kapauku woman digs up sweet potatoes daily, collecting as much as her family needs that day. The growing plants are left in the ground, and a plot may be dug over three or more times before the pigs are let in to finish the harvest. Taro and manioc are also dug as they ripen, and as they are required, and green vegetables are collected in the same way. As Pospisil emphasises, the Kapauku gather their produce in much the same way and with as little ceremony as one would treat a perpetual kitchen garden.

The Iban harvest begins, in a sense, at the time of planting, for different strains of rice are sown with the sacred *padi pun* at the centre, and quick-maturing varieties on the outside. Reaping starts at the edge and moves slowly towards the central sacred rice which is brought home last. Numerous rituals accompany each stage, with particularly important ones at the beginning of the main harvest and during the reaping and carrying in of the *padi pun*. Freeman's description conveys strongly the ceremonial, festive and above all religious atmosphere of the Iban rice harvest (Freeman 1970, 202-15; cf Dogon agricultural ritual, discussed briefly below, p. 229).

After harvest, storage. Obviously those farmers who can gather their produce as it is required for eating, do not need any storage facilities. But where the harvest is an annual event, which is normally the case with cereals and in temperate climates, both the seed crop and that which is to be eaten must be kept safe from vermin, rain and raiders. There are many ways of solving the problem, from the underground storage pits of the Maori (Fox 1976), to the elaborate mud-built granaries of the Azande (Evans-Pritchard 1971). Some peoples store grain in pots and jars or baskets, and the Iban keep their rice in bark-bins in the rafters of their longhouses, practices that will leave less obvious archaeological trace than pits or granaries.

The production team engaged in these agricultural operations is often the family. 'Family', however, covers a number of different arrangements and one finds production organised on anything from a village to an individual basis. The plots of the Yanomamo, for example, are all concentrated together in one village 'garden'. Anything relating to the garden as a whole, such as choosing and setting up a new site, is carried out by the men of the village together. But within the garden, each man works his own plot independently, helped by his wife or wives. The Iban unit of production is the *bilek* family, a small group of about 3-7 closely related people. Each *bilek* family works independently of all the others in the longhouse, unless it is a question of firing adjacent plots. The Bomagai-Angoiang appear to work more on a partnership basis. A person may have several plots, each cleared and cultivated with the help of different male and female partners. The partners are not necessarily closely related, and although man and wife will work together, both will also work separately with other people. Huron men cleared the fields, but after this agricultural work was the women's responsibility, except for the growing of tobacco which was cultivated by the men (Trigger 1969).

Movement

The aspects of primitive cultivation which are probably of most interest to archaeologists are the way land is used, and the movement of farmers into new areas. There are two sorts of movements involved in shifting agriculture, which may be termed local and pioneering. Local movement takes place within a home territory, whereas pioneering shifting agriculture entails (as the name implies) the colonisation of new land. Relevant ethnographic studies include several of those already mentioned, such as Chagnon's *Yanomamo*, Freeman's *Report on the Iban* and *Iban Agriculture*, Trigger's *The Huron*, and Clarke and Pospisil's work in New Guinea. Chagnon and Freeman are perhaps the most useful, as they discuss long term pioneering movements as well as local shifts of field. Local movement can take place within a long-term pioneering trend.

Local movement

Local movement can be relatively haphazard. The Yanomamo simply abandon one end of their plots and take in new land at the other, front end as required; the rate of movement is determined largely by the growth of weeds and scrub at the rear end. Thus, slowly, the whole village garden creeps forward.

The Kapauku system is more organised, and varies according to the local environment. On the steep hill slopes surrounding the valley in which they live, where they grow mostly sweet potato, one year of cropping is followed by 7-8 years fallow. In the valley, mixed and single crops are alternated, then the plot may be cultivated for up to 8 years, using fertilisers. When the farmer thinks that the soil has got 'cold', the plot is abandoned, for about 8 years, but the actual length of fallow varies because the land may be needed earlier, or the farmer's memory is at fault. Sometimes the Kapauku judge whether or not a plot is ready for recultivation by the amount and height of secondary growth it carries.

The various local cycles of the Iban are well-defined. Plots cleared in virgin forest are cultivated for two years in succession and then left for between 10 and 20 years. Plots cleared in secondary forest are cropped once only, and left for at least 15 years if possible. Occasionally the land is used more heavily, but then the lengthy fallow of 15-20 years is all the more necessary, for overcropping at this stage would destroy the land for any future cultivation. This system requires a large acreage, and the Iban find that within five years or so they have used all the land within easy reach of their long-house. The settlement then splits into several smaller units, consisting of 3-4 *bilek* families, who build subsidiary longhouses or *dampas* in adjacent primary forest, moving to a new site every 5 or 6 years. Contact is maintained with the original longhouse and after about 20 years, when the land around it has sufficiently regenerated, the Iban leave the *dampas* and return to live in the longhouse for a few years.

The Huron, who were among the most northerly of North American cultivators, would take several years to clear land before using it to grow crops. The intake of new fields seems to have been a continual process and every ten to twenty years a village would be moved a few miles, to an area of fresh woodland where fuel, building materials and the land for new fields would once again be available in plenty. The new village sites were kept within the general region of Huron settlement, probably re-using old locations though this was not done on any systematic basis, and Trigger stresses that 'a move into virgin territory would spell disaster for any sizable group' (Trigger 1969, 27-8).

Long-term movement

The Iban, by contrast, prize virgin forest very highly for a variety of reasons, including the timber and game it holds, the weed-free land it yields and the prestige and wealth to be gained in felling it. The Iban have therefore a certain incentive not to return to their original longhouse, but to keep moving outwards into new territory. This results in long-term movement, which may be described as pioneering shifting agriculture.

In many ways, the whole of Iban culture is oriented towards the outward movement, encouraging it so successfully that the rate of migration has been calculated at 50-100 miles per generation, and a man may die 250 miles from his birthplace (Morgan 1968). The Iban, who have not surprisingly been dubbed '*mangeurs de bois*', moved into their present area of Sarawak in the 1800s. By the beginning of this century settlement was quite dense, and migration had proceeded rapidly, although the rate fluctuated in response to political changes, and not, as one might have expected, to population growth or soil exhaustion.

The pioneering nature of Iban agriculture, their urge to move outwards, may also be found among the Yanomamo, although for rather different reasons. The Yanomamo move because they have to, to escape from their enemies. They live in a state of chronic intervillage warfare, and settlements are continually threatened by raiding parties. For a while, a village may defend itself by making alliances with nearby settlements, and by encouraging adult men to settle, thereby increasing its fighting strength. But either the allies quarrel, or dissension breaks out within the village, and then the only way to escape hostilities is to move. Fig. 22, Chagnon's map of recent moves, shows the apparently random trajectory of one village. However, there is some method behind the moves, which take the village either close to an ally or out of reach of an enemy, and always to a good defensive site not too close to a main river. In only one case

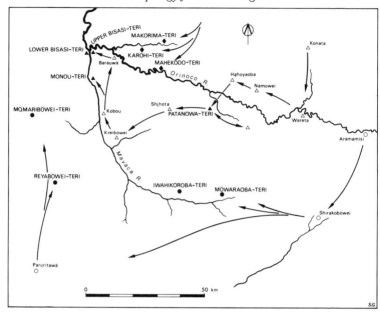

Figure 22. Yanomamo village moves. The settlement which started at Konata
(open triangle) arrived at Lower Bisasi-teri some seventy-five years later. Reasons
for moving: from Konata to Wareta away from enemies to take refuge with allies,
from Wareta away from new enemies; from Namowei away from old enemies who
had harassed Konata; from Hahoyaoba because of poor soil in the area; at
Patanowa the village split, and one part remains, the other settled first at Shihota
and then moved to Kreibowei to escape Patanowa hostilities. Here, southern
villagers massacred them at a feast and the survivors fled to Mahekodo, over the
Orinoco, to live with allies whilst they established new gardens at Kobou. On
leaving Kobou the group split again, some settling at Monou-teri where they lived
for over a decade but suffered increasing Patanowa harrassment. The others
settled first at Barauwa and then split yet again to settle either side of the river at
Upper and Lower Bisasi-teri (Open symbols indicate abandoned villages, filled
symbols inhabited villages. Chagnon 1968)

did the village move because of soil exhaustion, and that because a
hurried retreat had led the farmers to settle in a particularly poor
area.

   What the map does not show is that in the long run, the
Yanomamo villages gradually colonise new areas of forest. Chagnon
comments that only villages on the periphery of the Yanomamo
tribal area move into new territory, acting as pioneers who push the
frontier forwards. Villages in the interior, with no frontier, move like
the Huron to gaps within the established tribal area. They never

pass beyond the outer settlements to become pioneers themselves. Chagnon suggests that this distinction may be found in all pioneering situations (Chagnon 1968b).

There are several points here of interest to the archaeologist. First, neither the Iban nor the Yanomamo move into new territory because of soil exhaustion, rather they move for social and political reasons. Secondly, the difference which Chagnon notes between central, relatively static settlements and peripheral highly mobile settlements may be of interest, and has certain political repercussions to be discussed later. Thirdly, a point which has not been discussed in detail so far, it appears that the pioneering cultivators come from those farming populations with the *lowest* population density, not the highest as one might expect. Very roughly speaking, the Yanomamo density is about one person to every 12 sq km, the Iban about 37 for the same area, and in New Guinea 200 people or more (New Guinea population densities vary enormously: see Table 3, p. 128).

This suggests that pioneering shifting agriculture is a phenomenon of the early stages of colonisation, that farmers move into new areas before infilling settled territory to capacity, and that the ready availability of fresh land fosters certain cultural developments which encourage migration. On the other hand, if surrounding territories are already occupied, whether by other villages of the same tribe as for the central Yanomamo, or by other similar tribes as for the Huron, cultural developments would appear to discourage migration though local movement continues. The results of this pioneering agriculture amount to the very rapid colonisation of large areas by a scattered, sparse population that lives in small and fairly temporary settlements. This is followed by infilling, and the emergence of larger, more stable villages as the frontier recedes.

Archaeological implications

The archaeological implications of the above are considerable. First, those of the local cycle of cultivation will be discussed, as they can affect long-term events. One can distinguish various factors governing the choice of land for cultivation, which may provide some clue to the interpretation of land use in the past. For example, it is clear that primitive farmers are aware of differences in the soil, and may use this knowledge to select the best soils for their crops. It is also clear that even the densest and heaviest forest can be felled. This suggests that the early Eurasian farmers could indeed have deliberately selected lighter soils for cultivation, as has so often been suggested, but it is unlikely that they were limited to these by their technology.

Much of the archaeological evidence for early farming in temperate zones comes from pollen diagrams. The ethnographic literature shows that when farmers move to a new area and have ample land at their disposal, clearings tend to be small and scattered and incomplete. Rapid regeneration is favoured by the nearness of the forest and the trees and stumps left growing in the so-called clearing. One wonders to what extent such very temporary and slight openings in the forest cover could be detected by pollen analysis, and whether in fact what we take to be the earliest evidence for agriculture does not come from a later, more intensive stage of cultivation. Several archaeologists and palaeobotanists have discussed this problem, and recent trends towards more sophisticated methods of pollen analysis may offer more scope for discovering localised clearances within a generally settled area (e.g. Turner 1975, Beckett and Hibbert 1978). Incidentally, given an archaeological timespan, land may be settled, cultivated and abandoned, and then resettled centuries later, by when regeneration is so complete that the newcomers, like the Yanomamo, are effectively dealing with virgin forest.

There may be other signs of agriculture, apart from the pollen evidence. One suspects that in any European or North American situation wild animals competed with farmers for their crops, and so it is likely that fields were protected with fences or hedges. This is the more likely in Europe, perhaps, where domestic cattle, sheep, goats and pigs added to the hazards. Because fencing is quite hard work, people may clear two or three adjacent plots, with shared boundaries. This is done by the Kapauku Papuans, and leads to a scattering of clustered fields in the area around a village (Fig. 23). Similar field patterns are well-known from prehistoric contexts, although they are generally thought to belong to the later stages of prehistory and more settled systems of agriculture (Bowen and Fowler 1978). Whatever their date, it may be suggested that they indicate not only agriculture, but also the presence of animals that need to be kept out of growing crops.

The technology of shifting agriculture can be very simple, and

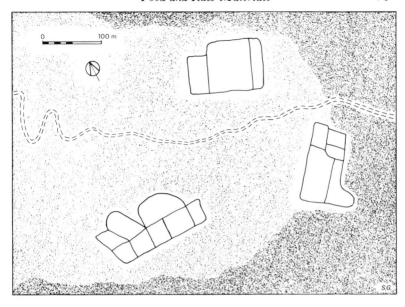

Figure 23. Kapauku fields. Clusters of fields, cleared in secondary forest and encroaching on the primary forest in a mountainous valley. The shared boundaries of the adjacent fields have cut down considerably on the labour of fencing. A path runs through the valley up into the uncleared forest (Pospisil 1972)

there may be nothing in the tool-kits of farmers to distinguish them from hunters. The latter, as we have seen, use stone axes and digging sticks; the former have bows and arrows, for they also hunt and fight. Farmers probably have more possessions than hunters, and they are more likely to use pottery, because they lead a more settled life. But the dividing line between the material equipment associated with the two means of subsistence can be very hard to draw. Fig. 24, the equipment of the Kapauku, when compared with the hunter's tools and weapons illustrated in Figs 9 to 15, demonstrates the overlap in the range of artefact types.

It also shows that the farmer's hunting equipment can be as diverse as any hunter's, suggesting that wild animals remain important to subsistence. In regions where wild animals are still present, primitive cultivators hunt to obtain meat, to eradicate pests and to acquire desired raw materials such as boars' tusks and birds' feathers for decoration. And they hunt because success brings

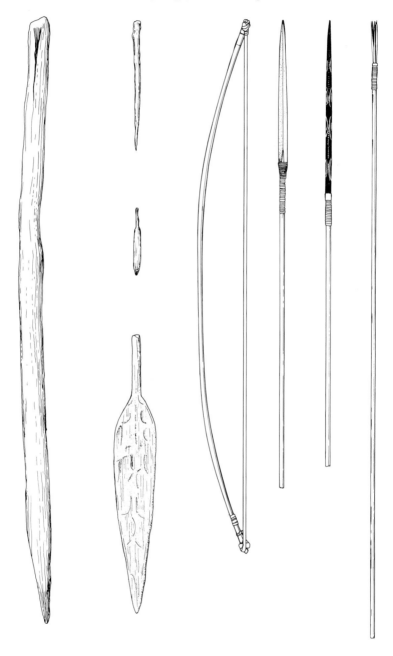

prestige. The suggestion that prehistoric farmers reverted to hunting only in times of hardship does not seem very plausible in the face of the ethnographic evidence that hunting is a normal pursuit of many farmers; and while fluctuating percentages of wild animal bones could plausibly reflect the economic situation, a range of other cultural factors such as those mentioned above will probably also have influenced matters. Moreover, there is ample evidence from the New World of the viability of hunting plus farming plus gathering, as a subsistence base (e.g. the Huron and Iroquois in North America, the Yanomamo in South America) and we should include the Hunter-Farmer in the spectrum of possible prehistoric economies. Admittedly, the New World situation is strongly influenced by the paucity of domestic animals, especially domestic herd animals which could yield food and raw materials alive as well as dead, but despite this one should consider the possible evidence for hunter-farmers in early Eurasian and African contexts because it is often a *pioneering* mode of subsistence, in contrast to mixed farming which appears to flourish largely in settled contexts. (For hunter-farmers see Trigger 1969; and references in Rogers 1970a and 1970b.)

All told, primitive farming can be quite diversified, and this characteristic certainly applies to the crops grown. Even where production is concentrated on obtaining a surplus of a single main crop for trade, other plants are grown. Some of these are weeds from a strictly economic point of view, but they have uses other than food, ranging from medicines to magic. Other plants have unexpected food-values, and it is these that the archaeologist may fail to recognise. After all, cultural ideas about which plants are edible vary almost as much as ideas about animals, and when one realises that the Kapauku grow tomatoes mainly because they are decorative, and the Elizabethans in England grew that most pernicious of weeds, ground elder, for food, one can appreciate the danger of preconceived ideas.

Soil exhaustion has already been mentioned several times, and it should be clear by now that in many primitive farming situations, the question of exhausted land simply does not arise. Land is

Figure 24. Kapauku artefacts. Left to right: wooden planting stick; root-crop harvesting stick, wood with flint inset in tip; wooden weeding stick; wooden earth-knife for digging ditches; palmwood bow with rattan string; arrows for hunting wild-boar, for use in warfare and for hunting small game, all with hardwood or bamboo heads. The planting stick is *c.* 2m long (Pospisil 1972)

abandoned before exhaustion, very likely because of weeds, or for political and ideological reasons. In the long term this has beneficial results, for it ensures that the land is not destroyed for future use. It also means, naturally, that more land is needed by any one group of people than if a given area were exploited more intensively. In archaeological terms, these factors probably contributed to the rapid spread of farming cultures, to a fairly sparse population in the initial phases of settlement and to relatively little alteration of the landscape while *pioneering* shifting agriculture was practised. It follows that palaeobotanical evidence for forest clearance probably indicates that the pioneering phase is passed, and farmers are either engaged in localised shifting agriculture which involves the fairly regular re-use and regeneration of the forest, or they may be even more settled and beginning to fossilise the landscape in a pattern of crop-fields, pasture, managed woodland and forest stands that will endure with little drastic change for generations.

The study of shifting agriculture prompts one question of particular interest to the prehistorian. Can the ethnographic evidence suggest why farming developed in the first place, and why it replaced hunting and gathering as a means of subsistence in many parts of the world? After all, it was argued earlier (p. 30) that hunting represents a singularly successful adaptation on the part of man, enabling him to live in more varied environments than the farmer, and probably working less hard for his living. On the other hand, it was seen that hunting entailed certain limitations such as few possessions and low population density. With farming, a more settled life is both possible and necessary. As a result, people can accumulate more belongings, since they no longer have to be able to carry them all at once. For the same reason they can have children more often. In the long run, this means that a farming family will probably rear more children, than a hunting one, and so one has more potential farmers than hunters (Orme 1977). Admittedly, farmers are more dependent on the land than hunters, and cannot recover so quickly from disasters. But, given an historical perspective, one must allow that whatever the affluence of the hunter, where farming is possible it supports more people and more possessions in more permanent settlements and therefore may well have seemed desirable. What made it first *possible* is another matter, and one that probably depended as much on social as on technological and economic developments (see Chapters 2 and 3).

Farmers' animals and mixed farming

So far, very little has been said about animal husbandry, except in the negative sense of noting that many farmers who practise shifting cultivation keep few, if any, domestic animals (other than dogs, that is). Those who do keep animals often do so for reasons other than their food value, and even where the animals supply scarce protein their cultural value may be primarily prestigious or ritual rather than dietetic. If small-scale societies do depend for subsistence on animals, then they are more likely to be pastoralists than cultivators; where equal importance is allowed to both plant and animal husbandry, the farmers are probably relatively settled in a permanent cultivated landscape, and quite possibly linked to some more complex economic system. A few examples will serve to illustrate these variations.

The Iban keep chickens, which they do not eat but which need feeding. Both the birds and their eggs are used as ritual offerings, some birds are kept for cockfighting, and a large flock is to a certain extent a demonstration of wealth.

Pigs in Melanesia are certainly a demonstration of wealth, and we have already noted the prestige and political power that their ownership can bring to Kapauku men. Pospisil discusses the role of pigs in Kapauku society at some length (Pospisil 1972), and in *Pigs for the Ancestors*, Rappaport presents an analysis of another New Guinea culture where pigs are essential to ritual life, and ritual serves in the long run as a mechanism to keep man in balance with his environment. Moreover, the Tsembaga, the people in question, do eat all their pigs that are ritually killed, and Rappaport stresses the importance of pork in Tsembaga diet (Rappaport 1968).

Likewise, the Nuer eat all the cattle that they sacrifice. These cattle-herders from the Sudan are more properly described as pastoralists than farmers, in terms of their cultural values and their own appreciation of their economy, but they do grow crops in a system of shifting cultivation, and also fish. Evans-Pritchard discussed at some length the Nuers' preoccupation with their cattle. 'The Nuer ... not only depend on cattle for most of life's necessities but they have the herdsman's outlook on the world. Cattle are their dearest possession and they gladly risk their lives to defend their herds or pillage those of their neighbours. Most of their social activities concern cattle and *cherchez la vache* is the best advice that can be given to those who desire to understand Nuer behaviour'

(Evans-Pritchard 1940, 15). Cattle provide milk and cheese and blood, and although not killed for meat, sacrificed animals and those which die naturally are eaten. They are also a most important source of raw materials; 'Their skins are used for beds, trays, for carrying fuel, cord for tethering and other purposes, flails, leather collars for oxen, and for the tympana of drums. They are employed in the manufacture of pipes, spears, shields, snuff-containers, etc. The scrota of bulls are made into bags to contain tobacco, spoons and other small objects. Tail-hairs are made into tassels ... Bones are used for ... armlets, and as beaters, pounders and scrapers. Their horns are cut into spoons, and are used in the construction of harpoons.

'Their dung is used for fuel and for plastering walls ... and to protect wounds. The ashes of burnt dung are rubbed over men's bodies, and are used to dye and straighten hair, as a mouth wash and tooth powder ... and for various ritual purposes. Their urine is used in churning and cheese-making ... tanning ... and bathing' (Evans-Pritchard 1940, 29-30).

The social uses of Nuer cattle include sacrifices for religious purposes and at times of illness, sacrifices which amount to fines for quarrelling or otherwise breaking the law, and the giving of cattle as marriage payment. There is almost no aspect of their life, from the mundane to the sublime, where the Nuer do not depend on their cattle.

If, culturally, the ritual, prestigious and social aspects of cattle herding are stressed by the Nuer, there is little doubt that they also form an essential element in the mixed economy of crop-growing, fishing and herding. Evans-Pritchard emphasised that without the food provided by their cattle, the Nuer would not survive in their present environment – and this is a situation common to pastoralism where subsistence in a harsh environment is made possible by herd animals (see Chapter 6). In this sense, as well as in their own eyes, the Nuer are more pastoralists than farmers.

Where one does find mixed farming, in the sense of an economy where people grow crops and keep a *few* animals of various sorts, the farmers belong to more complex societies. To take one example, the Hausa of West Africa live under a sophisticated urban administration, by farming and engaging in a wide range of part-time specialist occupations, and by trading extensively with the pastoral Fulani who rule them. They grow guinea corn, millet, maize, rice, various rootcrops and vegetables such as onions and peppers, and indigo. They manure and fallow their fields, and practice a system of crop rotation; some of the manure comes from the herds of the Fulani and some from their own few cattle, horses, donkeys, goats, sheep and poultry (Smith, M.G. 1965, 124-5).

To the European archaeologist, Hausa economy at first glance resembles that of the Middle Ages, or maybe parts of the Roman Empire, rather than anything earlier. We generally assume that the farmers of prehistoric cultures practised simple shifting agriculture for several millennia, and perhaps developed a more settled régime by the 1st millennium b.c. But many of the indications in the archaeological record, when interpreted against the background of an ethnographic survey of shifting agriculture, are for something more settled and varied. This is a problem that involves more than an understanding of subsistence bases, and one that we shall return to in the final chapter.

2. Settlement

Together with food, shelter is one of the basic requirements of man's life; like food, it is relatively well-documented archaeologically. Man alters the local environment, builds structures to make shelter, and concentrates his activities in and around the shelter area, thereby creating a place to live, a settlement. Archaeologically, it is the physical aspects of settlement such as walls and doors which are best documented, whereas the ethnographic record tends to emphasise social aspects such as residence patterns on marriage. As a result both sides have been known to deny any useful rapprochement, although the dichotomy of interest is perhaps more apparent than real. In practice archaeologists do speculate about the social organisation of past settlements (sometimes to an alarming degree), and ethnographers acknowledge the possibility of changing settlement habits, which can be traced by archaeological fieldwork when no other documentation exists (Green, Haselgrove and Spriggs 1978; Lauer 1970). From the archaeologists' point of view, many of the physical aspects of modern primitive settlement are neglected, or dismissed in a brief but tantalising sentence; yet there is a great deal of useful information available in the ethnographic literature. Several recent publications suggest a trend towards more detailed recording of the material evidence relating to settlement, together with some discussion of the possible correlations between structures and living arrangements. The following pages attempt to show what sort of ethnographical information about settlement may be useful to archaeologists; this survey is deliberately incomplete, for its aim is not to be comprehensive but to demonstrate the *potential* value of ethnography to archaeology.

Structures

In almost every human society people use some sort of shelter, at least for part of the year. The structures built by non-industrial societies for this purpose are varied, and what follows is only a cursory glance at the known diversity, which ranges from the flimsy temporary windbreaks of the Yamana to the massive adobe conglomerations of the Pueblo Indians.

Temporary shelters

Temporary shelters are built by hunter-gatherers in the normal course of their lives, and occasionally by farmers as well. The purpose of the shelter is the same in either case: protection against sun, wind, rain or cold. The materials used to build such a shelter depend on the immediate local environment. Thus the Hadza, living in an area of desert scrub, use branches and grass, while the Esquimo, to cite perhaps the most obvious example of all, use snow to build shelter against the Arctic winter. Neither takes long to gather the materials and build their hut: an igloo may take under an hour and a half to make, using a snow-knife. The use of snow is, however, exceptional, and most of the more temporary primitive shelters consist of branches, grass and leaves fashioned into windbreaks, lean-tos and beehive-shaped huts (Fig. 25).

Where nomadic and semi-nomadic people live in an environment affected by seasonal change, they frequently build different types of shelter at different times of year. Many of the North American Indians vary the size, the fabric and the style of their huts throughout the year, as was recorded of the Athapaskans. Donald Thomson's article 'The seasonal factor in human culture' (Thomson 1939) demonstrated the archaeological significance of such variation: basing his argument on a description of the Wik Monkan of northeastern Australia, Thomson showed that several different kinds of shelter were used, which varied according to the weather, the number of people gathered together, and the locality being exploited (Fig. 26). The diversity was such that an archaeologist might deduce the presence of two or more cultures. We will return to this important point again later.

In whatever manner a temporary shelter is built, the potential archaeological traces are likely to be slight. In some cases, stakes are pushed into the ground, and may leave recognisable holes. In others, a ring of stones acts both as a support for the uprights and as weight for the covering, and these stones may remain undisturbed when the shelter is abandoned. But with the majority of temporary shelters,

Figure 25. Temporary shelters. (a) camp of a Kayan hunting party, Sarawak (Royal Anthropological Institute. (b) Lake Pomo fishing camp, California (Curtis)

Figure 26. Wik Monkan shelters. Left to right: sleeping platform covered with bark, smoke fire below, used early *ontjɪn* (see Table 2) after rains, for protection against mosquitoes; large house covered with bark strips, used in savannah forest in wet season; simple wet-season shelter of bark strips over a ridge-pole; large wet-season house covered with bark strips over a sapling frame, up to 18' diameter; windbreak, used on beaches and sandbanks; shade-shelter used in hot weather; small wet-season house of bark-strips on sapling frame; fork to hang bags, food, etc. out of reach of dogs, and a rest for spears and firesticks (Thomson 1939)

evidence is likely to consist only of accumulated debris, a compacted floor, sleeping hollows and perhaps a hearth.

Tents are a form of temporary shelter, with certain distinctive characteristics that warrant their being discussed separately. Some tent types are illustrated in Fig. 27, giving an indication of the

Figure 27. Tents. Left to right: Bedouin tent, covering of strips of goat-hair cloth, wooden poles, guy ropes and metal pegs; Netsilik tent, sealskin covering and thongs, one pole, stones to secure covering; Kirghiz yurt, felt covering on willow framework tied with leather thongs and horsehair rope, inside lining of woollen rugs and reed matting; Blackfoot tipi, buffalo hide covering on wooden poles

variation in size, ground plan and use of poles from one group to another. However, all the tents have one or more poles, a stretched covering, and weights to hold the cover down. They are used by groups who move fairly often, as for example the Athapaskan during the late winter, which is their season of greatest mobility. One does not find sedentary peoples living in tents, for they are a response to the need for shelter coupled with mobility, particularly where there is much wind or rain. The tent's advantage lies in the ease with which it is erected and dismantled; its main disadvantage is that it must be carried from site to site. Weights are often left behind, and only the poles and the covering taken to the new site. These are still heavy: a Blackfoot tipi was made of 40 bison skins. It is hardly surprising, therefore, to find that most primitive peoples who live in tents have some means of transport. The Plains Indians have possessed horses since the time of European contact and had previously developed the travois to cope with heavy loads when they only had man- or woman-power. More northern groups, such as the Lapps and the Yukaghir of the Old World, use domestic dogs and reindeer both to carry packs and to pull sleds. The people who rely most heavily on tents are the pastoral nomads, who normally have ample means of transport, whether it is provided by the camels of the Tuareg or the horses and cattle of the Kazak.

More solid temporary shelters, akin to houses rather than windbreaks, are ethnographically well-documented. Such structures may be used for several weeks or months, and possible re-used from one year to the next. Their relative permanence is due partly to the use of more solid materials than for the shelters described above, and partly to a greater structural complexity: in other words, they are more carefully built. For example, both the Mbuti and the Andaman Islanders live in a hot, forested environment. The Mbuti's slight hut of leaves and branches is not intended to last beyond the few weeks any one settlement is occupied. The Andaman Islanders lead a more settled life, staying at one site for several months at a stretch, and returning to their main camp for several years in succession, and they build accordingly. Although in a sense no more than elaborate lean-tos, their huts are well made; the uprights are solid poles, more poles are used as cross-ties, and the roof is made of waterproof palm-leaf matting (Fig. 28). The Andaman Islanders keep their huts repaired, even when they have temporarily abandoned them, to exploit other sections of their territory, and one hut will have a life of several years.

Figure 28. Andaman shelter, built of bamboo poles and palm leaf-matting, to last for several years (Radcliffe Brown 1922)

The Andamanese are not exceptional as hunter-gatherers in building relatively substantial shelters. The Ainu of Hokkaido built an intricate house of bamboo poles and reed matting: the Alaskan Esquimo made half-sunken wooden houses with an earth-covering, that sheltered them for several years in succession (Fig. 29).

Figure 29. Hunter-gatherer houses. Two relatively substantial and permanent buildings: (a) Ainu house, built of thick planks and bamboo poles with matting and rush walls and a thatched roof, bound with cord and bark strips. (Starr). (b) an Alaskan Esquimo village on Hooper Bay, photographed in the early 1900s, houses built of wood and earth (Curtis)

Figure 30. Permanent structures. (a) the frame of a Kwakiutl house. The walls and roof are made of planks which can be used temporarily for other structures, and brought back to the main house when it is re-occupied (cf. figure 31). (b) terraced houses of the Zuni, south-western North America (Curtis)

Just as hunter-gatherers may live in relatively permanent houses, so farmers may at times build temporary seasonal shelters. The Nuer need shelter while living in their summer cattle camps, and make windbreaks and beehive-shaped huts, the hunter-farmers of North America built seasonal shelters, as well as permanent dwellings, and examples may also be found among the farmers of South America and New Guinea.

Permanent structures

The above descriptions indicate the variety and adaptability of primitive man's dwellings, but the full sophistication of his building techniques is only revealed when one examines more solid and permanent structures. Then, the complexity of the hunters' and the farmers' architecture appears as great as that of industrialised man. Consider, for example, the great timber halls of the Kwakiutl and Zuni conglomerations (Fig. 30).

Where wood is abundant, both log-built and plank-built houses are common. They are usually rectangular or square in plan, with vertical sides and a pitched roof, a style which is probably dictated by the materials used. Fig. 31 illustrates a large plank-built house of the Nootka, and Fig. 32 a smaller Kapauku plank-house. Planks are normally split, rather than sawn, from a tree trunk, and may be held together by binding and wedging, by sewing, or by jointing. The roofs of plank-houses are normally carried directly on the walls, and if the span is large there may be interior supporting posts. Roofing materials vary: for example the North West Coast Indians use planks and shingles, whereas the Kapauku, with equal access to wood, make a thatch of pandanus leaves.

If a house is to be built of small timbers, rather than planks or heavy logs, it is likely to be round rather than having straight sides. If the timbers are pliant, the roof and wall may be continuous, giving an appearance not unlike the classic African hut of story-books. Sometimes even poles are unavailable, as for the Nuer, who use considerable ingenuity to get round the limitations imposed by their environment. They bind millet stalks together to make 'poles' for the framework of their huts, and they build up the walls with a daub-like mixture of mud, dung and ash; the roof is covered with leaves.

Stone is not a common building material among modern hunters and primitive farmers – that is to say, a few stones may be used as

Figure 31. Nootka house interior, north-west coast of America as seen by John Webber; artist to Cook's 1778 expeditions (redrawn by S. Goddard). Compare with figure 30, Curtis' photograph taken over 100 years later of the framework of a similar structure

Figure 32. Kapauku house, New Guinea, built of planks and posts (Pospisil 1972)

weights or foundations – but walls are rarely built entirely of stone. Nomadic pastoralists, and some farmers with a marked pastoral bias make greater use of it, for their permanent structures; this suggests a possible correlation between the use of stone as a building material and environment and means of subsistence. Where wood is abundant it seems to be used in preference to stone, for permanent as well as for temporary structures, and in an abundantly wooded environment pastoralism is unlikely; where wood is scarce, it is unlikely that slash-and-burn agriculture will be practicable, and hunting or more sophisticated mixed farming with manuring and irrigation of fields, or pastoralism, are possible subsistence strategies; people living by these means may build in stone if available, and if they want permanence. The barren and stony environments of the western fringes of Europe can provide many examples of undressed stone structures, from the prehistoric villages of the Orkneys and Shetlands to some still inhabited dwellings of western Scotland and Ireland, all built of dry-stone walling. An example from another equally stony environment, that of Luristan, will be examined in more detail below, but here let us note a few common details. Walls are generally very thick, enclosing a more or less rectangular space, with a narrow roofspan due to the shortage of timber. The roofing material may be straw or reed thatch, heather, or turf. Any increase in size is dependent on solid internal sub-division of stone, to support the roof, creating separate rooms. In a timber-built house, such sub-divisions are not always necessary, as extra posts can be set up which do not necessarily form partitions. Unless one starts erecting classical columns, the span of stone houses can only be increased by adding walls of solid stone, in default of timber uprights. The consequences in terms of living-space are shown in Fig. 33 where an open-plan wooden North American house is contrasted with both a recent and a prehistoric stone house from Scotland (cf. also Fig. 31).

In view of the rather specialised use of stone in modern non-urbanised and non-industrial contexts, its frequency in the archaeological record poses some awkward questions. Undoubtedly its present abundance can partly be explained as a distortion of past conditions: very few wooden houses will leave visible traces for the archaeologist to discover, in contrast to those of stone whose ruins

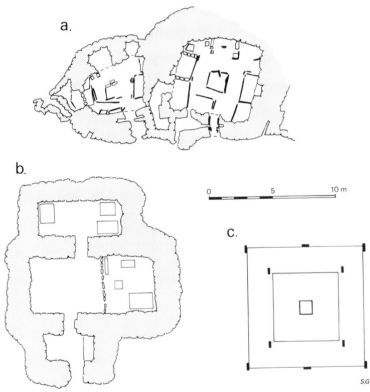

Figure 33. Stone and wooden house-plans, to show difference in internal space. The wooden house (north-west coast of America) has posts, but no internal dividing walls and consists of a single large enclosed area (cf. figure 31) whereas the stone houses (Skara Brae, Orkneys, Neolithic and recent Scottish Black House) have sturdy internal walls and several small rooms

may stand visible for millennia. But where stone was used, was this due to local scarcity of wood? And if so, was shifting cultivation practicable or were other means of subsistence employed? This is not the place to attempt a full discussion of such problems, but they may serve to demonstrate that the use of stone needs questioning, for it is not a normal, but an exceptional, building material.

The use of mud, or wattle and daub, imposes some of the same restrictions as stone, and produces houses with separate rooms rather than communal halls. Sometimes, instead of a single dwelling, each room may be built separately, giving a free-standing hut for each living-unit, be it nuclear family or adult individual and further huts for cooking, storage, etc. Such free-standing huts should really be regarded as a 'dispersed house', and not as separate houses in their own right, for they do not function economically or socially as such. Many examples of this approach to building may be found in Africa, whereas in America, builders in mud and wattle have tended to keep their dwelling units nucleated, and may even join several together. The contrast in visual effect between the two styles of building is obvious (Fig. 34), and the contrast in their archaeological remains will be equally marked. It is therefore important to remember that differences in economic and social terms between the dispersed and the nucleated styles may be no more real than between any two types of 'dispersed houses'.

The above survey, brief though it is, reveals primitive man capable of building many different types of shelter and housing, using a wide range of materials. The diversity reflects differences in the properties of local building materials to a certain extent. It is also a response to local culture requirements, in that settled peoples find it more worthwhile to invest in solid and permanent structures than those who move frequently, and those who live in large communal groups need a bigger enclosed space than those who lead more solitary lives. Weather conditions exert some influence too, on both the choice of materials and the shape of the structure, giving perhaps variety within a group from season to season, as well as from one culture to another.

The diversity of buildings made by any one group will be given further examination in the examples towards the end of this chapter, but let us note a few preliminary points here. Most archaeologists are aware of the range of buildings to be found in complex societies and civilisations, indeed it is one of their hallmarks. But how many would expect hunter-gatherers living in marginal conditions to make

Figure 34. Extended building. (a) compounds of separate round units, Serowe town (Schapera, Royal Anthropological Institute). (b) Hopi conglomeration of rectangular units, forming a continuous structure (Curtis)

five different types of shelter, as Thomson describes for the Wik Monkan of Australia? Seasonal variation in house types is in fact well-documented ethnographically, and it is a possibility which archaeologists should undoubtedly allow for in the interpretation of settlements, in hunting, and farming and pastoral contexts.

One may also find examples of more complex variations. Freeman describes how the Iban build a longhouse as their characteristic dwelling. The longhouse may be abandoned towards harvest for temporary huts in the fields, so that the farmers can guard their crops. This gives large substantial houses and small temporary huts inhabited by the same people. After about five years residence in their main longhouse, the Iban have exhausted most of the cultivable land within easy reach. At this stage, they abandon their home, the group splits into three or four smaller units, and each of these builds a subsidiary longhouse, known as a *dampa*. The *dampa* is inhabited for four or five years, and then it too is abandoned for a new house in new territory. After twenty years or so, the scattered families return to live in the original longhouse, as the land around it has by then recovered sufficiently to be cleared and cultivated anew. The longhouse was never totally abandoned, being visited and repaired from time to time, and used for certain festivals. In this one society, therefore, there are large permanent dwellings, smaller dwellings occupied for a few years, and temporary seasonal shelters. The diversity is the result neither of class structure nor of different economic strategies, nor of culture change. They are all in simultaneous use by a single group of people following the same subsistence pattern. Moreover, there is more house space for the population than it requires at any one time, and population estimates based on total floor-space, or the number of structures or hearths, would be misleading.

Living arrangements

An examination of the living arrangements within houses can be quite illuminating, for people do not always live in a simple family group, or even in straightforward extended families, as one might expect. The correlation of nuclear families with dwellings does exist, but there are various other possibilities, such as bachelors' houses, men's houses, separate houses for a man and for his wife or wives and children, and the many various combinations which can loosely be termed 'extended families'. And then there are other house-like buildings to consider: dance-houses, council-houses, club-houses, houses for the dead and houses for ghosts. Rather than cite scattered examples from the whole range of ethnographic reports, the living arrangements of a few groups of people will be discussed below, in the hope of conveying some impression of the range of possibilities.

Some of the different types of *Athapaskan* house were referred to above (p. 79). As the types vary, so may the social units. For example, several related families may live together in one of the rectangular summer houses of the Upper Tanana region, whereas a temporary lean-to shelters only one family. The Ingalik, Athapaskans of the Yukon, build both large and small winter houses, and also *kashim*, or men's houses, which are used by the men for sleeping and working, for sweat baths and for both secular and religious ceremonies (Van Stone 1974, 36). The most common secondary structures of the Athapaskan are drying racks, set up within a settlement, to cure fish. Caches or raised store-houses are also built, and burial platforms, both of which are raised on posts. The posts, stakes and poles used in building secondary structures may fall within the size range found in house-building, and their arrangement is not necessarily any more haphazard. Therefore, the archaeological evidence in terms of postholes may not enable any distinction to be made between various different types of structure, or, perhaps more likely, different types may be recognised, while their function eludes interpretation.

The *Ainu*, who live as settled hunter-fishers in Hokkaido, have three types of building. The largest is the living-house mentioned above (p. 85) and illustrated in Fig. 29. This house is a family house, and each married couple and their children will have their own such dwelling. The Ainu also build store-houses, which are small versions of the living-house, set on four posts to raise them well above ground level. The third type of structure common to Ainu settlements is a sentry-box-like shelter for latrines; such shelter is rare in primitive contexts, but one imagines that if prehistoric man indulged in like luxury, interpretation would be facilitated by evidence for a latrine-pit.

The pastoral *Somali* have only one type of structure, the small family huts to be seen at their main grazing encampments. If a Somali man has several wives, there will be a hut for each woman and her children. Co-wives do not necessarily live in the same encampment, and if his wives are scattered a man may officially be resident in several hamlets. Boys over seven or eight years of age live outside the camps, herding the camels, and they have no hut or shelter whatsoever. Here, then, is yet another example suggesting that population estimates cannot be based on the number and size of the dwellings.

The Somali depend for their subsistence on their herds and flocks, and care for them most solicitously; yet they do not build any shelter for the animals. They make pens to retain the animals when necessary, but that is all (Lewis 1961). In this, they are unlike the Nuer who might be described as less nomadic pastorals, and who probably depend less on their cattle than the Somali do on their camels. The Nuer build large byres to protect their animals from insects, and perhaps also from raiding parties. Architecturally, these cattle byres are like living-huts, only larger, and they contain hearths where smoky fires burn incessantly to keep the insects away. What with the fires, and the use of dung to build living huts, and the similar arrangement of posts, a Nuer cattle-byre might appear archaeologically as a superior living-house, belonging perhaps to the dominant member of the community. This is not far from the truth, of course, given the high esteem the Nuer have for their cattle (Evans-Pritchard 1940).

The various living arrangements of the *Bomagai-Angoiang*, who farm in the Bismarck Mountains of New Guinea, are summarised in Figs. 35 and 36. Note that shelter for animals is incorporated into the houses, but only into those occupied by women since it is they who care for the animals. If a woman is not responsible for any pigs, it is quite likely that her house will have no side-compartment. Women's houses are further distinguished by having an inner dividing wall, which is not found in men's houses. Women's houses are normally inhabited by one woman and her children and her pigs, men's houses by up to three or four adult men and boys over five years old. In Fig. 36 the siting of houses within a hamlet is shown, and this figure also reveals the influence of animals and of sex on living arrangements. The fence surrounding the hamlet is to keep pigs out, and the women's houses are built near the fence, so that the pigs have direct access to their compartments and can not enter the hamlet 'compound'. Less obvious is the fact that all the men's houses are built on slightly higher ground than those of the women, since it is wrong and improper for women to walk, or to live, higher than men. (Clarke, W. 1971).

Some New Guinea peoples build separate shelters for their animals. The *Dugum Dani*, for example, build large rectangular pig-

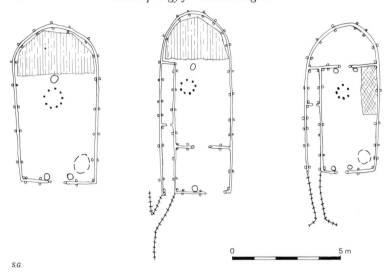

S.G.

Figure 35. Bomagai-Angoiang houses, floor plans. Left to right: men's house, slept in
    by two to three men and several boys, no separate compartments; woman's house
    for one woman and two pigs – the pigs live in the compartments at the side, with
    their own entrance from outside the compound, and the main house is divided
    into two areas, the inner part for sleeping; family house occupied by a man, his
    wife, two small boys, three girls, and four pigs – the pigs sleep in the side
    compartments, the man on the platform in the central part of the house, and his
    wife and children in the inner part. The shaded areas are bamboo sleeping-
    platforms; circles of black dots, hearths; broken-line circles, earth ovens; and
    small open circles, ridge poles (W. Clarke 1971)

houses with separate compartments inside for each pig. As for
people, a woman and her children live in their own small round
house while all the men live together in a single large round house.
Large rectangular family cooking-houses are also built within the
village, and outside it very high watch-towers are set up, on several
poles lashed together, and these watch towers have small shelters
built at their foot (Fig. 37). The Dani, therefore, have six different
types of structure; they build round and rectangular houses at the
same time, and both large and small ones. Yet theirs is an
egalitarian society on the whole (Heider 1970).

Archaeologically, the above information may seem beside the
point or even a deterrent to interpretation, for it would appear that
the function of structures bears little relation to size or internal
features such as hearths, and the number of structures may not

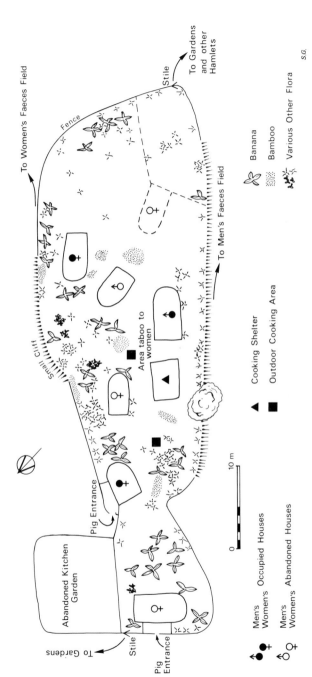

Figure 36. Bomagai-Angoiang hamlet, showing men's and women's houses. Note that several of the houses are empty or abandoned and the seven extant buildings house two men, two women and two children. The numerous plants growing within the compound fence have economic, ritual or decorative uses, and many are privately owned. The fence keeps pigs out of the compound, and the women's houses are sited on the perimeter so that the pig compartments open directly to the outside. The paths lead to gardens and other hamlets, and to faeces-fields (W.C. Clarke 1971)

Figure 37. Dani structures. (a) rectangular pig-sty under construction, with plank walls and internal passage way and compartments for the individual pigs. (b) construction of a rectangular cook-house, similar in outline to the pig-sty, but without internal divisions, and with a hearth for each woman of the compound. Used by all members of the compound for cooking, chatting, working, eating. (c) view of compound with round and rectangular structures, showing construction of woman's sleeping-house with sleeping loft. There may be a clay hearth built on the wooden floor of both storeys and a pig-compartment on the ground floor. Men's sleeping-houses are also round, somewhat larger, and without pig compartments or wooden floor. (d) watch-tower and watch-tower shelter, both used by men when on guard-duty at the frontier.

reflect the number of people. However, viewed in another way, the examples can be put to good use: archaeologists need not expect every hut with a hearth to be for people, nor every large house to belong to a chief. As for the excessive number of structures built by some people, in relation to their own numbers, this is a reminder of the wealth of many primitive groups in terms of space and materials. It is more than likely that prehistoric man, living in a less populated world, could afford a similar lavish provision of structures.

Some of the points raised here have been discussed in more detail by Flannery (e.g. Flannery 1972) who puts forward a strong argument for the influence of social factors on domestic architecture. In particular, he associates round houses and compounds with individual living units brought together in an extended family, and rectangular houses in hamlets or villages with nuclear families. He suggests that people living in round houses tend to be nomadic and those in rectangular houses tend to be sedentary. In some of the cases we have examined, such correlations do occur, but in others there are people who confuse the issue by building both round and rectangular houses, and in others still the paramount influence does seem to be the raw material used for building. It is likely that any correlations are rather more complex than anything detected so far, and the subject is one that requires much further work.

Storage structures

These occur mainly, but not exclusively, in farming contexts. As noted above, various nomadic people such as the Ainu and the Athapaskan build store-houses for keeping surplus food. On the other hand, farming communities exist where no special provision is made for storage. Tubers and roots are 'stored' in the fields, and grain may be kept in baskets and pots and bark bins within ordinary dwellings. Grain, such as maize which will stay on its stalk, can be quite simply hung in the rafters, along with a variety of other plant foods, and cured meats and cheeses. Any smokiness will help preservation.

More elaborate methods of storage fall into two categories: above ground and below. Among the former, one often finds a store-house raised on posts, with an overhanging floor, to keep out vermin. The floor area is therefore greater than the space enclosed by the posts, and yet the whole structure may be lower and less imposing than the sometimes massive posts would suggest (Fig. 38). Other above-

Figure 38. Lapp store-house built on a tree-stump to raise contents beyond reach of vermin, with log-ladder to be set up for human access (Severin 1973)

ground stores look very like ordinary dwellings, or at least, the arrangements of posts and entrance and floors might leave archaeological traces similar to those of a living house. Thus, although a Hausa grain silo looks very different from a house, its floor plan is not dissimilar. Therefore, above ground storage facilities will not always be archaeologically distinctive, and even if distinct types of non-dwelling structure are recognisable, burial platforms and the like will still confuse the issue.

Below-ground storage presents fewer problems of recognition, no doubt because the features are more likely to be well-preserved, and also because men rarely live in underground pits, or even dig holes

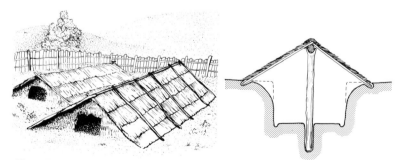

Figure 39. Maori storage, roofed underground storage pits for tubers (Fox 1976). See figure 42 for storage huts raised on a single post, similar to Lapp method

with the primary intent of burying rubbish. Paradoxically, archaeologists may be more aware of storage pits than ethnographers, since the latter may see no more than a hump in the ground, or perhaps not even that when a pit is carefully concealed below the floor of a house. Traditional Maori society used both underground and raised structures for the storage of sweet potatoes, and it seems that both may have been in use at the same time on some sites, but the early Europeans in New Zealand commented only on the raised stores even though their illustrations of the *pa* show what are probably the roofs of underground storage pits (Fig. 39; Fox 1976).

Settlement patterns: duration

The nomadic Fulani of West Africa live in small temporary camps, soon abandoned as they move with their herds in search of fresh pastures; at intervals, they make their way to the large, permanent towns and cities of the Hausa, there to trade the surplus products of their animals for the specialised goods of the settled farmers and craftsmen. Within the single region there are two co-existing cultures, each with its own characteristic pattern of settlement; these patterns are formed partly by the size and the duration of the individual settlement units, partly by the way in which these are distributed over the landscape, and also of course by local topography and raw materials which influence the type of structure built (see preceding section). It is the first two of these influences that we are mainly concerned with here, the duration of settlement from temporary camp to permanent city, and the distribution of these varying types within the homeland of the cultural groups producing them. It is these factors, duration and distribution which form the basis of settlement patterns.

In the recent flood of settlement pattern studies, seen first among geographers (e.g. Chisholm) and latterly among archaeologists (e.g. Green, Haselgrove and Spriggs 1978), the emphasis has usually been on the second factor of distribution, with its concomitant aspects of size of unit, size of territory exploited, access to resources, hierarchies, and communication. Duration has received less attention, except perhaps for the recognition of a simple division into temporary or permanent settlement, and for the valiant efforts of Palaeolithic archaeologists in particular to determine the length of occupation of sites.

The following pages will explore these two aspects by considering the general pattern of variation to be found in modern and recent ethnographic societies, and then looking at the resulting long-term settlement patterns in selected examples. The implications of this survey for the archaeologist will then be discussed in an attempt to highlight those aspects of settlement which ethnography shows to be impcrtant and which the archaeologist may reasonably hope to recognise in his material.

It is only catastrophes such as a famine, earthquakes and modern war that give rise to homeless, aimless refugees, people who have no pattern of settlement. In normal circumstances, all human groups show a certain regularity in their patterns of movement and settlement, and this is as true of nomadic peoples as of those who are sedentary. They do not wander at random over the face of the earth, but instead move purposefully within an established homeland at predictable intervals.

Temporary camps

There are few, if any, instances of people being constantly on the move, year-in and year-out, stopping only to sleep overnight. In most cases, even the most nomadic of peoples settle for a few days between moves or after a short run of over-night halts, and they may stay put for a week or two in auspicious circumstances. All these moves will be made within a known territory, and are likely to follow an annual pattern bringing the group back to the same vicinity at more or less the same season each year. The main factor causing and directing movement is the availability of food and water, for people in the case of hunter-fisher-gatherers, and for the herds of pastoralists; when these resources are far-flung and not over-abundant one finds a pattern dominated by temporary halts, as in the Australian Central Desert or in the pastoral lands of the Turkana of East Africa. The temporary nature of settlement encourages equally temporary structures, as does the generally denuded background landscape and these influences also keep the size of each settlement unit small, a single family or maybe two, and rarely more than 20 people together for any length of time. It must be stressed however that there are very few groups who live in such a manner with no respite, and it is far more common to find a seasonal break in the settlement pattern, the small temporary camps being abandoned in favour of a larger and more permanent site (see below,

Seasonal Movement). It is also likely that many temporary camps arise from the seasonal wanderings of otherwise sedentary groups; this is particularly true of semi-nomadic pastoralists exploiting temporary abundance at the extremes of their territory, but also happens when, for example, a section of a farming community sets out on a hunting or trading expedition. There are indeed manifold occasions when essentially sedentary peoples camp out in small scattered groups for a few days or a few weeks, and from the archaeologists' point of view it is this which one should remember, that the temporary small camps may form part of a larger, varied settlement pattern, and that they are not the sole prerogative of nomadic peoples, nor are they necessarily a sign of impoverishment.

Seasonal movement

The majority of hunter-fisher-gatherers move from site to site according to seasonal variation in the availability of food (see the account of Athapaskan food quest in Chapter 1 above and the analysis in Jochim 1976). The length of occupation of each site is governed by the food supply, and also by other economic and by social factors, so that the pattern of movement may be an irregular one: spring moving around in the foothills, summer by the river, a month back in the hills and winter by the coast. However, the pattern is repeated from year to year allowing for minor change in response to climatic variation, and in many cases it appears that the same settlement sites are reoccupied from year to year. This is particularly likely when a nomadic group has a traditional and lengthy camp based on the exploitation of an abundant and localised but seasonal food supply, as for example the salmon runs which have provided similar opportunities for settlement to peoples on both sides of the Pacific (Watanabe 1968, Wood 1973).

Most pastoralists conform to a seasonal pattern of settlement, moving from one ecological zone to another in the search for grass at all times of year. This is the essence of their way of life, movement to exploit seasonal abundance, and it will be discussed more fully in the later chapter on Pastoralism. For the present we should note that pastoral settlements tend to be farflung, perhaps among the settlements of other peoples, or else they may occur at different altitudes within a relatively small area of steep slopes: in either case it is likely that the sites of one and the same people will be found in a range of different ecological zones, and there will be corresponding variations in the size of the settlement and in the raw materials used for building.

Farmers, cultivators of crops, may also conform to a pattern of seasonal movement, despite the innately sedentary way of life imposed by their means of subsistence. Curiously, it seems not to be the crops so much as the animals which keep farmers at home, for it is in America, where one finds so few domestic animals, that farmers are prone to abandon their permanent settlements for a few weeks or months of nomadic subsistence based on hunting and gathering, perhaps precisely because they have no domestic animals. The Indians living around the Great Lakes of North America show something of the many ways in which farming can be incorporated into a pattern of seasonal movement. The Huron lived in semi-permanent villages of varying sizes, from where the adult men might set out for quite lengthy hunting, trade and warfare expeditions in the autumn, but the people as a whole appear to have been relatively sedentary (Trigger 1969). The Algonkian tribes, living generally to the north and the east of the Huron and other Iroquois, were also farmers, who relied extensively on hunting and fishing. Some tribes, such as the Winnebago and the Menomini, lived in settled villages for most of the year except for the autumn when they departed for a season of buffalo hunting on the prairies. Others, the Ojibwa and Fox among them, settled in villages only for the summer season and for the rest of the year lived in small family groups, hunting and fishing (Rogers 1970a and 1970b).

Once again, the aspect of seasonal movement which is of most importance to archaeology is the variety to be found within any one group, variety in type of settlement unit, variety in size and variety in length of occupation. Variation along these lines is exceedingly common for hunter-gatherer groups, and not as rare as one might have expected for people subsisting by other means; it frequently gives rise to a multiplicity of settlement sites, in themselves permanent but occupied only temporarily. Thus within the homeland of a particular group there may be three or four main types of settlement which neither represent three or four cultural units or subunits, nor provide a reliable guide to population density, for only a proportion of them are occupied concurrently. Archaeologists dealing with the Old Stone Age are well aware of such situations, but once one moves into the study of sedentary farming peoples the possibility of multiple seasonal sites is too often neglected or ignored, except perhaps for the specialised case of transhumant pastoralists. Even here, the subject is bedevilled by the usual manner of identifying the presence of pastoralists through an *absence* of settlement sites (an absence which we shall see later to be unlikely). Hence the present stress on the seasonal movements of farmers and of pastoralists, who may be possessors not only of second homes but of a third equally permanent house, and also tents for a brief summer camp in the hills (see examples below, and Chapter 6 on Pastoralism).

Semi-permanent settlement

Any division between semi-permanent and permanent settlement must necessarily be blurred, varying according to individual prejudice from a decade to a generation to a century before permanence is granted. In the present context, 'semi-permanent' is used for those settlements which are occupied for several years at a stretch but not for as long as a generation, and where most adult inhabitants will have lived elsewhere previously, and will expect to move again before they die.

Settlement units of semi-permanent duration are normally associated with the practice of shifting agriculture, an association which is well-recognised in the archaeological literature. The farmers build themselves relatively substantial houses, usually of wood but mud and straw will serve in default of a forest to supply the timber. The settlement units are continuously inhabited for as long as the land within working distance is held to be cultivable; the actual duration of occupation may vary within a culture as well as from one people to another, for it depends on such factors as soil, crops, weeds and the availability of wild resources, all of which are likely to change from one settlement territory to another. It depends also on less predictable variables, such as sickness or warfare: people who do not expect to die in the village where they were born are predisposed to movement as a solution to many problems, and their means of subsistence, slash-and-burn or *shifting* agriculture, is well adapted to such a strategy. Many farming communities therefore move sporadically over the decades, and they may at times return to an old site, but this will normally be decrepit and decayed after several years abandonment and it will not be re-inhabited in the same sense as a seasonal dwelling.

There is one semi-permanent pattern of settlement which is especially relevant to the study of prehistory, namely pioneering shifting agriculture where a group of farmers moves onwards and outwards with every new site, colonising land new to their culture and abandoning the old settlement for ever. In recent and present contexts, pioneering shifting agriculture is the most commonly-found vehicle for the colonisation of new lands, more so than hunting or pastoralism; archaeologically, it is generally held to be the means whereby farming spread from various centres of origin over the face of the earth. Normally, while the pioneering settlements move outwards, other settlements of the same culture remain to consolidate the nuclear territory, and to fill in the land behind the pioneering groups. Two points should be noted here: first, that this is a settlement pattern typical of an expanding population, and secondly that although the pioneer farmers abandon their old settlements, the territory is soon occupied by a more sedentary element of their own culture. (This has been so even with modern, complex pioneering movements such as the European settlement of North America.) Archaeologically it may not be possible to distinguish a pioneering pattern of settlement from that of the follow-up, although a very *low* density of farming settlement should suggest the former.

Permanent settlements

Permanent settlements are those where people expect to stay put, where families live in the same house from generation to generation, as part of the same settlement unit. Towns are the most obvious, but by no means the only, setting for permanent occupation, for farming villages and hamlets may stand as long as any urban settlement, and in some regions the buildings of pastoralists are equally enduring. Permanent settlement is not linked to any one means of subsistence, nor is it confined to those cultures that have attained urbanisation. Nor is it necessarily a static state: a village may spread and sprawl with the years, expanding on one side, contracting elsewhere, rebuilding houses to new designs on new alignments, yet maintaining that continuity of occupation that defines it as a permanent site. In dealing with such settlements, the ethnographer is at a disadvantage when compared with the archaeologist or historian since he rarely has the facilities or the training, and perhaps lacks the inclination, for a study through time. There is relatively little in the ethnographic literature to elucidate the nature of permanent settlement in primitive societies, and it is more likely that archaeologists, geographers, historians and ethnohistorians together will define the constraints and the potential of such settlement patterns – indeed there is already a trend towards such studies.

Size and distribution of settlement units

The next determinants of settlement pattern to be considered are the size of the units of settlement and the manner in which they are distributed throughout a territory. The two factors of size and distribution are considered together because to a certain extent the former is dependent on the latter: the units of a dispersed settlement pattern are naturally small, while nucleation implies a concentration of people and an increase in size.

Dispersed settlement

Units of settlement are rarely smaller than a family or a working party of hunters or some other action-group of two or three people. Even in the most scattered societies it is unusual for a person to live alone for any length of time. The units of dispersed settlement are often temporary, as befits a pattern which is typical of hunter-gatherers. Dispersal, however, can be adopted by any society that lives in a relatively bland and uniform environment, with an even distribution of key resources. In the latter case, settlement units are likely to be scattered across the landscape within sight of each other, and each unit will probably be a family farm as was the case with Azande homesteads in the Sudan before nucleated settlement was imposed by the government (Evans-Pritchard 1971). But where dispersal occurs as a reaction to *limited* resources, the units will be far-flung and out of daily contact with each other, probably not scattered at random through the territory but associated either with a particular topographical feature or with particular food resources as these become available seasonally. Pastoralists in search of grass, or hunter-gatherers living off scarce and scattered foods (whether animal or vegetable) therefore tend *not* to settle within reach of another unit, for this would obviate the advantages achieved by dispersal. The discovery of archaeological evidence for a scattering of small, temporary sites, within hailing distance of each other is therefore unlikely to represent adjacent camps in simultaneous use. Instead it may be supposed that the sites represent successive occupations of a particular territory. There may be a problem distinguishing between such an accumulation of successive isolated sites, and the pattern exemplified by the contemporary Azande settlements, and it will be relevant to determine what resources were being exploited, and how these were distributed. It should also be noted, a point to be discussed more fully later, that whenever the resources of nomadic peoples allow for agglomerated settlements the opportunity for socialisation is seized, and such peoples are inherently unlikely to live, like the Azande, in small close-set settlements scattered evenly across the land.

Loose agglomerations

These are distinguished from dispersed settlement in that it is possible to recognise areas of settlement that contrast with vacant areas within a given territory; the vacant areas may be exploited but they are not inhabited, and they are more clearly distinguished from the settled areas than in the case of dispersed settlement. Within the areas of settlement, buildings are spread around with room for movement, and there is no clearly defined nucleus or central area. This arrangement is particularly suitable for people with animals, who need some room for manoeuvre, and pastoralists may settle in such a manner either for a season when they are living in relatively close concentrations, as, for example, the Kazak do in winter, or living more or less permanently in one area as do the Nuer. Seasonal concentrations of hunter-fisher-gatherers are also likely to conform to this pattern, given the opposing influences of sociability which draws scattered units together, and a social organisation which has not been evolved to cope with living at close quarters. Therefore, when a sudden glut of food makes it possible for hunters to live together, they are likely to do so, but the settlements do not exhibit any degree of nucleation or centralisation. Loose agglomerations of this nature will leave patterns of archaeological evidence that shade into the range of scattered temporary camps accumulated over the years: how is one to determine between the evidence left behind by twenty families co-existing for a week and that left by one family in the course of twenty successive week-long halts. Once again, it will be relevant to assess the resources available and any indication of temporary abundance should weigh the argument in favour of the sociable agglomeration.

Settlement units of this nature tend to be associated with particular landscape features in a territory, and in some cases the pattern would doubtless be more dispersed except that the terrain thought suitable for settlement is limited in extent. Nuer houses straggle along the low ridges that crop out above the surrounding plains, confined to the higher ground because of seasonal flooding. Elsewhere, access to different zones within the territory may influence siting, along with social factors such as intervisibility: the Bomagai-Angoiang live in a scattered group of compounds and houses in the New Guinea Highlands, perched on ridges and spurs above the river system where each household can see what is going on.

Village settlements

The majority of communities living in nucleated settlements live in villages, small collections of houses distinct from the surrounding land, perhaps set in a forest clearing or amid cultivated fields. The village settlement is typical of farming, both semi-permanent shifting agriculture and more permanent forms. It is also occasionally associated with hunter-fisher-gatherers, especially where fishing is important, and with some pastoral groups and people living by other specialised occupations such as mining or pot-making. Most villages have at least fifty inhabitants, and probably not more than three hundred: below fifty, there are not enough adults for corporate works and defence; above three hundred, the social structure of village life is no longer adequate to cope with every day law and order.

Each village will have an associated territory, though in the case of people who move seasonally this will not always be a single coherent block. The village settlement pattern of a farming community conforms more closely than any other pattern to the basic notions of site catchment analysis, individual units being well scattered throughout the culture area and each surrounded by its own land containing a cross-section of vital resources. In practice, local topography and the accidents of history may distort the pattern from time-to-time, and cultural values will certainly affect the spacing of villages. The maps (Figs. 40 and 41) indicate how village settlement may appear on the landscape; Fig. 40 incorporates the added distortion of semi-permanent settlement sites and Fig. 41 illustrates the strong influence of local topography.

It is also appropriate to include here such specialised forms of nucleated settlement as royal courts and warrior settlements. These are not villages in the subsistence sense, but they do give rise to a collection of buildings distinct from the surrounding landscape. In these instances social organisation has in fact replaced subsistence as the dominant influence in determining how and where people live, and the effect may be illustrated by the following accounts of a Zande royal court, cited by Evans-Pritchard:

> All that here met my eye was evidently on a scale and in a style that proclaimed the power and greatness of a really formidable African ruler. The number of huts, the size of the well-kept open space, and of the assembly hall, all surpassed my expectations,

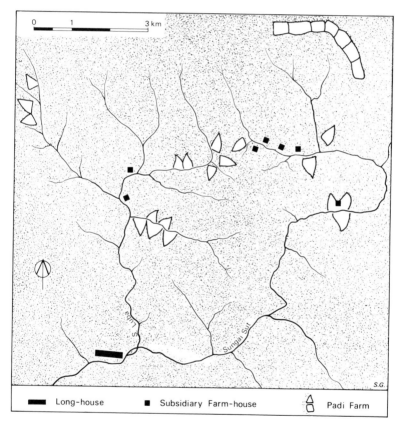

Figure 40. Iban settlement. Long-houses and subsidiary dampas confined to river valleys, with fields cleared on steep hill slopes in primary forest. The row of square fields runs along a ridge-top (Freeman 1970)

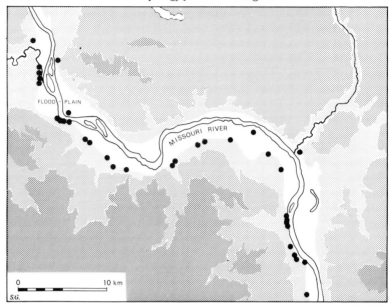

Figure 41. Missouri River villages. Horticultural Plains Indians such as the Mandan
settled along the edge of the flood-plain, growing crops in the valley floor. Villages
were very rarely located in any other situation, and settlements of intruders such
as the Cheyenne were also found along the flood-plain edge. Shading indicates
flood-plain edge, and 1800' and 2000' contours (Wood 1974)

and even exceeded everything I had yet seen at the headquarters
of any native potentate. The mbanga and its surroundings still
bore the genuine stamp of the powerful old Zandeh dynasty,
which, in the northern territories, had already entered on a
period of decadence.

The royal huts spread over a free space of about 1000 yards
east and west, with a breadth of perhaps 500 yards, but
narrowing somewhat westwards. Probably some 200 huts for the
female slaves were disposed in two long rows on the edge of the
open space, the broader east end of which, serving for the daily
gatherings, was carefully kept free from grass. Here Bakangai
usually sat under a large tree, while the assembly took their seats
on long tree-stems at distances ranging from forty to seventy-five
yards from the prince.

Close by stood the assembly hall, which afforded complete
shelter from sun and rain, and which was sixty-five by twenty-five

yards, or about the size of our riding-schools. Its roof, artistically constructed of foliage, rested on innumerable poles, a central row supporting the ridge, and several side rows the two slopes. The hall was enclosed by mud walls five feet high, so that, despite the doorways on all four sides, the interior was always gloomy. In one corner was an enclosed space, whither the prince withdrew from time to time.

Nor was there any lack of ornamentation, for an accomplished Zandeh artist had covered the walls with all manner of natural and other objects, drawn in rough outline, but perfectly distinct. I noticed that the *pinga* [*kpinga*] or many-bladed Zandeh throwing-knife, was most frequently represented; but simple drawings of tortoises, birds, and snakes also occurred. The building, however, was effective only from its great size, for in the manner of its construction it could bear no comparison with the fine artistic structure of the Mangbattu people.

The Zandehs, in fact, lack the sense of proportion, and the patience for time-consuming details. The mud-floor in the vast hall had not even been levelled, so that the two ends stood considerably lower than the central part, while the roof-ridge described a curved instead of a straight line.

Several other large huts stood round about the assembly hall, all (Zandeh fashion) round with mud walls and conic roof. At the west end of the open space the private dwelling-houses of the prince were visible above a pallisaded enclosure. A similar fence stretched southwards beyond the long rows of huts occupied by the female slaves, and here stood the dwellings of Bakangai's favourite women, in the shade of the trees and neighbouring banana groves. (Evans-Pritchard 1971, 174-5)

Tightly nucleated settlements

At the opposite end of the spectrum from dispersed settlements are the villages and towns defined, or confined, by a wall, and the settlements so markedly nucleated as to consist of a single building bringing the whole community under one roof. These tightly nucleated settlements are often a response to defence, though not, of course the only such response (Rowlands 1972). The majority of examples come from farming communities, from groups practising endemic warfare such as the Maori with their hill forts (Fig. 42) or the Yanomamo who live in a single oval shabono (Fig. 43), to those whose

Figure 42. Maori pa. A settlement nucleated and palisaded for defence (Severin 1973)

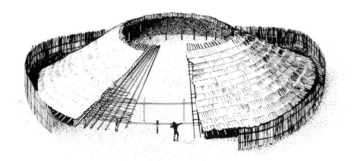

Figure 43. Yanomamo shabano, a village built as a single structure for defence
(Chagnon 1968)

present bellicosity is less apparent but who traditionally engaged in battle, such as the Iban of Sarawak.

Local terrain may occasionally give rise to a similar tightknit form of settlement, whether island and coastal communities where there is little land suitable for housing, or in some mountainous territories where the more land is used up for housing, the less there is available for cultivation.

Towns are the chief remaining settlement type, by definition areas of dense housing with focal, communal places in almost every case. Towns are a rarity among *small-scale* communities, perhaps because implicit in the definition of urban life is the presence of a complex society. However, town life can be supported by non-industrial communities whose farming technology is no more sophisticated than that of village cultures. Some of the most interesting and complex of 'farming' towns are to be found in West Africa, the settlements of people such as the Yoruba and the Hausa. The nature of such towns will be discussed briefly below in relation to the Yoruba, and the topic will recur in other contexts.

Duration and distribution

The interaction between duration and distribution is a complex subject, and not one that lends itself to categorisation. Therefore, while the above descriptions have been deliberately kept very general, the next section will be devoted to a few examples only, selected in order to illustrate both the variety of ways in which categories of duration and distribution may be combined and also the variety of settlement types that any one culture may adopt. This last point is of particular importance since archaeologists have traditionally defined cultures partly by uniformity of settlement type (e.g. Childe 1956), but if the present argument is accepted, the converse should also be sought: a pattern of settlement made up of diverse degrees of dispersal or nucleation, inhabited by groups ranging in size from a family to a tribe, who remain at home for varying lengths of time. A second 'anomaly' to be explored, and which will be described in one of the examples below, is the imposition of more than one cultural pattern on a given territory, as with the Hausa and the Fulani referred to initially. The examples that follow are not typical of a particular means of subsistence or level of social organisation, but have been selected to illustrate the range of possibilities for human settlement.

The Yoruba (source: Lloyd 1965)

The Yoruba kingdoms of West Africa are spread across savannah and tropical rain forest, with a total population of about 6 million, the majority of whom live in towns. These towns have a long history, some being documented at the time of Portuguese contacts in the early sixteenth century, and they are certainly indigenous and not the result of European trade influences. Each kingdom has a major town that is walled, and contains within it the walled royal palace with its many courtyards, and the compounds of chiefs and lesser inhabitants; the population of a major town may be anything from twenty to fifty thousand. Within a kingdom there will also be subordinate, smaller towns and all the towns have a number of associated hamlets which serve as outlying residences to the urban farmers. For the Yoruba are farmers, with 70 per cent or more of the adult male population being engaged in agriculture, and their fields are far distant from the town as is bound to be the case with populations in the tens of thousands. The radius of cultivation of a major town may be as much as 20 miles; the smaller subordinate towns have fields spread up to five miles from the centre. The farmers consequently build themselves a secondary, less substantial and less permanent home in a hamlet in the immediate vicinity of their fields. The settlement pattern therefore shows an excess of housing in relation the adult male population – but not perhaps so much so in relation to the women, for Lloyd notes that a man may have a town wife and a country wife. One cannot interpret this as a rural population supporting an urban one, for they are one and the same people (except for some wives). Lloyd makes one further comment which should be noted here, and that is that two of the Yoruba kingdoms have a slightly different pattern of settlement, with villages of permanent residence as well as the major towns.

Even this superficial description of Yoruba settlement brings out certain aspects of relevance to archaeological interpretation; these are the rural subsistence base of the quite considerable urban centres, the possession of more than one dwelling per adult male, and the presence of exceptions to this pattern within Yoruba culture itself.

The Yanomamo (sources: Chagnon 1968a and 1968b)

These hunter-farmers of the northern part of South America are repeatedly providing illustrations of points relevant to archaeological interpretation, perhaps because they have been so excellently studied and described by Napoleon Chagnon both in print and in film. The matter of settlement patterns is no exception. The Yanomamo live in villages which consist of single large oval buildings, with a central open space (Fig. 43). These villages are situated near rivers, but not within sight of them for fear of attack by enemy villages, and for the same reason they are usually well-spaced, at least 2-3 days walk apart. The distribution of settlement units is therefore influenced primarily by considerations of defence, and their size is also regulated by the same considerations.

The Yanomamo are constantly at war with each other, and every village must be a viable fighting unit if it is to survive, which necessitates at least 10 to 15 warriors and therefore a total population of not less than forty people. But there is also an upper limit to size, and beyond about 150 inhabitants or exceptionally 250 the villagers quarrel and split into opposing factions which in due course separate to form independent units; the reasons for this upper limit are not entirely clear, although one can say that it is not a question of land shortage, but possibly related to the lack of authoritarian rule in Yanomamo society, and to quarrels arising from the shortage of women (see further discussion below, p. 197-8).

As for duration, the villages are semi-permanent and two patterns of movement may be observed. In the core area of Yanomamo settlement, where the villages are surrounded on all sides by others of their own kind, moves are relatively infrequent (exactly how often is not stated in the literature) and always within the same area. On the periphery however, where Chagnon made his study, villages move frequently as a form of defence, and one settlement is recorded as making nine moves over a period of seventy-five years; peripheral moves eventually lead the Yanomamo into new territory, spiralling outwards from the initial area of settlement, in contrast to the inner villages that moved on a closed circuit. Fig. 22 illustrates the pattern of recent movement in one peripheral area, and it should be noted that only one of these moves was dictated by subsistence (soil exhaustion), the rest were culturally-motivated by the bellicosity of the people.

The Wik Monkan (source: Thomson 1939, 209-221)

The value of Thomson's paper on the Wik Monkan of Northern Australia has already been emphasised. Thomson intended to demonstrate the close links between Wik Monkan life and seasonal change, with emphasis on those aspects which he thought the archaeologist might neglect, ignore or misinterpret; the information was summarised in a table, given here as Table 2, and Thomson's main theme may be expressed in his own words: '... the camps and

Table 2: Thomson's analysis of the annual cycle of activities, based upon, and regulated by, seasonal

SEASON (Division of year – Wik Monkan Tribe)	CORRESPONDING CALENDAR MONTHS (Approximate; varies with seasons)	CHARACTERISTICS OF SEASON	ACTIVITIES
Ontjin { *ontjin many* ('little' *ontjin*) / *ontjin min* ('good' *ontjin*) }	The *ontjin* extends from about the middle of March to late July; subdivided on basis of food harvest. Mid-March to mid-May. Mid-May to late July.	Period immediately succeeding rains, beginning of 'dry' season, characterised by South-east winds; climate becomes cooler, especially in May and June; 'cold weather' period. Flood waters recede rapidly but surface water still abundant. Country clothed at first with long grass, mosquitoes numerous and troublesome; travel difficult. Bark canoes, *tonn*, manufactured in 'wet', still in frequent use on rivers. This is *the* greatest vegetable harvest season.	Wet season camp sites abandoned with cessation of rains. The first camps in early *ontjin* are generally established on open ground exposed to South-east winds, for protection against mosquitoes. Nomadic movements delayed until grass begins to burn. Fish fences and traps constructed extensively in streams carrying receding flood waters. Fish also taken with nets in sheets of shallow water on plains. Bark canoes freely used for transport on rivers, on salt arms and estuarine reaches of streams. Large camps break up and nomadic period commences.
Kaiyım	July (late); transitional period. August. September. October (part).	Height of 'dry' season; cool at first, growing hotter towards *turrpak*. Vegetable foods abundant at first, becoming scarcer and more difficult to obtain as vegetative parts wither and dry. Water courses drying up.	Final break-up of large camps into small parties of one to several families now general. Great nomadic period. Vegetable foods of *ontjin* fully mature, but become progressively difficult to find. Netting of fish practised. Great 'grass burn' period in which grassed areas are systematically burned in conjunction with hunting drives. Many mammals – wallabies (*Macropus*), native cats (*Dasyurus*), 'goannas' (*Varanus spp*) and snakes obtained.
Turrpak	October. November. December (early).	Climate hot; South-east winds cease and wind commences to blow from N.W. quarter. Water courses dry; surface water scarce and confined to deep holes and wells. Lightning, followed by thunderstorms, denotes approach of wet season.	Nomadic movements now much less extensive. Burning of grass, carried out on large scale in *kaiyım*, proceeds systematically in conjunction with hunting and with kangaroo 'drives'. Poisoning of fish, which are now concentrated in deep permanent lagoons. Rain making ritual practised when food plants commence to shoot, before onset of rains.
Karp	December (late). January. February. March (part).	'Wet' or rainy season, extending over a period of 4-4½ months during which the great part of annual rainfall is precipitated. Season sets in with heavy thunderstorms and country becomes flooded rapidly. Period of maximum growth of vegetable foods. Following heavy rains, bark of 'Stringy-bark' (*Eucalyptus tetradonta*) can be stripped freely for construction of houses and canoes (*tonn*).	Nomadic wanderings much restricted and local, except for special purpose at onset of *karp*. Bark of *Eucalyptus tetradonta* stripped for house building and for canoes (*tonn*) for use on rivers, also for food vessels (*ıkka*). Fish capture by spears, and nets, important activity. Women collect shellfish in large quantities. Also quest for eggs of geese jungle fowls (*Megapodes*) and crocodiles (see 'Foods').

OCCUPATIONAL SITES	HOUSE TYPES (see fig. 26)	PRINCIPAL FOODS *Note:* In the absence of suitable common names for many of the food plants, the use of scientific names is unavoidable.
Camp sites on open ground away from jungles (*ark itta*). Open wind-swept beaches, raised beaches and sand pits on coast; sand banks on river courses and well drained open ground on edges of big plains and salt pans. Windswept areas afford some protection from mosquitoes following rains.	*Types 1, 5 and 7* Type 1, sleeping platform, is used chiefly in *ontjin many* for protection from mosquitoes. Type 5, the break wind, is used in the typical dry season camps on open beaches and exposed areas as a protection from cold South-east winds. Type 7, a dry season, cold weather house type.	Fish abundant (see 'activities'). Great vegetable food harvest of *ontjin min* commences. Large number of vegetable foods obtained, chief of which are: White mangrove (*Avecinnia marina* var *resinifera*). Black mangrove (*Bruguiera Rheedii*). Long yam (*Dioscorea transversa*). Round yam (*D. sativa*). Water lily tubers and seeds, sp. such as *Nymphaea gigantea*. Leguminous roots of many species, especially *Eriosema chinense, Vigna vexillata. Vigna canascens*. Arrowroot *Tacca pinnatafida*. Rootstocks such as *Typhonium Brownii*.
Nomad camps; temporary camp occupied for a few days or a few weeks only.	*Types 5, 6 and 7* For protection against cold, wind, and sun respectively.	Same vegetable foods as in *ontjin*; less abundant, but now more mature. Long yams (*D. transversa*), greatly relished, become scarce; also such foods as *Typhonium Brownii*, and the legumes *Vigna vexillata, V. canescens*. A round yam (*D. sativa*), requiring elaborate preparation, remains staple vegetable food for some months. Nonda Plum (*Parinarium Nonda*) becomes important food. 'Sugar bag' honey, an important food, also becomes more plentiful. In late *kaiyim* tubers or corms of a swamp plant *Heliocharis sphacelata*.
Nomad camps at first, gradually becoming established close to permanent water, generally that nearest to food supply.	*Types 5 and 6* Many of the camps during nomadic wanderings consist of a fire and a few branches as a breakwind and for privacy. The fork shown in no. 8 is frequently used for hanging dilly bags, as a spear rest, and to protect possessions from children and from dogs.	Vegetable foods relatively scarce and difficult to obtain on account of shrivelling of foliage and burning of grass. Nonda Plum (*P. Nonda*) still obtained in quantity. Certain foods, especially Round Yam (*D. sativa*), water lily bulbs or tubers stored from *kaiyim*. 'Sugar bag' (wild honey) abundant and good. Tubers of rush-like *Heliocharis sphacelata* become most important of all vegetable foods, especially on coastal plains, where they support large camps. Some burning of grass still, in conjunction with ambushing of wallabies. Fish obtained by poisoning inland waterholes. Second vegetable harvest of limited character occurs in late *turrpak* when plants shoot before wet.
More or less permanent camp now established, chiefly on well-drained ground, especially within patches of dry jungle near rivers, or in dense cover on raised beaches fringing coast. A favourite site for the large communal wet season house *ngorkal pi'in* (type 4) is under shade of a large Banyan tree. Chief object in *karp* is protection from great storms of wind and rain.	*Types 2, 3 and 4* When 'wet' breaks tea tree bark only is available for construction of camps until bark of *E. tetradonta* can be stripped. House types 1-3 are built on high ground in open savannah forest during *karp*. Type 4, covered with *Melaleuca* bark, is constructed in jungle and sheltered situations, *e.g.*, under Banyan Fig tree.	Vegetable food season virtually finished but some fruits available, especially a small sweet fruit like currant, *Flueggea microcarpa*, in great abundance; Black Fruit (*Vitex glabrata*); 'Lady Apple' (*Eugenia suborbicularis*); fruits of certain *Ficus*. Numerous 'casual' foods, each obtained in small quantities. Matchbox bean (*Entada scandens*) not relished, used as stand-by. Some Nonda Plums (dessicated) and some Round Yams (*D. sativa*) carried over from *turrpak* and *kaiyim*, in early *karp*. Fish, shellfish, crabs, become important. When wet breaks, eggs of Megapodes, waterfowl, turtles and of crocodiles furnish much protein food. Large kangaroos, the Red (*Macropus rufus* var.) and Grey (*M. giganteus* var.) more easily approached under cover of high winds.

the house types, the weapons and the utensils, are of a specialised type and related to the seasonal life, so that viewing these independently at different periods of the year, and seeing people engaged in occupations so diverse, an onlooker might be pardoned for concluding that they were different peoples' (p. 209). The seasonal change in settlement pattern has been abstracted from the rest of the material for the present purpose though obviously all the different elements shown in Table 2 are closely interrelated.

At the beginning of the dry season, the Wik Monkan embark on a life of nomadic hunting and gathering, wandering ever more freely and in smaller family groups as the forest savannah dries out and grass is burnt. Camp sites are initially situated on open, breezy ground to minimise the effects of mosquito plagues; windswept beaches are particularly favoured. Each site is occupied for a few days or weeks only. This period of dispersal lasts for three or four months and then, as conditions become progressively drier and water becomes scarce, people begin to congregate in larger and more settled groups near permanent water supplies. With the onset of the rainy season, the Wik Monkan settle in large permanent camps near rivers or on the coast and much of their subsistence during this phase is based on the exploitation of fish and shellfish. The settlement pattern of the Wik Monkan is therefore characterised by a dry season of high mobility, spent largely in small temporary camps in the inland areas and a wet season when large sedentary groups are to be found living coastally. And, as Thomson stresses, the archaeological evidence might suggest two separate cultures so different is the material from the different seasons.

The detailed pattern of Wik Monkan settlement is closely adapted to *local* conditions, and one should not presume to apply it in detail to any past hunters and gatherers. But one can apply, as typical of hunter-gatherer settlement in general, the contrast between a phase of dispersal when people live in small mobile family groups, and a phase of concentration when they come together as one large public and sedentary body.

The Tuluaqmiut (source: Campbell 1968)

The Tuluaqmiut lived in inland north Alaska, in a cold and dry environment virtually devoid of plant life. They are included here for the rare precision of detail which Campbell gives about their movements around their territory, and for his comments on the delimitation of that territory. The Tuluaqmiut were one of a number of bands forming the Nunamiut tribe of Alaskan Esquimo; the band was about 80 strong and occupied an area of approximately 3,200 square miles. The Nunamiut territory was defined by an essentially economic boundary 'which separated the resources most suited and necessary to the Nunamiut from either unoccupied lands or those resources that were less suited, and which were being exploited by Eskimos or Indians with different basic economic orientations and technologies ... Each band had its own home territory, the boundaries of which ... were only vaguely recognised if at all by its members, and which were never considered inviolate. Nevertheless, such boundaries existed and encompassed the geographical space necessary to provide each band with food, fuel and clothing' (p. 3-4).

Campbell defines six settlement types for the band (see Fig. 44). Type I was the headquarter locality of the band, consisting of a dozen caribou-skin houses which were moved around the site during the periods of occupation, which were April-May and August-October. The site was permanent, its position determined by the availability of fuel in the vicinity (a large willow thicket) and access to lake trout and also caribou hunting. Although the caribou provided the major source of food and raw materials, Campbell stresses that *no* site could be occupied for more than a few days unless it was near a willow thicket, and the headquarters were located near trout lakes because this fish was abundant all year and provided an emergency food supply when other game was scarce or failed.

Type II settlements were inhabited by two or more families from November to January or March. There were therefore several of these settlements for each band, in contrast to the single headquarters site. Location was influenced by the availability of fuel, the need for shelter from fierce winds, and access to caribou and Dall sheep which were the main source of foods for these winter months. Such conditions could be found in sheltered valleys just within the forest boundary or in the mountains in the tundra zone. Sites would be reoccupied off and on for up to 25 years.

Type III settlements were outposts from I and II, hunting and fishing camps occupied by small groups of men for two to five days, potentially at any time of year and most frequently in February-March and June-July. They were situated higher up the valleys and mountains, nearer the caribou and sheep than the larger and more permanent Types I and II. Type IV settlements were similar in size and duration to these hunting camps and used by people collecting

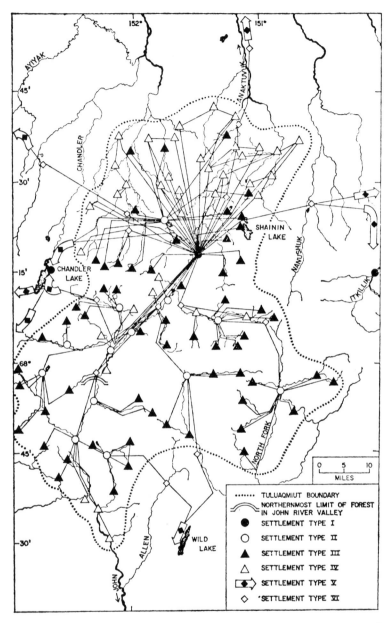

Figure 44. Tuluaqmiut settlement, Alaska. The map shows the varied types of settlement used by the Tuluaqmiut throughout the year, the pattern of moves from one type to another, and the variation in number of the different types (Campbell 1968)

resources other than food; they might be occupied at any time of year, and if a particular resource was available year-in, year-out the same site would be reoccupied: permanent, though inhabited only for a very brief period each year.

Type V settlements were camps of the Tuluaqmiut in other people's territory, frequently combined with the camps of other bands for trading purposes. They were used at all times of year, as were Type VI, overnight camps used on journeys between any of the other settlements.

The number and location of these different settlement types is summarised in Fig. 44. The variety of settlement size and duration that may pertain to any one group has already been emphasised, and Campbell brings out one aspect of this variety which creates a particular problem for archaeologists. This is the differential survival rate of the different settlement types. The headquarters and the extra-territorial trading/visiting camps (Types I and V) leave far more cultural débris than the other types, and are more likely to be recognised archaeologically. But as Campbell emphasises, the other settlements form an integral part of the overall pattern, and one should therefore allow for a category of undiscovered site when reconstructing past settlement patterns (cf. Simonsen 1972).

The Tikopia (sources: Firth 1936 and 1939)

The Tikopia live on a small island in the Western Pacific, isolated from most outside influences at the time of first European contact and dependent on their own efforts at cultivation and fishing for their existence. The island was estimated by Firth to have a population of about 1,280 people, and being only three miles across with a large lake in the middle the density was in the order of 400 people per square mile. The whole of the island was under cultivation, except for a few rocky cliffs. The inhabitants lived in permanent villages which were sited coastally to give ready access to fish and to the sea for ease of communications by canoe; the lack of villages along the northern coast was attributed to the poor fishing facilities there. Supplies of fresh water also affected village location to a certain extent, and the lack of settlement around the lake may be explained by its brackish water. There is little doubt that the permanence and density of the Tikopia population was made possible by the abundance of fish as a food supply to supplement the cultivation of vegetables. Fig. 45 indicates the size and location of

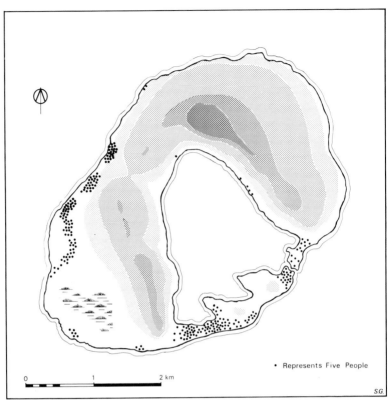

Figure 45. Tikopia settlement. The island rises from sea level to 1200', and settlement is largely confined to the low coastal strip, near good fishing waters, and avoiding the marshy region in the south west; all the island is used for agriculture (Firth 1939)

villages; what it does not show is the amount of subsidiary housing, which yet again one finds over and above the basic needs of a household, and this time in a sedentary farming population that is involved neither in seasonal nor long term moves and which, on an island three miles across, can scarcely find the trek to work arduous. Yet, as Firth notes, 'partly due to their desire to have shelters where they can spend a night or longer in their various orchards, partly to their custom of converting an ancient house where many of their dead have been buried into a temple, the Tikopia have many more houses than are necessary for bare accommodation, and a man of rank may have three or four in different parts of the island' (Firth 1936).

The Mandan and Cheyenne (source: Wood 1974)

The Mandan, along with the Hidatsa and the Arikara, were settled village farmers living along the Missouri river in the Northern Plains region of North and South Dakota. Unlike the Great Lakes tribes they were not hunter-farmers, but engaged predominantly in horticulture. Villages were placed on the terraces above the Missouri flood plain, or along major tributaries; they seem to have been confined solely to such locations, because, Wood suggests, this was the optimum in terms of access to the valley for garden plots, to the treeless terraces and to the uplands, giving access to a wide range of resources (see Fig. 41). Each village site was in a good defensive position. To this neat settlement pattern must be added that of the nomadic Cheyenne hunters who exploited the plains and also had seasonal village settlements in the same region as the Mandan, and traded extensively with them. Wood argues two consequences of this trade, one being a common material culture for the two separate tribes and the other the specialisation of each group, on the one hand as farmers and on the other as hunters in the knowledge that they would acquire the surplus of their neighbours through exchange. In a purely archaeological context, with no help from ethnohistorical sources, one wonders whether such a dual settlement pattern would be recognised. (The archaeological problems highlighted by the Mandan-Cheyenne interrelationships will be discussed further in Chapter 4, pp. 187-8.)

Kurds and Lurs of N.W. Luristan (source: Edelberg 1966-67, 373-401)

The Kurd and Lur inhabitants of northwestern Luristan studied by Edelberg were farmers, growing crops in a river valley surrounded by mountains and keeping a few horses and donkeys, cattle, sheep and goats. Some fields were irrigated and yielded two crops a year; those that were not irrigated yielded only one crop and were left fallow in alternate years. In the summer, the farmers lived in three villages set at about 5km intervals along the valley, close to the river (Fig. 46). The two best-documented villages consisted of several hamlets, and each hamlet was formed by about half-a-dozen households, that migrated as a single unit with each seasonal move. The summer villages were occupied for about four months, from June to the end of September, and the dwellings were built with rush-mat walls and flat roofs.

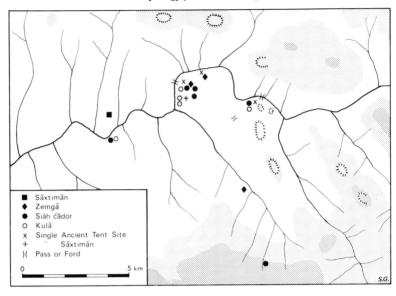

Figure 46. Settlement in north-western Luristan, showing the very restricted area within which seasonal moves to different types of settlement are made. Zemga: winter stone houses; siah cador: tents occupied spring and autumn; kula: summer shelters; saxtiman: village of flat-roofed mud houses (Edelberg 1966-67)

October was spent living in tents, in groups of 5-6 households corresponding to the summer hamlets. Normally the tents were set up at old-established campsites in the foothills of the mountains, where animals could graze and fodder be collected for the winter. The greatest recorded distance to an autumn camp was just under 10km, and the move was accomplished in less than half a day.

In winter, each household moved into a stone-walled house, grouped in hamlets usually just above the cultivated land. Part of the house was roofed with oak poles and branches and thatched with straw, but the main living quarters were under the tent covering that was stretched across the walls. The stone houses were occupied from November to March, and re-occupied year after year; they were the most permanent *structures* of the region, though no more permanent as *sites* than the summer villages or campsites.

In spring, the households took to their tents again for a couple of months, either moving with their animals into the mountains or staying close to the cultivated land.

The farmers' migrations took place within an area where the

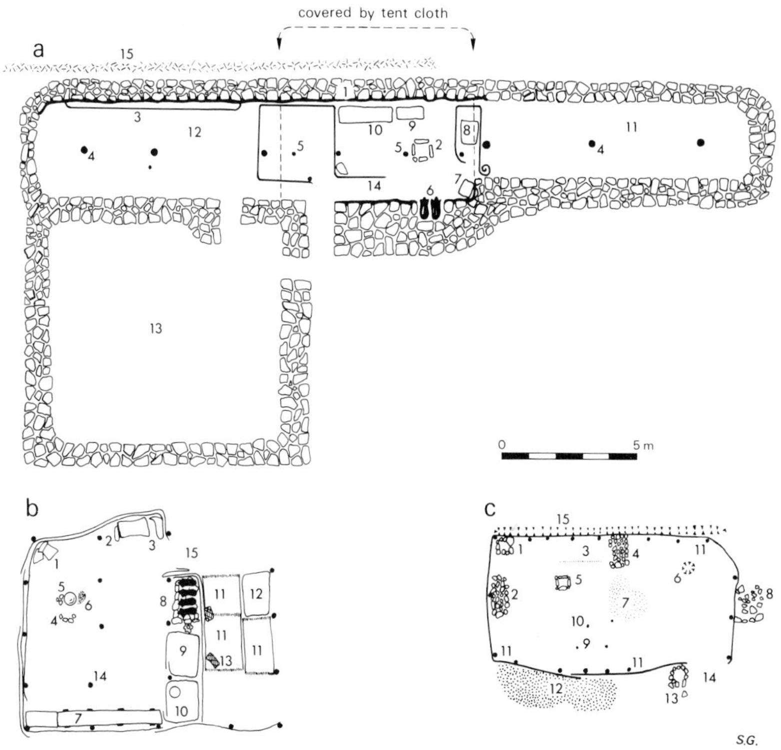

Figure 47. Luristan house-types (Edelberg 1966-67)

(a) Zemga
1. Stone wall, plastered
2. Hearth in kitchen
3. Manger for oxen
4. Forked main posts for roof
5. T-shaped tent posts
6. Goat skins for water in a niche in the wall
7. Containers of clay for skin filled with ghee
8. Containers of clay for floor or grain
9. Box
10. Stand for bedding and carpets
11. Store for fodder
12. Room for livestock
13. Open yard for goats and sheep
14. Rush mats
15. Fence of dry oak-branches the leaves of which will rustle when touched by approaching wolf or thief (the wall around 13 is furnished with oak-branches too)

(b) Kula
1. Sack for wheat and horse bag
2. Wrought iron tripod, yoke and wooden jar for *xut*
3. Rolled tent cloth and string bag for carrying straw
4. Hearth in kitchen
5. Iron griddle for baking bread
6. Fuel consisting of droppings from goats
7. Stand for bedding
8. Stone platform with four water skins
9. Stone platform for milk products surrounded by rush matting
10. Stone platform for flour sack and bread plate
11. Carpets
12. Felt covering hearth laid out for the reception of goods
13. Cushions
14. One of the forked posts
15. Entrance

(c) Siah cador

1. Stone recess for broody hen
2. Stone platform for waterskin
3. Stone bed for carpets and bedding
4. Stone platform for flour sack and skin containing ghee
5. Hearth in kitchen
6. Hearth in guest room
7. Droppings from lambs and kids
8. Pile of stones indicating where children have been playing
9. Peg used to tether oxen
10. Peg used to tether calf
11. Sticks for attaching rush mats
12. Manure from oxen
13. Stone recess for dog
14. Entrance
15. Furrow for draining rain-water from tent cloth

(Edelberg (1966-67))

Table 3. Population Densities

People	Density (per sq. mile)	Comment
Nunamiut, Alaska	0.02	Environment dry, cold and barren. Hunting and fishing subsistence basis. Herd animals (caribou
!Kung, Kalahari	0.1	Environment dry, hot and semi-desertic. Gathering subsistence basis, plus some hunting.
Yanomamo, Venezuela and Brazil	0.2	Environment dense forest. Vegetable cultivation subsistence basis, plus a little hunting and fishing. Pioneering shifting agriculture.
Tiwi, Melville and Bathurst Is., N. Australia	0.3	Islands of mixed desert and swamp. Hunting, fishing and gathering.
Azande, Sudan	4	Environment variable, probably increasing savannah at expense of bush/forest with time. Subsistence now primarily agricultural, historically much hunting and gathering. Localised shifting agriculture. Mixed cereal, vegetable and fruit crops.
Nuer, Sudan	5-6	Grassland environment, periodically flooded. Subsistence mixed crops, pastoral and fishing. Mostly cereal crops.
Jie, Uganda	11.2	Semi-desert and upland savannah. Subsistence basis pastoral, plus some crop cultivation (cereals).

Table 3. (continued)

People	Density (per sq mile)	Comment
Iban, Sarawak	9-20	Dense forest with rivers. Subsistence basis crop cultivation, plus some fishing, hunting and gathering. Pioneering shifting agriculture. Dry rice and some vegetables and fruits.
Huron, Great Lakes	25-43	Temperate forest. Subsistence basis mixed crop cultivation, hunting, fishing and gathering. Localised shifting agriculture. Cereals predominate.
Iatmul, Kapauku, Chimbu, New Guinea	10-15 100 320	Environment varies from lowland swamps to highland forest and grassland, predominately forested. Crop cultivation and pig-raising; some hunting in the more forested areas. Kapauku rely heavily on gathering and collecting to supplement farming. Chimbu riverine settlement, fishing important. Both localised and pioneering shifting agriculture. Root crops and vegetables predominate.
Yoruba, W. Africa City of Ibadan	c. 200 350	Savannah and forest. Subsistence based on cultivation of crops; localised shifting agriculture. Mixed crops; roots, cereals and legumes.
Tikopia, W. Pacific	400 or more	Whole island under cultivation; subsistence based on mixed crops plus fishing. Sedentary agriculture and fallowing of fields.

(Figures based on total land area wherever possible)

contrast between river valley and mountains offered different ecological niches with different resources to exploit as each season came round, but as Edelberg stresses their moves were restricted, 10km at most and sometimes no more than a few hundred metres, which can hardly have been necessary to take advantage of seasonal variation in resource distribution. Edelberg also discusses the very different nature of the dwelling-types. What archaeologist would expect people to live in long, thin but very solid stone walled houses and in slight square pole and mat houses and in tents, all in the space of a year and all within at most a couple of hours walk of each other (Fig. 47)?

Population densities

It has proved extremely difficult to calculate population densities for the above groups on a comparable basis. In some cases insufficient information is available even for a very rough estimate, and often, especially with the farming groups, no clear distinction is made between estimates based on cultivated land alone, estimates based on total territory exploited and estimates based on total territory available. In general, however, the more nomadic of the hunter-gatherers have the lowest densities, while those who settle seasonally and particularly those who rely on fish have a higher density. Similarly the mobile, pioneering farming groups are more thinly scattered than the sedentary cultivators, and again access to fish seems to permit an increase in numbers. Generalising grossly, farming supports more people per given area than either hunting and gathering or pastoralism, but there is considerable overlap in the ranges of variation. Secondly, the greatest densities are found where settlements are permanent, but this need not entail marked nucleation (see Table 3).

Settlement patterns: some archaeological implications

In the preceding pages reference has been made to the relevance of certain features of the ethnographic settlement patterns to the understanding and interpretation of archaeological evidence. The more important of these are now brought together for discussion.

Perhaps the most striking point to emerge is the affluence of many ethnographic communities in terms of housing. Whatever the environment, subsistence basis or social organisation, time and again one finds that people have two or three or even four houses per household and these may all be permanent structures, or at least permanent sites of occupation. For hunter-gatherers, such affluence is to be expected and it is generally acknowledged in the archaeological literature though its implications are only rarely worked out in detail. What one must recognise is that along with the number of sites there is also diversity in the size of the settlement unit, in the type of structure used from one settlement to another, and in the ecological setting of the different units. The possibilities are best illustrated by Campbell's analysis of Tuluaqmiut types with a range from the large permanent lakeside settlements to the small temporary hunting camps of the valley heads and mountainous areas. The archaeologist searching to define the settlement patterns of prehistoric hunters and gatherers should be aware of this diversity: it can exist for a single tribe and within a single territory, with the possibly very different units being in contemporary (but not simultaneous) occupation. The problem of the differential survival rate of different types of sites also emerges from the Tuluaqmiut study; it could be a let-out for the archaeologist who cannot find sites appropriate to all seasons of the year and this is a reasonable if defeatist use of the ethnography. More positively, one could make due allowance in all models of hunter-gatherer settlement for small and temporary units which have left no archaeological trace.

Affluence in terms of housing and settlement sites is not solely the prerogative of hunters and gatherers, but achieved likewise by farmers and pastoralists. Of the latter, more will be said later; for the former, two aspects of this abundance should be noted. First, even the most sedentary of farmers are prone to build themselves extra houses, whether it be the Yoruba in their distant fields or the Tikopia on their tiny island; this phenomenon is referred to repeatedly in the ethnographic literature, and many causes are given ranging from the practical such as distance from home base to fields to the ceremonial such as houses for the dead or for feasts and celebrations to the sheer comfort and convenience of having somewhere to go when you don't like your relatives. The implication here is that in a settled landscape, population cannot safely be calculated on the basis of house numbers as it is unlikely that every house contained a full complement of inhabitants at all times, or even any inhabitants for a lot of the time as was the case for the Luristan dwellings. Archaeological evidence for outlying isolated dwellings should be studied with this in mind, and perhaps interpreted as pertaining to the main settlement rather than being independent units in the manner of modern farms set at a distance from villages.

Secondly, it emerges that many farming communities indulge in seasonal hunting and gathering when either the whole population or perhaps only the adult males leave the main settlement to live in a series of temporary camps no different to those of hunter-gatherers. Indeed for a season they are hunter-gatherers to all intents and purposes, and there is often no indication in the material evidence from these seasons for the farming aspect of their lives, nor perhaps any obvious link between the two types of settlement which make up the overall pattern. The possibilities for misinterpretation are obvious, particularly since the temporary camps tend to be situated in a different terrain to the base sites, and are probably outside the obvious catchment area of that site (within it they would not be strictly necessary but might all the same be used). However, this last-mentioned difficulty could perhaps be looked at from another angle and used to avoid misinterpretations: temporary hunting camps confined to a single ecological zone should have their complements in another zone for their temporary nature is indicative of scarce resources, and to find new resources a new zone must be sought. If contemporary farming sites exist and there are no other contemporary hunter-gatherer settlements, then a reconstruction linking the hunting and the farming sites in a single pattern would be plausible. These points will be relevant to the problems of interpreting some of the more enigmatic of the early Neolithic sites in Europe whose inhabitants appear perhaps to be mesolithic, i.e. hunter-gatherer or else particularly impoverished farmers; Franchthi in Greece and Coppa Nevigata in Southern Italy are two such sites which could have been seasonally occupied by farmers. Given the above possibilities, a further hypothesis can be advanced, that prehistoric farming cultures can and should be expected to have indulged in seasonal hunting and gathering in territories marginal to their farming activities.

A further consideration must be that for all types of community there is the possibility of variation in settlement pattern *within the culture* at any point in time; somehow this has to be distinguished from the situation, where two different peoples exploiting different aspects of the environment live together in a single territory. How, archaeologically, can one distinguish the Great Lakes settlement patterns created by people who are both hunters and farmers, from the Missouri pattern which results from the co-existence of nomadic hunting people and settled village farmers? There is no easy solution, but the interpretation of archaeological evidence can only benefit by an awareness of the possibilities.

There is one frequent variation in settlement pattern which has as yet received little attention, and this is the occurrence of large communal sites, bringing together a number of major settlement units for a short time. The purpose of the gathering may be trade, or a funeral or a feast, or simply the exploitation of a sudden abundance of food; often several or all of these causes may be combined and their occurrence is likely to be annual, though possibly less frequent where resources are scarce. Such a phase of concentration is seen clearly in many hunter-gatherer settlement patterns, and is abundantly documented by Sahlins in 'The original affluent society' (Sahlins 1974) and by Jochim in *Hunter-gatherer subsistence and settlement* (Jochim 1976) as well as in one example cited above.

Jochim explores the causative factors behind these periods of concentration, and attributes them largely to localised and temporary (i.e. seasonal) abundances of food (Jochim 1976, 67-9). He allows that people may have a strong desire to come together for social reasons, particularly when they have been isolated from all but their immediate band for months on end, but still takes abundance of food as the main cause of concentration. In some respects, however, the food is merely permissive in that without it people could not all live in one place for more than a day or so, and the motivating factors of concentration appear to be more cultural than Jochim admits. The Tiwi may delay funerals until there is enough food to feed the mourners, but they deliberately seek to build up their stocks of food for the event and do not wait for abundance. And peoples living in an essentially bland environment magnify small seasonal variations in resource availability in order to have a pattern of concentration and of dispersal in their lives. Despite Jochim's refutation (ibid., 77), the purely cultural nature of this division is seen best of all in Turnbull's analysis of the Mbuti. We shall return later to a discussion of the cultural factors that cause this typical pattern of a phase of dispersal and a phase of concentration for hunter-gatherer settlement.

What is less frequently recognised is that the same pattern can be detected in a great many other cultures, particularly in those where the normal large settlement unit does not exceed 2-300 people. New Guinea farmers congregate for religious festivals and pig feasts, North American hunter-farmers meet in vast trading camps, pastoralists assemble for annual herd round-ups and they all seize the opportunity for much social and political activity (Rappaport 1968, Wood 1973, Leeds 1965). Such gatherings often serve to define coherent cultural units: the tribe consists of those bands or those villages who meet and interact, and thereby achieve a homogenous spread of cultural traits. All these gatherings will be discussed in one or more subsequent chapters, for like those of the hunter-gatherers they serve a variety of purposes and are not primarily caused by subsistence factors. For the present, the main implication in terms of the archaeological study of settlement patterns must be that which has been stated above, namely that within a single culture there is likely to be variety in the size and duration of settlement units.

3. Social Organisation

According to archaeological tradition, social organisation is more difficult to interpret from the surviving evidence than either subsistence or settlement, because it has less tangible manifestations. The tradition is undoubtedly based on fact, and social organisation does have fewer *direct* connections with material things than do food or dwellings. This makes it all the more necessary for archaeologists to make themselves aware of the manifold ways in which pre-industrial societies may organise themselves, and to open their minds to interpretations of social organisation beyond those familiar through their own cultures. The need stems from another factor also, in that as spheres of activity becomes less closely tied to the material aspects of life, they are probably more prone to variation. This exaggerates the problems facing the interpreter, and increases his need for a cross-cultural awareness of the possible variables. A few archaeologists have ventured into the realms of social organisation, with sufficient and increasing success to show that it *is* within the grasp of archaeological studies, but many still need convincing of the possibility.

The anthropologist on the other hand has felt no qualms in studying the varied faces of social organisation; indeed the discipline has been sufficiently developed for 'social' anthropology to be distinguished from 'physical' anthropology. The subject has received more attention both in the field and in the literature than either subsistence or settlement, and its study has developed to a more sophisticated level. It is therefore likely that any social anthropologist who reads the following pages will consider their content old-fashioned and elementary if not over simple, for no attempt will be made to tread the higher flights of anthropological theory. Yet the deliberately basic level of approach has its reason in the needs of the archaeologist, who must be equipped with some knowledge of social systems before he can begin to search for their manifestations in the past: he will not recognise the slight traces that do exist unless he is familiar with the possibilities.

One consequence of the great development of anthropology in the social field has been the rise of different schools of interpretation, to a far greater extent than for subsistence or settlement, where work has remained largely at a descriptive level. Much of the literature dealing with social organisation is dominated by an evolutionary outlook that harks back to the nineteenth century and continues in the works of Lowie or Sahlins, to name but two of those who tend to see one means of social organisation developing from another in ever-increasing size, complexity and efficiency. While it is evident that the more advanced systems of social organisation known to the world did not appear out of the blue, archaeologists should be very wary of the influences of the evolutionary approach. It has a certain seductiveness, and the archaeologist is studying the *evolution* of human culture, and the natural bent of the western mind is to categorising things in an hierarchical manner. Therefore what could be easier and better fitting than to apply chronologically in ascending manner the present diversity of social systems, neatly ordered from those which are simple and therefore early to those that are complex and therefore late. It is so easy, and so simple, as to be dangerous, and nothing illustrates this better than Sollas' faux-pas in *Ancient Hunters* (Sollas 1911). Moreover, classic evolutionary determinism is not unchallenged by the anthropologists themselves (e.g. Burnham 1973), and it is probably wiser, as well as safer, for archaeologists to recognise that there are conflicting views and then to avoid the controversy until they have some information of their own to contribute.

What follows will be selective, for two reasons. First, few scholars, let alone an outsider, can hope to cover all the literature of social organisation, and secondly, the archaeologist has specialised interests within the field, being more concerned at first with the material attributes of power than the rules of in-law relationships (though these may eventually turn out to be relevant). Therefore the bulk of this chapter will deal with one particular aspect of the subject, that of leadership and the alternatives to leadership, with some reference to group size and particular attention to the material manifestations that are linked, however indirectly, with power. The organisation of several societies will then be examined, before turning to a brief discussion of the questions and implications raised for the archaeologist by the ethnographic evidence.

Finally, in these introductory remarks let it be noted that the anarchic primitive society beloved of evolutionists as the first condition of mankind is a contradiction in terms. All human communities are by definition organised and in possession of a social system. This need not entail leadership or hierarchy but does in all cases define a network of relationships that contain people as a group.

Group classification

The common categorisation of groups starts with the band as the smallest and simplest unit; then comes the tribe, a somewhat larger grouping, and then the chiefdom, bigger still and with a higher degree of organisation, and eventually one reaches the complexities and political sophistication of the kingdom, scarcely a primitive state. This classification is based on criteria of size (the number of people belonging to the group), of leadership in terms of the degree of personal authority, and of political organisation, though not all these criteria apply to every class and the implicit upwards evolutionary trend from band to nation masks many complexities such as seasonal variation from band to tribe and back to band again, or the functioning of one category such as the tribe within or alongside the larger unit of the nation. Moreover, there are various other means of classification, one of which is potentially of special interest in the present context for it relates closely to settlement size. Parallel to the band and the tribe, and perhaps integrated into the larger units, there can be grouping by family, by neighbourhood, by village, and by village confederacy. It is advisable, therefore, to maintain a flexible approach to the classification of groups and to recognise that the neat terms of band and tribe cover many diverse situations.

One problem with human groups, of course, is that people belong to different communities according to the circumstances of the moment and the focus of affairs, but in this state of flux there can normally be distinguished a dominant active unit as, for example, the farming village which takes action as a unit and can be picked out from smaller or cross-cutting and relatively passive component family, clan and age groupings or larger and equally passive tribal units. This distinction is mentioned here because it is relevant in the context of leadership, in that the size of the *active* unit is probably closely related to the level of personal authority in a community, whereas there does not seem to be any such correlation of size and power in the case of the passive units.

Power, personal authority and leadership

'There are chiefs because there are, in any human groups, men who, unlike most of their companions, enjoy prestige for its own sake, feel a strong appeal to responsibility, and to whom the burden of public affairs brings its own reward' (Levi-Strauss 1944; in Cohen & Middleton 1967).

Activity leadership

Given that all people are not equal in every respect, and given the implications of Levi-Strauss' remarks that some people are natural organisers of others, it is not surprising to find that every community has at least a minimal level of leadership, revealed in the course of the major group activities. Thus for a group of hunter-gatherers, be they family or band, there will be one among them who directs any communal hunting; this position rests on his acknowledged skill as a hunter and also, no doubt, on his ability and willingness to direct others. Similarly a leader of ceremonies has both to be familiar with the occasion and prepared to instruct his fellows. Leadership at this level is confined to the event and does not necessarily confer a similar role in other spheres of life, though a person may be repeatedly found in charge of a particular activity for as long as his skill and experience warrants. Activity leadership is likely to be a role that most adults experience, temporary and ephemeral – a stage in life – and probably changing from one activity to another with maturity and old age.

Minimal leadership of this nature is not hereditary, nor is it a position giving power and authority over other people. The mechanics of leading will vary from group to group and according to the particular situation, but in no sense does an activity leader have the power to coerce his fellows. He can explain and advise, he can exhort and insult, but he cannot command; and his best hope of getting a job done is to do it himself (Levi-Strauss 1944, Chagnon 1968a).

All communities have people who are temporary leaders in some contexts, however sophisticated their social organisation, and whatever other authority may be present, and it is the dominant or sole means of leadership for small hunter-gatherer bands of, say, up to thirty to fifty people. Such a band is likely to be a flexible unit of varying size and activity, acccording to season, having perhaps a winter congregation for ceremony followed by dispersal to summer hunting in smaller groups. As the situation changes, so do the leaders; and of the total population a large percentage of the adults may be engaged in directing affairs at some stage – witness Colin Turnbull's accounts of the Mbuti pygmies (Turnbull 1961 and 1965; and see below, p. 150).

Being ephemeral and wide-based, activity leadership is unlikely to leave any archaeological manifestation in terms of the wealth of individuals, or distinct types of housing. After all, if most of the adults have been a bit of a leader for some of the time, none will be any more so than the others. Moreover, Levi-Strauss was much struck, in his study of the Nambi-Kuara (from which the above quote was taken), by the lack of material reward for leadership. It was this that led him to reflect on the essential bossiness of some human natures, for otherwise why would people take on responsibility without reward? It follows that the lack of archaeological evidence to differentiate leaders from others does *not* necessarily imply a lack of all leadership in the original society.

'Bigmen'

The term 'bigmen' comes from New Guinea, where it is used to describe the outstanding men of a settlement unit, who are leaders of their group but not chiefs. It is a useful term, and may be applied widely to distinguish the leaders of small groups such as villages or bands, whose role is greater than that of activity leaders but whose position is not dependent on birth and who do not wield the authority over others that a chief possesses.

The size of groups led by bigmen falls within the range discussed for villages in the previous chapter, from a minimum of about 40 people to a maximum of 300, with most groups being from 60 to 150 strong. One factor which distinguishes the 'bigmen' group from that with activity leaders is its relative permanence and stability; the members of the group belong to it and live together for an appreciable length of time, in contrast, for example, to the state of flux of a Hadza hunter-gatherer band. The type of settlement most frequently associated with bigmen is the village. Even where the settlement pattern is dispersed, as with the Bomagai-Angoiang, the active socio-political unit is 'village' in its size and level of complexity, and 'village' in its characteristic of all the members knowing each other well.

It is from among these members that the bigmen emerge. Their position is not hereditary but acquired, and acquired only in the prime of life through the acceptance of their fellows. A bigman achieves his status by being particularly good at the male activities of his culture, whether it be hunting or fighting or raising pigs or growing crops or a bit of all these. As a result of his skills a man grows wealthy, and he is expected to be generous with his riches if he wants to achieve the status of a leader: a miser will never rise above his peers. Nor, in most circumstances, will a quiet man – big men need the gift of oratory, and they need the extrovert character to exercise it whenever the occasion arises. Above all a bigman is a successful man, and he knows it and he shows it – a man slightly larger than life.

The duties of a bigman naturally vary from one cultural context to another. Thus a Kapauku man organises pigfeasts, while his Yanomamo counterpart negotiates alliances with a neighbouring village and the Cheyenne and Mandan leaders come together to arrange a trade-fair. The common factor in all these activities is the organisation of communal affairs, very often on an inter-community level and almost always associated with feasts, where the bigmen are duty-bound to demonstrate their generosity if they want to maintain their position. (For feasts, see also Chapter 5.) They are also likely to arbitrate in local disputes between members of their community, but any decision that they make can only be carried out with the agreement of most of their peers: if they violate custom they will not be bigmen, unless they are great indeed and possess enormous charisma, and then one has moved into another realm of leadership.

The need for consent and the rule of custom indicate the very limited nature of a bigman's power – he may command respect but he does not command men – he influences them. He has prestige, but no authority. Like the activity leader, he gets things done by example, by exhortation, and by the skilful deployment of the material benefits of his success, that is, by generosity in the right quarters. The ways in which the bigman game is played can be well appreciated through reading Pospisil's description of the Kapauku (Pospisil 1972).

The rewards of the game are sometimes difficult to disentangle from the prerequisites. Wealth is unlikely to accrue, since although a bigman is by definition successful and does particularly well in trading ventures, gift exchanges, marriages and the like, he must give as fast as he gets in order to maintain his position. Possibly he may keep the wives, and here we see one of the facets of leadership which, like generosity, reappears at all levels of authority in all but monogamous societies: the men at the top have more wives than their contemporaries. This is the case with the Kapauku, but again it is in some senses a prerequisite in that the more wives a man has the more pigs he can own and hence the more capital he has to influence others. So wives should perhaps be seen as an attribute rather than a reward of bigman status.

The material manifestations of polygamy, and some other facets of bigmen status, may be visible archaeologically: housing to accommodate the family, and shelter for the extra animals or storage for the extra crops that a bigman is expected to raise in order to give away. Artefacts are unlikely to accumulate: they too are given away and generally there are no objects or raw materials exclusive to the powerful and forbidden to others. Moreover, leadership of this nature is held only in the prime of life. Many will die not as bigmen, but as ordinary members of the community, and this may diminish the chances of their archaeological recognition. Still, it is not only a matter of recognising archaeologically the leaders of a culture, but also of interest to determine the nature of leadership that was present and as we shall see later the size of the coherent social unit may well be the most relevant factor here, and the association of bigmen with village settlement units should be borne in mind.

Village chiefs

In societies where position is hereditary and yet power is restricted to a physical extent similar to that of the bigmen, it seems appropriate to designate the leaders village chiefs.

The village chief is a man with authority or influence over a single unit of people, normally a settlement of 80-300 people as with the bigmen, or he may be leader of a clan or lineage dispersed through several settlement units. His position is partly hereditary, in that only certain families or lineages can provide chiefs and there will be many members of the population whose birth precludes them from ever holding this status.

Within the chiefly group, there may well be several candidates for the role of leader. Normally the successful man will be distinguished by qualities similar to those of the bigman: he will be a successful member of the group, whether as hunter, warrior, farmer, fisherman or trader; he will be generous and gregarious, a good public speaker and promoter of public events; he will have many friends and will form a number of alliances, possibly cemented by marriage and undoubtedly confirmed by the exchange of goods. Even more than the bigman, the chief will be the focal point of an extensive exchange network as, for example, in the Trobriand Islands where chiefly exchange provides the framework for the elaborate Kula system (Malinowski 1922; and see below, p. 181ff).

The duties of village chiefdom include all those already noted for leaders. Some, such as settling local disputes, may become more important and the chief may have the authority to determine and to enforce punishment, such as the payment of compensation for crimes against fellow members of the community. Diplomatic duties may also be more extensive and more complex than those of the bigmen, the chiefs negotiating with each other on behalf of the people they lead. Feasts may be more frequent and on a grander scale.

The distinctions between bigman and chief noted so far are largely ones of degree, and the various aspects have deliberately been treated summarily because there is unlikely to be a *clear* division archaeologically between, say, a feast given by a bigman in the New Guinea Highlands and one given by a chief in the Solomon Islands. What does create a distinction of particular archaeological interest is the addition of religious duties to the ceremonial and secular aspects of leadership. A chief is expected to perform certain rituals for his community – whether to secure good harvests, good fighting or good health does not matter: what is significant is that the rituals can only be performed by the chief. Firth has demonstrated this role of chiefs clearly for Tikopia (Firth 1936 and 1939), and other examples may be found from the tribes of the North West Coast of America (Drucker 1963). In so far as one can generalise, the ritual aspects of leadership are closely associated with hereditary power and there is a tendency for any increase in personal authority to be accompanied by a corresponding increase in the ritual and religious element of a chief's duties. With the village chief we see for the first time a version of leadership whose ultimate expression is divine kingship.

In some respect the rewards of the village chief are little more substantial than those of the bigman. He is given more than his peers, but is expected to be correspondingly more generous, so material goods need not necessarily accrue. However, where there are chiefly families it seems that they may well possess more than commoners, and perhaps live in bigger houses, not solely because of wealth but because the family itself is more numerous: chiefs have more wives than commoners, and more children of chiefs may survive thanks to the increase in food and in care that may result from the family's status. In death, too, the chief may be archaeologically recognisable since his position in society was hereditary and for life, and his status may be indicated by distinctive funeral rites and perhaps denoted by some difference in the nature and amount of grave goods compared to those of commoners (e.g. Northwest Coast chiefs).

While most of the examples above have been taken from societies where the village chief leads an autonomous political unit, many such chiefs are to be found in the lower echelons of power of larger states. This is particularly so in the African kingdoms, where each settlement unit may have a chief responsible to a governor or prince responsible to the king (see Swazi, below). The recognition of this situation archaeologically will depend on the recognition of the larger political unit, a matter of some importance (see Chapter 4).

Tribal chiefs

Tribal chiefs are those who lead a number of settlement groups, or a number of people dispersed through several sites. The people of the tribe do not necessarily have a common assembly, and they may not all know each other; these factors distinguish the tribal chief from the village chief whose control is based on face-to-face relationships within the local community.

Tribal chiefdom is hereditary. Leaders are drawn from one chiefly family, or alternate between two families; or possibly several families may provide candidates; but still the pool of potential chiefs is restricted. Laws of succession vary from group to group according to marriage and inheritance rules, but it is likely that there will be such laws, that they will be more restrictive than for a village chief, and that their effect will be not only to designate the chiefly candidates but also to rank the families or kinship groups within the tribal community. Most societies with tribal chiefs are more hierarchical than those of the village chief, the classic examples to illustrate this being the more complex stratification of most Polynesian societies when compared with those of Melanesia (cf. Malinowski 1922·and Best 1924).

Wealth and generosity, the requisites of success and adulthood, are as much expected of tribal chiefs as of any lesser leader, with a similar emphasis on the receiving and redistribution of gifts. However, some objects may remain with a chief if either the object itself or the raw materials used in its manufacture are forbidden to commoners. This is the case with the Maori jade *meru*, artefacts which are exclusive to the chiefs and which acquire some of the power of their owners and are therefore dangerous to people of lesser standing. Like the *meru*, many of the artefacts exclusive to chiefs are weapons and ceremonial objects derived from weapons; however, the archaeologist cannot rely on their presence to indicate chiefs, nor should he expect all chiefs to possess special artefacts of a warlike nature: Hawaiian chiefs have the exclusive right to wooden bowls decorated with the teeth of their enemies, and to wooden bowls with legs, variations in morphology which one might attribute to function or to fashion rather than to rank. The power of the chief's possessions is a reflection or an extension of his own power, and both have the same element of sacred danger, epitomised in the Hawaiian and Maori concepts of *tapu* (Steiner 1956) (Fig. 48).

The ritual role of tribal chiefs is greatly enhanced compared with that of the village leader, and a chief takes on permanently in his own person some of the attributes of supernatural power which transforms him into something essentially different from his contemporaries. This is often manifest, as with the Maori, in the separateness of the chief and perhaps also of his family: separate eating, separate sleeping, even the separation of the chief from contact with the earth lest his power seep into it inopportunely. The contagious nature of the power of chiefdom and the danger which direct contact with it holds for others as well as the danger of its being diminished naturally reinforces any tendency to exclusive possession of artefacts, and the archaeologist may legitimately expect a tribal chief to leave an archaeological record distinct from that of the commoners he leads.

Emphasis here has been placed on aspects of tribal chiefdom where there is some likelihood of archaeological evidence surviving for their existence, but naturally there are further factors to distinguish them from other leaders. Among these one may note

Figure 48. Artefacts for the Aristocracy. (a) Maori jade, reserved for chiefs. Top: 20 cm; bottom: 18 cm. (b) Hawaiian feather helmet (red and yellow), worn by chiefs (S. Goddard, Exeter City Museum)

more extensive duties as keeper of law and order, related to the greater number of people involved, and a corresponding extension of the leader's power to coerce and to inflict punishment, including the power to banish, enslave or kill offenders. Personal authority is considerable, but it is normally balanced by an obligation to listen either to a formal council or to respected adults of the community, those who in other circumstances would be the bigmen. The extension of authority is further checked by custom and tradition and even men with supernatural powers must act within the norms of their culture.

The rewards of leadership are implicit in much of the above: possessions, authority and the deference of the community. If wives are to be seen as a reward, then the tribal chief also enjoys these in greater measure than any leader so far discussed, and he will probably produce more children, command more housing, cultivate more fields and tend more herds than his followers.

Kings

The recognition of monarchy in primitive states is something alien to most prehistorians, who prefer to see kingship restricted to literate and civilised societies and tend to speak of Egyptian kings but Celtic princes. Yet at the same time (in the sixteenth and seventeenth centuries) as antiquaries were confidently giving their own ancestors only the status of chiefs, they were acknowledging the rulers of newfound lands in Africa, North America and Polynesia as kings and princes. This was due to a certain extent to the influence of one of the factors that distinguishes between kings and other rulers, namely the recognition and acceptance of a king's unique status by his subjects and by neighbouring groups. The antiquaries granted these newfound rulers the status accorded to them by their own world, but for the rulers of past worlds there was no one to speak.

Kingship exaggerates many of the features of tribal chiefdom. Kings are rulers over a number of settlement units, and frequently over a state that is subdivided into chiefdoms or substates, each with a subordinate ruler (see *Kede*, below). The position is hereditary, and probably has a more restricted field of candidates than for a chief, so that a king may be a juvenile, whereas for other leaders this is rarely the case. That a juvenile can function as king indicates the increased strength of another attribute, the ritual power and role of the leader. Not all kings are divine or sacred, but all function as the leaders of prescribed rituals for their subjects, and all act as figureheads for their nation. Thus the Queen Mother of the Swazi is Rainmaker, and the Oba of a Yoruba kingdom ensures its prosperity by proper attention to ritual. Archaeologically, a monarch will be indicated not so much by the size of the coherent social unit, or by the size of settlements such as towns, but by the regalia of the crown and the king's palace or court. While tribal chiefs possess some sacred and exclusive objects, kings are laden with them – literally so in the case of some West African monarchs (Fig. 49). Kings are also burdened with, or enjoy, large families, countless wives, councillors, courtiers, bodyguards, and the housing required by all these people. Hence the palace or court, be it the magnificence of urban Benin or the rural sprawl of the Azande (see pp. 111-13 for description). Where a king has military power in addition to his ritual and judicial roles, it is likely that the army will be quartered with him, an advantage that Chaka was quick to perceive and which added to his strength as king of the Zulu (Gluckman 1940).

These attributes of monarchy contribute to the creation and maintenance of distinctive royal settlements and regal artefacts, which may be mirrored in distinctive royal burial grounds and grave goods of death. The vagaries of burial custom are wellknown from Ucko's survey (Ucko 1969); nevertheless in ranked societies headed by a monarchy, where artefacts have become part of the essence of power, distinctive burial rites may be expected for kings, designed to maintain their unique status in death as in life. These rites may sometimes be extended to the royal family. Sutton Hoo is a royal burial recognised archaeologically because of literary evidence (Bruce-Mitford 1968); yet the chariot burials of La Tène Europe, which are equally distinctive, are not given quite the same accolade.

This has been a very summary treatment of kingship, biased in favour of those aspects of status and power which could leave tangible archaeological evidence. However, as one purpose of this book is to persuade archaeologists of the advantages to be gained from a knowledge of *complete* societies, and not simply the material aspects, the nature of kingship will be further explored in later pages, and those interested will find additional information in works such as Evans-Pritchard's *The Azande*, or the second part of Lucy Mair's *Primitive Government* (Evans-Pritchard 1971; Mair 1962).

Figure 49. Artefacts for the Crown. Oba Atenzuwa II in full coral regalia, with carved
   ivory bracelets. Two of the chiefs also wear strings of coral beads, as signs of their
   rank, and one wears a bronze mask at his waist (R.E. Bradbury)

Other systems of social organisation

It would be wrong to suppose that all primitive and prehistoric
societies were organised solely in terms of leaders, chiefs and kings;
it may come nearer the truth to argue that all communities are held
together by means other than leaders, and some but not all have the

additional cohesive force of a figurehead. Those other means will now be examined briefly, and some space will be devoted to them in the examples that follow, since an awareness of the alternatives to the centralisation of political power may help the archaeologist to a better understanding of the questions implicit in perennial problems of interpretation, such as 'Who built Stonehenge?' As the alternatives are explored, it should also become apparent that there is no logical and pre-ordained development through a hierarchy of increasingly powerful leaders: this will be relevant to some of the main themes of prehistory.

Kinship

One of the dominant forces of social cohesion, one so important that no social anthropologist would have left it till now to discuss, is kinship. The subject is too often neglected by the archaeologist, who gets bogged down in the jargon of another discipline without perhaps realising that behind it there lies a wealth of information relevant to all his studies. I do not mean that he needs to become an expert in the niceties of in-law relationships, or that it matters to him whether or not the members of a particular community could marry their mother's brother's children but not their father's sister's (although there are recent suggestions that such items could be of the greatest importance and interest). I mean that in every human community biological kinship is recognised and it delimits the basic units belonging to the community, for it is primarily by such blood-relationships that people gain their membership. They are *born* Mbuti, Mandan or Mundurucu, Andamanese or Zulu, and the limits of the group are the limits of kinship, limits which may also be defined by the limits of marriage: Zulu marry Zulu, not Swazi, and Kede only marry Kede (but Nuer marry Dinka and cause much anthropological confusion; e.g. Southall 1976). Where a community is small, as on Tikopia, all people are closely related and it is not surprising that these relationships are used to structure the social organisation, but equally where a community involves thousands, as for the Nuer, the framework of society can be based on kinship, and degrees of social cohesion can be measured in degrees of blood relationship (see below, p. 151).

Where kinship is a functioning subsystem of a community, and not merely a passive feature allowing membership, it can be used to mobilise people as the Nuer example will demonstrate, and students of the Scottish Highlands or the Mafia on either side of the Atlantic will acknowledge the potential power of a mobilised kinship group. With the leadership of a clan chief, such a system can have considerable military force; it also has, even without any leader, potential for communal action.

Where kinship is the sole, or main, organising framework of a community it is likley that the settlement units will be small: nuclear and extended family groups (as for so many pastoralists) or small villages. Permanent settlements of more than about 300 people suggest that some other factor is involved, because at about this level the limits of close kinship and of face-to-face relationships are reached.

Age-sets

Kinship may be reinforced by the institution of age-sets, which are particularly formalised in Africa but which in practice contribute to the ordering of society in many places. Roughly speaking, all male members of a group, be it settlement, clan or tribe, are born into a particular named age-set that will span up to ten years: those born between 1900 and 1909 would belong together throughout their lives in one set, and those born between 1910-1919 would belong to the next set. At intervals, all the members of a set are initiated at one and the same ceremony and then they move together through a series of roles or occupations for which a typical sequence would be: warrior, then farmer and family man, and finally elder. Each stage carries with it certain duties and responsibilities that vary from society to society, but frequently the young adults are responsible for defence, the next age-set deals with civil and secular organisation, and the elders deal with the ritual aspects of life. Alternatively one may find rule by a gerontocracy, as for the Tiwi, whose power increases with age.

Age-sets combined with kinship can hold together large tribes, but again it is unlikely that any individual permanent settlement will exceed the size of a village, unless there is also an element of personal authority in the society.

Religious leaders

In archaeological literature, religious leaders are from time to time proposed as alternatives to the secular political hierarchy, particularly where the apparent focal point of a culture has the appearance of a ritual centre as does the Avebury complex in Wiltshire (cf. Kehoe and Renfrew 1974). However, before making any such interpretation we have to contend with the vagaries of preservation and realise that the evidence may appear central because it alone has survived. Furthermore, even if the archaeological evidence is being correctly interpreted, I would argue that institutionalised religious leaders are so similar to their secular counterparts as to be indistinguishable to the archaeologist. The distinctions are further blurred by the religious functions that accrue to many chiefs and kings, and in some cases, of course, the two roles are deliberately combined as with the Kede chief or Swazi monarch (see Chapter 5 for further discussion of this point).

The religious leaders who may be significant are of a different order. They are the prophets and the wild men out of the wilderness who suddenly unite a people in a common cause, a cause that is in all likelihood violent, destructive and explosively expansionist. Such leaders have often emerged in historic times from tribes who have come into contact with European rule, and who have been in some measure oppressed by it. Examples may be found from among the Indians of North America, from African tribes including the Nuer, and especially in the cargo-cults that have sporadically swept through Melanesia since the nineteenth century (Burridge 1969; Worsley 1957). In all these cases, a leader has come to the fore in a society which has no marked degree of personal, centralised authority in normal circumstances. The man's position has been based on or justified by religious sanctions. Power of this nature is ephemeral – were it otherwise, the prophets' role would soon be secularised – but while it lasts it can bind a group of people together more surely than any other means, and they may wage wars, build monuments or destroy all their possessions and crops according to the inspiration of the moment. The direct archaeological implications of such phenomena cannot be fully explored here, but, in the present context of social organisation, it is relevant simply to note the existence and the meteoric power of such religious leaders.

Examples of political and social organisation

In contrast to the previous chapter, the range of examples used here is deliberately restricted: all the peoples described are African. The reasons for this are twofold: first that there is abundant literature concerning African political systems, and secondly to demonstrate a fraction of the variation that can occur within one continent at one time. On the whole, the examples do not neatly illustrate the categories discussed above, but they show how functioning societies can blend together different aspects of leadership and government.

The Mbuti (sources: Turnbull 1961 and 1965)

The Mbuti pygmies live in the Ituri forest of the Congo, as hunters and gatherers, with some contact with settled village agriculturalists (of which more later). Their manner of subsistence demands a basically nomadic life, moving camp every month or so, but there is no urgency in this movement as food supplies are plentiful. People live together in sufficient numbers to hunt effectively, about 30-50 in the case of net-hunters and 10-15 for those who hunt with bow and arrow.

The essence of Mbuti social organisation is fluidity, and there are no full-time leaders. A hunting band consists of a number of families, in all probability related to each other, but inter-family relationships are not used to structure the group. Each family normally consists of an adult man and his wife and children (occasionally two wives); marriage outside the band is preferred, but not invariably enforced, and residence is likewise normally but not always with the husband's band. All the qualifications in the above sentence are necessary because Mbuti families are free to move from band to band, and band membership and blood relationship are not synonymous.

Hunting activities of the band need to be co-ordinated where nets are used as every active member of the group takes part: women and children drive the game through the forest towards a line of nets set up by the men, who wait there with their spears. There is no individual leadership of the drive and all decisions are reached through communal discussion, though the opinions of good hunters will be given more weight than those of the younger, inexperienced men. Gathering needs less group co-ordination, and is more or less a matter for individual action.

For two months of the year, it will be remembered, the Mbuti abandon their normal subsistence activities to collect honey, and at the same time the net hunters abandon their band organisation, splitting up into independent family units. When bands reconvene after the honey season, membership is likely to have changed. This pattern of splitting and reforming in different groupings is one means whereby tension between group members is reduced, in that people who were antagonistic towards each other beforehand are likely to join different bands for the next net-hunting season. The need for formal law and order is lessened by this fluidity. Furthermore, if people quarrel at any time, or if someone does not fit into a band, the option to move away and join another group is always open. Therefore the Mbuti have not needed to invest any one person with the authority to arbitrate in disputes, because those in conflict do not have to remain living together. Such a situation can only exist for nomadic groups with ample resources, and all settled communities will need some institutionalised means of maintaining the peace. The Mbuti illustrate one end of a spectrum of law and order whose opposite may be seen in complex urbanised kingdoms, such as those of the Yoruba.

Fluidity as an alternative to the development of authority has been emphasised because of its particular interest to prehistory, and Turnbull has underlined this function of the hunter-gatherer's freedom of movement by showing how the Mbuti who are archers also use the honey season as a time for adjusting relationships, though for them it is the period of amalgamation and not dispersal. Other aspects of Mbuti organisation to note, since they reappear in other contexts, are the almost institutionalised role of the band clown, a man who acts as butt and scapegoat for his fellows, and the great importance of the communal performance of ritual which affirms the unity of the group and its separateness from the village farmers. The Mbuti show minimal evidence of personal authority, with nothing more than occasional activity leaders, but they provide ample evidence for the social organisation of a community: for them as much as for the most hierarchical of kingdoms, there is no anarchy.

The Nuer (sources: Evans-Pritchard 1940a and 1940b)

In his studies of the Nuer, Evans-Pritchard pays considerable attention to the interplay of resources, subsistence, and social and political organisation. The Nuer, like the Swazi, have a mixed economy with a strong cultural orientation to pastoralism – it is argued that they could not subsist without their herds. Settlement is in villages on long low ridges above the flat plains for the wet half of the year, and in cattle camps by water sources during the dry months. Evans-Pritchard distinguishes three means of socio-political organisation which fit in with the subsistence and settlement pattern: the tribe, the clan, and the age-set.

There are a number of Nuer tribes, and from Evans-Pritchard's description of their distinguishing features it becomes clear that the tribe is best defined as a territorial unit, for Nuerland is divided into a number of territories each of which belongs to and is inhabited by a different tribe. Each tribe can be divided into two main segments which are in turn subdivided and subdivided yet again, and broadly speaking each tribal division corresponds to internal territorial divisions, the smallest unit of any political significance being the village. Seasonal changes in settlement allow for a certain fluidity of residence, in that all the people from one village need not go together to the dry season pastures, but will probably disperse to a number of camps within the territory of the tribal subsegment that their village belongs to. Neither village nor tribal segment nor tribe has a leader, and the forces which hold groups together appear to be common culture, residence, and opposition from outside. A village feuds against a neighbouring village, but the two unite against another tribal segment, and all the units of a tribe will come together as one against another Nuer tribe or against foreigners.

While tribal membership appears to stem from residence and not descent, the clan system of organisation is based entirely on the latter principle. There are about twenty Nuer clans, and as with the tribes each clan is divided and subdivided and divided yet again, in this case into maximal, major, minor and minimal lineages. At each stage the people comprehended in any one unit are more closely related to each other than to persons in other like units. Clan divisions do not correspond to tribal division, but each division of the land is associated with a particular clan, and Nuer who live within the tribal area associated with their own clan are regarded as 'aristocrats', though they will not have this distinction if they live anywhere else. Likewise the subdivisions of tribal territory are associated with particular lineages (i.e. sub-divisions) of the tribal clan, but the system does not appear to confer any privilege or authority upon the people concerned. Despite the fact that members of any one clan may be dispersed through a number of tribes, Evans-Pritchard sees the segmentation of both as being closely linked, with the bonds of kinship reinforcing those of residence, particularly at village level. It would also seem, though he does not stress the point, that the dispersal of the clans through the tribes serves to unite those tribes together as the Nuer nation.

The third organising factor is the age-set, which applies to males only. Each village or district initiates its adolescents yearly for about six years, and the initiates belong to the same age-set. Then for four years there is a pause and the next series of initiations creates the next age-set. Bouts of initiation are co-ordinated within the tribe, and more or less so between adjacent tribes, so that a man will recognise members of his set wherever he goes within the country, and he will have a closer bond with them than with members of older or younger sets.

None of these Nuer organisations have institutionalised leaders, not even the clans despite the acknowledgment of some lineages as 'aristocrats'. There are some men distinguished from their fellows as 'Men of the cattle' and others as 'Leopard-skin chiefs', but their roles are ritual and involve neither leadership nor government. The former are concerned with initiation and the latter with the formalised settling of feuds. For all common activities, certain people emerge as activity leaders, but they do not retain any status beyond the moment. Historically, the only Nuer to have held power over their fellows were the prophets, men whose authority (as their name implies) was based on religion and whose leadership was against the pressures of Arab and European incursions into Nuerland.

The Nuer show us a culture which is clearly definable as a political and social unit, but which has no leader. The lack of leadership no doubt prompted Evans-Pritchard's references to the 'anarchic state' (Evans-Pritchard 1940, p. 272) of the Nuer, but it is clear that the society is ordered and organised at all levels, and in ways that cross-cut and intermesh sufficiently for anarchy to be a far from apt description.

The Karimojong (source: Mair 1962)

The Karimojong of northeastern Uganda are farmers who, like so many peoples, lay greater cultural stress on their cattle than on their crops. They are included to illustrate the role that age-sets can play as a means of political and social organisation.

The mechanics of the Karimojong age-set system are fairly straightforward. In each neighbourhood of up to 30 or so households, small groups of boys are initiated by their elders as they become old enough, and every five or six years the initiates of the whole country are grouped into a set with a common name. Successive sets are ranked according to seniority and there are two recognised generations of five sets each, the senior generation of elders and the junior generation of warriors. Every thirty years a ceremony is held at a particular spot in the northeast of the country, which is reserved for this purpose alone; all the Karimojong attend, and the senior generation formally retires, while the junior generation move up into the senior grade.

Through the age-sets, every adult Karimojong male has his position defined in relation to others: those of his set, throughout the country, are his equals, those of senior sets are to be respected and deferred to, those of junior sets show him respect and obedience. In a dispute between equals, i.e. men of the same set, any man of an older set may arbitrate. Men can recognise the age-set of strangers by the ornaments they wear, if attribution is not immediately obvious by age alone. The elder generation as a whole may act on behalf of all the people in some circumstances. For example, it is the elders who decide when cattle should be moved to dry-season pasture, and no man may move his beasts until the elders have declared their decision by performing the requisite ritual.

Within each neighbourhood, it is the duty of the elders to arbitrate in disputes between local inhabitants. However, it is common for one among them to stand out as 'spokesman' or leader of the discussions and leader of local opinion, and this man achieves his status in much the same way as a bigman; indeed his position is very similar. He is likely to be successful, to have married well, to have lots of sons and lots of cattle, and to be a good talker. These neighbourhood bigmen are the only leaders of the Karimojong. Recognition of a common bond is achieved through the nationally co-ordinated system of age-sets, and through the very important handing-over ritual between the generations which all attend, and which helps to define those who are Karimojong.

The Kede (source: Nadel 1940)

Nadel's account of the Kede emphasises the close relationship between environment, economy, settlement, history and the ensuing state of political organisation, thereby providing a study of particular interest in the present context.

The Kede are a riverain people of Northern Nigeria; their country lies along the banks of the Niger and its tributary the Kaduna, and they form both politically and culturally a section of the Nupe tribe, albeit a fairly autonomous section. Kede territory is inhabited by many non-Kede (but Nupe) peoples who were probably the prior inhabitants of the area but who are now ruled by the immigrant Kede, though the latter are in a minority of about 1 to 5. The non-Kede live by farming and fishing, while the Kede live entirely off the river, as fishermen and as canoemen ferrying goods and people up and down and across the Niger.

Riverside villages normally contain people of both Kede and non-Kede groups, living in separate areas of the settlement or perhaps living on either side of the water. Only the 'capital', Muregi, is inhabited solely by Kede, and it is the most permanent and probably the oldest settlement in the territory. Other villages have more-or-less permanent houses, depending on how long they have been settled, and it seems that the Kede were recently an expanding group, turning seasonal trade outposts into new villages, once these commercial footholds in new areas had become well established. The banks of the Niger have thus been strung with Kede villages, with only a few gaps where strong settlements of other Nupe peoples existed before Kede colonisation and still survive.

The extent of Kede settlement delimits the extent of Kede power, excluding any seasonal trading sites yet to be consolidated. The Kede state is ruled from the administrative centre of Muregi, the one pure settlement. The chief, known as the Kuta, lives here and from here exercises powers not unlike those of a king, except that he himself owes obeisance to a higher external authority, the Emir of Nupe. His position is hereditary. Briefly, the chief is aided in his rule by a number of officials resident with him at Muregi, and by titled delegates who govern other settlements in his name. These delegates collect taxes, maintain law and order and pass on the chief's orders in matters affecting the whole state (e.g. communal action for warfare).

The non-Kede pay taxes to the delegates which are eventually passed on to the Nupe Emir. The Kede pay an income-tax, and dues to the delegates where they trade; the delegates keep a proportion of this and pass the rest on to the Kuta, who keeps the bulk of it and sends on one-fifth to his overlord, the Emir.

The strong financial position of the Kuta is not mirrored by his legal role, for most major crimes are dealt with by the Emir. However, in religious matters the chief is a true leader of his territory, performing rituals on behalf of Kede and non-Kede alike, though the latter, unlike their rulers, are not Muslims.

The chief, the officials and the delegates form the upper class of the state, and all other Kede are ranked closely behind them socially, leaving the non-Kede as a demonstrably poor lower class, culturally impoverished in Kede eyes. The subservience of the majority of the population, particularly a conquered majority, demands some explanation. In the present climate of autonomy and home rule, it may be hard to appreciate the influence of tradition and shared history, in that Kede and non-Kede are alike Nupe, and Nupe history decrees that the one should rule the other. The historical sanction is bolstered by the chief's ritual activities on behalf of *all* inhabitants, and by the lack of direct economic competition between farmers and canoemen. Unlike some of the other systems discussed, the government of the Kede state does not rely on the right of one person or one group of people to dictate the life and death of others. Its power is economic rather than military, more akin to that of the village chiefs than to their tribal counterparts. Yet it cannot be denied that in some senses the Kuta of the Kede is supreme in his territory.

Nadel suggests that Kede rule is closely allied to their river-based economy, in that their mobility, control of trade, and efficient communications place them at an advantage, and that their economy could not flourish unless they had control of the river and authority over all who lived along its banks. It might be that the Kede with their distinctive culture could not exist except as rulers.

The anomalies of the Kede situation cannot be disentangled in so short a space, but they demonstrate that any rigid political classification and any hierarchy of rulers will have exceptions. Finally, the Kede, as relatively mobile rulers of a settled farming population, are like the Fulani who rule the Hausa, creating situations of cultural contact that will be discussed further in the next chapter.

The Swazi: a dual monarchy (source: Kuper 1963)

The Swazi are a Bantu-speaking people living in the southeastern part of Africa, the population being just under 200,000 when they were studied by Kuper, and their area of settlement 6,700 square miles (density *c*. 30 people per square mile). Traditional subsistence is based on crop cultivation and cattle, with the latter being far more carefully tended than the former; the Swazi, like the Nuer and the Karimojong, are pastoral in their cultural orientation though not so in practical terms. Settlement is in large family homesteads grouped loosely into villages.

There are three groups of people who form the Swazi: a nucleus of original invading clans, among them the royal clan; a group of clans subdued by the invaders early in the recent history of expansion (probably in the seventeenth century); and a group of immigrant clans who arrived in Swazi territory as refugees and settlers in the nineteenth century. These groups of clans retain some cultural differences, but they do intermarry and all owe allegiance to the monarchy.

The monarchy is hereditary, in a somewhat complex fashion. The reigning king has a number of wives, and among those who come from the nuclear invading clans, but not from his own royal clan, one wife will be distinguished from the others and designated as the future queen mother and she will be expected to have one son and then bear no more children. Her son is the heir to the kingship, and so too is she, for when the reigning king dies they inherit as joint monarchs. As rulers, the king and queen mother each have powers and privileges that act as a check on the other, and they habitually live in different parts of the kingdom with the queen mother settled at the main national shrine.

The king and queen mother are nominally all-powerful, but in practice their rule is tempered by the check each provides on the other, by the advice and counsel of the king's male kin, by a complex system of officials, and through local government by clan chiefs. Clan and lineage play an important part in local organisation, and they are supplemented by age-regiments for the men. Thus although the Swazi are ruled by king and queen mother, many other means of social organisation are active within the kingdom. Moreover, the political role of the monarchs is closely bound up with their ritual function, and with their responsibility for the prosperity and well-being of the kingdom. They are figureheads as much as leaders.

The material manifestations of the Swazi dual monarchy are of some interest. The king and queen mother have exclusive use of certain artefacts, mainly head-dresses, ornaments and royal 'medicines'. The king alone of all Swazi is embalmed at death. Their homesteads are more complex than those of commoners, and particularly conspicuous is the central royal cattle byre, which is the focus for the ritual life of the kingdom, and it is here that the annual ceremony of kingship is held. Swazi political organisation does therefore have some direct reflection in material terms; despite the rural, pastoral nature of the culture, some archaeological evidence for the political hierarchy could be expected.

Possible correlations

In the following section the relationship of two aspects of political and social organisation to the archaeological record will be discussed. The first of these is the possible correlation between settlement size and degree of political hierarchy; the second is the possible link between the development of socio-political hierarchies and the development of specialist crafts and industries.

Settlement size and political hierarchy

In the preceding sections, it has been emphasised that no society exists in a state of anarchy. But it is also apparent that some peoples have a very much less developed political and social organisation than others. Cultures with minimal organisation and minimal leadership generally live in small groups, in the manner of the Mbuti. We have noted Turnbull's suggestion that, for these hunter-gatherers, movement and the fluidity of group membership serve as alternatives to the development of authority, and one consequence is that settlements are small and transitory. If we take the reverse of this proposition, that permanent and stable groups can exist only with the development of authority, we have the beginnings of an interesting hypothesis.

Lee has developed this point further through his studies of the !Kung Bushmen (Lee 1972). He observed that the !Kung lived together in large groups for a part of the year and they apparently found this a mixed blessing: 'It offered the people a more intense social life but it also meant harder work and a higher frequency of conflict' (p. 182). As conflicts erupted between neighbours, the people who had quarrelled walked away from each other and went to live elsewhere, and so the large group ceased to exist. However, Lee observed one instance of a particularly large group of over 100 !Kung living together in relative amity for most of the year, alongside a group of Herero pastoralists. This new departure for the Bushmen was made possible partly by Herero food supplies, which meant that the hunter-gatherers did not have to walk far for their subsistence, and also, as Lee puts it, by the fact that 'the Herero provide a legal umbrella under which this large number of feisty Bushmen can live together'. In other words, the pastoralists were acting as arbitrators in disputes between !Kung, and their authority gave the group of hunter-gatherers a greater degree of permanence, such as would have been necessary to the initiation of settlement at village level.

Sahlins' essay 'The original affluent society' (Sahlins 1974) is concerned with food rather than authority, but it is mentioned again here to reinforce the possible conclusions to be drawn from the Mbuti and !Kung evidence. Sahlins shows clearly that hunter-fisher-gatherers of temperate and warmer regions are no more vulnerable to starvation than farmers, and he suggests that their food is relatively easily obtained. If Sahlins' arguments are accepted, scarcity of food cannot be taken as a key factor limiting the size and permanence of hunter-gatherer settlements, and more importance may be given to Lee's suggestion that there is a need for arbitration if people are to achieve a greater size and duration of group. Lee's particular instance of the !Kung and the Herero and Sahlins' general survey both bear out, in relation to nomadic hunter-gatherer societies, the proposition that for people to live together in any number for any length of time (usually over 40 people for half the year or more) there is a need for a recognised arbitrator, someone invested by the group with a degree of authority or influence over them. Both the Nuer and the Karimojong demonstrate this need, for though neither society has leaders as such one of the few roles differentiated by the Nuer in an otherwise homogenous and egalitarian society is that of the Leopardskin Chief whose function is to settle disputes. The Karimojong give influence to the elders and allow senior men to arbitrate between juniors through the system of age-sets and generations.

The relationship between group size and social control is explored by Forge in a survey of New Guinea societies (Forge 1972). Examining a number of New Guinea cultures, he notes that functioning residence units (i.e. the active social unit discussed above) rarely exceed 350-400 people and that in large villages of 1,000 or more, the inhabitants are subdivided into a number of smaller functioning residence units which rarely act together as one village. Forge suggests that given the basically egalitarian society of New Guinea, and given the ordering of that society through the competition among adult men to become bigmen, the optimum number of men in any one functioning group is from 30 to 80, as this allows all the men to know each other well and to adjust their relationships with each other through direct competition. With more adult men in a group, any one member is no longer able to know all the others well, and some institutionalised means of regulating relationships between people is needed or the community will fall apart. It would seem therefore that the bigman leadership is related to groups of about 150-350 men, women and children. Above this size, Forge concludes that some division of society along occupational and status lines is necessary, if order is to be maintained without the group splitting. Chagnon has observed similar factors at work while studying the Yanomamo in South America (Chagnon 1968b), which suggests that the arguments set out by Forge have more than local application.

The hypothesis to emerge from this is not particularly startling, but it is none the less relevant. It is that the initial development of permanent small settlements, and subsequent increases in the size of such settlements over certain population threshholds, must be accompanied by corresponding developments in social organisation, especially in terms of leadership and personal authority. One might almost suggest that the larger the settlement the more power is vested in fewer hands. (It should be remembered that we are talking here of settlements and not of tribal groups or cultures, whose growth is bounded by different parameters.)

These arguments may be used to shed new light on the Indians of the North West Coast of North America, who are traditionally cited as examples of tribes who break the rules of hunter-gatherer life. The Tlingit, the Haida, and their relatives are extraordinary (but not unique) among hunter-fisher-gatherers for their settled life: for much of the year they live in permanent villages built along the coast. These tribes are also exceptional in the degree to which they have developed systems of social hierarchy, systems which culminate in hereditary chiefs and which include the division of society into different classes including slaves. It is highly likely that these two exceptional traits developed interdependently, and that without the authoritarian framework of their hierarchy the tribes would lead a more nomadic life despite the relative abundance of their food supplies.

The spectrum of social and political development seen in non-industrial societies ranges from the simple and smallscale !Kung bands to the great complexity of large Yoruba towns, and the latter are fittingly ruled by kings. Yet the argument must not be pushed too far, and it should be remembered that one may find royal households in a village or homestead, and monarchs are not the prerogative of urban people – witness the Azande.

For the archaeologist, therefore, the size of a permanent settlement unit may well in itself convey information concerning the development of social organisation and political hierarchies. A village settlement like Stannon Down on Bodmin Moor in southwest England (Mercer 1970) is indicative of Bronze Age bigmen at least, and probably chiefs, for the site had a minimum of 70 houses and a likely population of 150-300 people. Larger and more diversified settlements would imply the existence of hereditary rulers, tribal chiefs if not kings, and here the evidence from fortified hilltop settlements of the Hallstall era, like the Heuneberg above the Danube (Kimmig 1975), confirms the suggestion noted at the beginning of this chapter, that the rich and unusual burials associated with these sites are those of royalty.

It was suggested above that developments in group or settlement size and permanence required a parallel development of social organisation, especially in terms of authority and arbitration. If so, then it is likely that the first moves towards permanent settlement were generated by changes in the social rather than the subsistence sphere. Flannery has shown that, in at least two of the focal areas for the development of farming, permanent settlement and the origins of agriculture did not go hand-in-hand. In the Near East, permanent settlements came into being before farming, whereas in Mesoamerica crops were grown for several millennia before farmers took to village life (Flannery 1972). Moreover, we know from abundant American examples, that farming does not *require* settlement – although it may facilitate it, which is a different matter. We know, too, that mankind has a surprisingly long history of large communal gatherings, which probably intensified during the Upper Palaeolithic (e.g. Moravian sites such as Dolni Vestonice and Pavlov) and which continued in Europe throughout the Mesolithic period notably along the Danube at sites such as Lepenski Vir and Soroki (Tringham 1971).

Undoubtedly, these settlements could not exist without an abundance of food, but the food could be hunted, fished and gathered as well as farmed: the means of production was not crucial to the initiation of settlement. Therefore we can return with renewed confidence to the hypothesis that permanent settlements arose as a result of more sophisticated systems of social control: human gregariousness gives people the desire to live in large and permanent groups, and this desire is increasingly satisfied as society becomes more hierarchical, stratified, organised and ruled.

To support such hypotheses, we need to establish a positive correlation between the development of settlements and an increase in organisation and authority. In the Near East, the search will be for archaeological evidence indicative of such developments very early in the Postglacial period if not before. It is most likely to be found in the complex burials of that era, which show that some people were buried with elaborate rites and ornamental grave clothes, a possible though by no means certain sign of developing social stratification (e.g. Mount Carmel). Evidence from after the event may also be relevant. The rapid urbanisation of some Near Eastern regions, with Jericho as the prime example of an early town contemporary with the early evidence for farming, suggests a long history of developing social organisation leading up to the establishment of urban centres. Many sites, and notably Anatolian ones such as Çatal Huyuk (Mellaart 1965), contain evidence for a large and highly organised ritual element in the activities of the settlement, and we have noted above the correspondence of religious and secular authority, and the increase in the ritual component of a leader's role as his position becomes more powerful. Again, the complexity of these developments suggests a lengthy history, in all probability predating changes in the means of subsistence (cf. Bender 1978, and see Chapter 7).

Chiefs and crafts

One recurring feature in the description of leaders from bigmen to kings was the frequent need for a man to be wealthy to qualify for a leading role. Once a leader achieved his status, he was required to be generous, to give feasts and food and riches to his fellows. This 'social generosity' has been required in many contexts, from the long-suffering leaders of the Nambi-Kuara to the flamboyant Kings of Beowulf's era.

Why the custom of so many cultures dictates that leaders should be generous is an unresolved matter, but one consequence that concerns us here is the resulting stream of gifts through the hands of men at the top of their hierarchies. In societies where there is no individual ownership of land and no money economy these gifts are likely to be people (slaves, wives, etc.) or precious objects, given by commoners to their rulers and redistributed by the latter to their followers (see Chapter 4 for further details). In addition, there is the diplomatic exchange of gifts between leaders of different groups; these will often be objects of especial quality and value. The diplomatic exchanges of valuables between sixteenth-century European kingdoms are an example of this phenomenon, as are the extravagances of the Potlatch or the complexities of the Kula. The more exalted the leader, the more numerous and the more varied are the gifts which pass through his hands. Polynesian social stratification is on the whole more developed than that of Melanesia, and a Maori or Fijian tribal chief has more power than a Trobriand village chief or Kapauku bigman – and Polynesian material culture is more complex and specialised than that of Melanesia. Many a museum curator has compared the carefully finished, very beautiful artefacts of the former region with the simpler and rougher objects of Melanesia. Now such a judgment depends on Western notions of value, but we can state objectively that Hawaiian culture produces more and more complex objects than that of the Dani, and that there is a greater degree of specialisation in the manufacturing process on Hawaii than in the Dugum region of New Guinea. The technology of both regions is similar, employing stone and bone and wooden tools but no metal. One of the factors responsible for these differences may be the influence which hereditary chiefdoms exert on manufacture, through the increased cultural demand for objects suitable for a ruler to give and to receive. Sahlins suggests this in his discussion of the redistributive role of chiefdoms, a point developed in archaeological contexts by Renfrew (Sahlins 1974, Renfrew 1973c).

Sophistication and specialisation in the manufacture of material culture may be correlated with general social complexity and not merely with leadership: hierarchical societies tend to have greater occupational specialisation than egalitarian ones as may be illustrated by the comparison of extremes such as the Yoruba and the Nuer. The distinction between Polynesian and Melanesian objects is less marked than this, but it too is complemented by a greater development of social hierarchies in the former context than in the latter.

The correlation of hierarchies and specialised skills is likely to be linked with the obligations of status. Rulers and members of a community have to be seen to be generous, and the greater the distinctions made between people the more likely it is for the such leaders and nobles to become patrons of the lower craftsmen, perhaps seeking rare and beautiful objects to enhance their own prestige. Therefore the emergence of leaders may encourage two linked developments which Forge suggested were inevitable if groups were to increase in size, namely the classification of people by occupation as well as by age and sex, together with the diversification of skills and specialisations practised by members of the group (Forge 1972).

Although the nature of the relationship between leaders, hierarchies and material culture is far from clear, sufficient examples can be quoted to show that development of material culture can be related to these factors and not to subsistence and technology alone. The Haida, with their nobles, commoners and slaves, do not have a metal-based technology, but their possessions are far more complex than those of most hunter-gatherers. The Azande Kingdom boasts many skilled craftsmen, despite subsistence and settlement closer to that of the egalitarian Nuer than the hierarchical Yoruba.

If the above tentative correlations are tenable, they give rise to an hypothesis that can be applied to archaeological evidence. If the variety of crafts and specialist skills in a culture is a function of its social complexity, then a study of material culture should provide some indication of the degree of social stratification. In this light, one might re-examine the artefact evidence from the Wessex burials and compare it with contemporary evidence from other regions of the British Isles. Or one might compare the artefact evidence from different regions of La Tène Europe and test the conclusions drawn against local evidence for settlement size, and where possible against the historical evidence available in classical literature. Both these suggestions require lengthy research, not to be dabbled in lightly here. They are put forward in the hope of tempting some prehistorian to prove or to refute them, thereby testing also the value of the ethnographic evidence.

4. Contact

The possible subject matter of this chapter is vast, worthy of a book
in itself. Therefore, as with social organisation, the treatment is
bound to be summary and selective and once again the bias is
towards aspects of contact which relate most closely to the interests
of the archaeologist. Transport will first be examined briefly, as the
essential means to contact, and the bulk of the chapter will be
concerned with both peaceful and hostile meetings between
primitive communities.

The extent of the subject matter is a reflection of the amount of
time and energy devoted by primitive peoples to contact with the
outside. Self-sufficiency and isolation are far from the norm, and
there is barely a group of people that does not establish some link
with others. Archaeologists have at times treated their evidence as if
the contrary were true, as if people had dwelt in discrete units,
almost as remote as the Lost Worlds of Conan Doyle and Rider-
Haggard; they have regarded imports as freaks, and any quantity of
foreign material the result of an invasion. Few archaeologists, it is
true, consistently carry interpretation to such extremes, but many
seem unaware of the potential for contact between primitive
communities. It is hoped that this chapter will begin to remedy
matters, by displaying the great richness and manifold means of
contact between peoples, from the simple barter of foods to the
wealth of redistribution achieved by ceremonial exchange cycles,
from the peaceful co-existence of two small cultures to the empires of
successful conquerors; from this it is hoped to demonstrate the
integration of the various means of contact into the total culture of a
society, affecting in one way or another all the major aspects of life.

Some explanation is due for the inclusion of exchange and
warfare in the same chapter, strange partners in many ways. This
has been done because they are discussed as two facets of the same
phenomenon, namely contact. Exchange is not purely economic but

often motivated by either prestige or diplomacy, and frequently by both. Likewise warfare is not pure aggression, but also a matter of prestige and diplomacy. Moreover the one is not inconsistent with the other: in some contexts they are to be found as different points on a spectrum of contacts such as those that take place between Yanomamo villlages, or between the Nuer and the Dinka. In other contexts one may find two peoples at war with each other, and yet trading extensively at the same time, as did many of the Plains Indians.

Transport

We are concerned here with the transport of people and of goods in the context of meetings between peoples. This does not directly include the day-to-day transport of nomadic peoples whether hunter-gatherers or pastoralists, nor the movement of people and objects within a settled community; however, in practice, most of what is described may be taken to apply also to these situations.

The means of transport available has a direct effect on the range and intensity of people's contacts, and may also influence the nature of contacts. Terrain is similarly influential. Thus we shall find that hunter-gatherers usually lack the mobility to bring sufficient people to one spot speedily enough to engage in warfare, and so their contacts with each other are peaceful. The exceptions, the warriors, are hunter-gatherers with horses or with boats that enable them to overcome the drawbacks of a sparse and scattered population: speed is of the essence for warfare. Other hunter-gatherers who move more slowly will probably assemble for peaceful contacts in the nature of barter and ceremony. It is therefore relevant to an examination of contact to consider the range of primitive transport and its potential for the movement of people and goods over the face of the earth.

The outstanding means of primitive transport is manpower, people walking and carrying loads. There is little to describe since walking is an activity with which most people are still familiar, but there are a few points to note. Not only is it the most important, it is often the sole means of transport. The majority of hunter-gatherers walk to their reunions, to the big tribal ceremonies, to funerals and to fairs. Farmers like the Kapauku or Dani walk to inter-village pig-feasts, walk over the hills to trade pork, walk or run to fight their enemies. Cattle-herding warriors may possess beasts of burden, but it is their own two feet which carry them to the battlefield, and the conquests of the Azande and the Zulu were walk-overs in the literal sense. The distances covered by people on foot are all too rarely recorded, and vary considerably according to terrain and cultural orientation to travel. Fifty miles could be a day's journey across the flat open country of the Nuer, or a week's travel through dense forest undergrowth in western North America.

People may use artefacts to increase their mobility and carrying power. In northern latitudes the development of snowshoes has made walking over snow easier and faster than journeys over bare land, and the Athaspaskans and the Lapps make their longest journeys on foot when the ground is snow-covered. Snow is also a good terrain for hand-pulled sledges, and any open and fairly flat ground is suitable for dragging loads, whether on a skin or with a travois. The Plains Indians dragged their own loads on the latter, before the introduction of the horse (Fig. 50).

Carrying power is most notably increased by the use of packs, parcels, nets and other containers. Richard Lee's comments on the importance of containers to human evolution are by now well known (Lee 1968), and may be remembered when surveying the results of

Figure 50. A horse-drawn Blackfoot travois. The earlier version drawn by people was smaller, and the load lighter, but the basic design and function were similar (Curtis)

human ingenuity in this respect. Parcels made of hide or leaves are common; nets tend to be restricted in distribution, and are particularly used in New Guinea by women; pails and boxes are largely the product of temperate zones; baskets, like parcels, are very widely employed, and often most beautifully woven (Fig. 51 and see also Fig. 13). Very few of these artefacts will leave archaeological evidence of their existence, except in rare conditions favourable to the preservation of organic material.

Animal power is available in some cultures to augment manpower, to increase the range of human contacts and the weight of goods carried from one society to another. It may be sufficiently important to alter the nature of human contacts. Most domestic mammals except the pig can be trained to carry packs, and the bigger ones will also carry people. Fig. 51 and Fig. 52 show some of these animals and their equipment.

All these animals will carry quite heavy loads relative to their size, and the larger of them, the donkeys, cattle of various sorts, horses, camels and elephants carry people. As load carriers, they often make it possible for people to trade food and salt and manufactured goods in sufficient quantity to provide a real contribution to subsistence, in situations where the lack of such animal transport might restrict the range of human settlement and the variety of human occupations. This point is very clear in the case of those Himalayan traders, the Tarali, who carry salt from Tibet across the mountains and down into the plains of India where they barter it for grain. 'Possession of a flock of goats and sheep accustomed to carrying loads is an indispensable condition for the operation of this barter-trade ... Only castrated males are used for carrying loads ... Each animal carries two small bags containing rice, barley, buckwheat, millet, maize or maize-flour, and this grain is exchanged for Tibetan salt.' The traders return with the salt to their village and then set out to take the salt, in 30lb. loads, to lower-lying peoples. 'Two or three traders may join together and move with 300-400 pack animals [9-12,000 lbs. of salt] ... to Rukumkot, Musikot and Jajarkot. In those areas they exchange salt for grain ...' (von Fürer-Haimendorf 1975). Although pack animals move much more slowly than people, taking 5 days to cover the same ground as a laden man will cover in one, a flock of 400 animals carrying 12,000 lbs of salt or grain needs only 12 men and one or two dogs to shepherd it. Acting as middlemen and dealing in large quantities thanks to their animals, these trader-pastoralists survive more comfortably and in greater numbers

Figure 51. Animal transport. (a) Fulani oxen carrying traders and goods to town market, Kukawa, Nigeria. (b) pack-camels watering, Tor al Tubaig (Gertrude Bell, Royal Geographical Society)

Figure 52. Animal transport. Horse in gala trappings, Nigeria(Royal Geographical Society)

through the exploitation of contacts with other groups than they could do by farming alone. Pastoralism in itself is often dependent on the availability of animal transport for the successful exploitation of widely-scattered resources, a point which is discussed more fully in Chapter 6.

The swift animals, the horse and the camel, are the only ones to make a notable contribution to warfare. They may even promote the development of this activity in regions where population is sparse; the introduction of horses to the Plains Indians gave them at one and the same time something to raid for, and a means of reaching the enemy (i.e. their fellow tribes), and there is little doubt that the scale and frequency of warfare escalated with the availability of horse transport.

Roads are rarely necessary for the means of transport described above, and more likely to be an adjunct of wheeled vehicles. However, transport across difficult terrain may be facilitated by tracks or pathways. These are likely to be well-defined where the choice of route is confined, or where the path can only be created with much labour. Trade and migration routes through mountain passes such as those of the Zagros and Himalayas afford examples of the first type, while the routes cut through dense forest cover in both the Atlantic and Pacific forests of America (Mellars 1976) illustrate the second. Elsewhere, the creation of pathways may derive from political needs, and Evans-Pritchard describes how the Zande kings established and maintained a network of pathways and hence of contact and authority throughout their kingdoms. 'Paths led from the king's court to the courts of his governors, and it was the responsibility of each governor to see that these arteries were maintained. When the grasses were high they were pressed down on either side of the paths by means of a pole worked by the feet ... The layout of each province was on the same pattern ... at the centre was the court of the ruler, and from that ran the paths, the veins of the kingdom, which led to the courts of his deputies' (Evans-Pritchard 1971; Fig. 53). Rivers may be crossed by bridges though more commonly people and animals will swim or wade or cross in a boat.

The information available concerning water transport is quite extensive, since boats of every description from simple dugouts to elaborate Kayaks are used by primitive groups, and a number of writers have been fascinated by the subject. What interests us here is the context of such transport, and the ends it achieves, as much as the details of craft construction. All modes of subsistence and every continent provide examples of the use of boats, especially of dugout canoes. Australian hunter-gatherers are known to have made dugouts. North Americans are famous for their birch-bark canoes and the Esquimo for their skin-covered vessels. Peoples such as the Kede, living on the Niger, make their living by carrying goods up

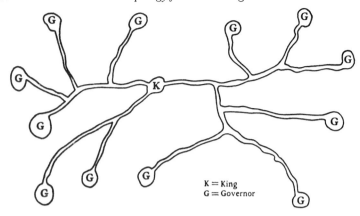

Figure 53. Azande paths. Evans-Pritchard's diagram of the crucial communications
network through which kings controlled their kingdoms (Evans-Pritchard 1971)

and down that river, their boats being the equivalent of the
Himalayan flocks as the means of transport and hence a means of
exploiting further or different ecological niches. As boats and
animals in one respect fulfil the same function, that of transport, it is
not surprising to find the former least common in pastoral contexts;
they are used, for example by the Nuer for fishing, but not on the
whole to carry people or goods from one place to another.

The environment which most favours the use of boats is an island
one, and many island peoples are renowned as long-distance
travellers and probably establish more contacts with other groups
than land-dwellers. Trade, diplomacy and warfare have all been
facilitated in areas such as Polynesia, or the Pacific coast of North
America, by the ease of water transport. The arrival of Chinese
mainland pottery in Australia, albeit through several exchanges,
shows what can be accomplished across a chain of islands (Hutton
1951); cultural flourishes such as the ceremonial exchange cycle
known as the *kula* have developed through and are dependent on
long-distance water transport (Malinowski 1922); Maori and
Kwakiutl warriors alike make use of large war-canoes to reach enemy
settlements, and both have made their boats into display and
prestige objects as well as functional means of transport (Best 1924;
Drucker 1963). Indeed, boats being swift and fairly silent are an
ideal way of moving warriors around, and their presence has
assisted the development of warfare in hunter-gatherer contexts, just
as possession of the horse has done.

As with containers, illustrations will convey the variety of boats in use by primitive communities better than words. Figs. 54 and 55 give some of these; further material may be found in such publications as Sanderson n.d.

The value of boats is very similar to that of pack animals, in providing power to carry loads for trade, and hence the means for people to set themselves up as middlemen (cf. Tarali and Kede). Their possession also encourages warfare, as does the ownership of swift horses or camels, and for much the same reasons (cf. Maori and Mongols). However, boats are very much more widely used than animals for transport; they are easier and quicker to produce, and much less demanding to look after.

Wheeled vehicles are rare, except in urbanised contexts such as the Indian sub-continent, and most peoples discussed in this book make little use of them. Wagons are fairly expensive of labour to make, they need costly and hungry animals to pull them, they are slow, and they need built roads. That they existed in prehistoric Europe therefore indicates something of the cultural complexity achieved (see below and Chapter 7 for further discussion).

Such a very brief survey of primitive transport does no justice to the subject, but it should nevertheless show that no primitive community is or has been kept in isolation for lack of transport. All land-dwellers can walk to meet other groups, and they do. Many have improved upon their own power, and some have done this so successfully that they have become transport specialists. All island-dwellers, or virtually all, first reached their homes by means of boats, and they are likely to be travellers *par excellence*. It is as likely that prehistoric peoples had the means of contacting other groups at all stages in the evolution of human culture. Whether and why they had the desire so to do is what we shall examine next.

Peaceful contacts: exchange

Economic anthropology is a developing subject, and one which is making its influence felt among students of industrial nations by demonstrating that economies at all levels of cultural complexity do not function solely along commercial lines, but may also provide a framework for social and diplomatic relationships and prestige games. For every straightforward barter exchange, there are innumerable exchanges dictated by social conventions, such as marriage gifts and funeral presentations. This is partly why it is

Figure 54. Boats. (a) reed boat on Lake Pomo, California. (b) Yurok dugout canoe, N. California (Curtis)

Figure 55. Boats. (a) wooden boat on the Skokomish river, near Seattle, Washington. (b) skin whaling-boat, Alaskan coast (Curtis)

legitimate to treat exchange as a means of contact, and in the present context just this aspect will be emphasised, for the archaeological evidence is often adequate for tracing the movement of objects from one culture to another, but only very rarely can any commercial value be assigned to the objects, or the full material transaction be traced. 'We do not know what went the other way' is a common archaeological statement, but no cause for defeatism if, instead of trying to assess the profits and loss of a past culture, the archaeologist turns his attention to some of the less commercial facets of exchange described in the following pages.

Subsistence exchange

We have already seen, in the section on transport, that there are people who subsist through being middlemen, and the highly significant role of exchange in the subsistence of pastoral communities will be examined later (Chapter 6). To these should be added many instances of barter exchange for food and manufactured goods, which enable settlements to be established in areas where man cannot be self-sufficient, and which encourage specialisation. Malinowski cites the barter of fish for vegetables in the Trobriand Islands, where coastal communities obtain food from inland in return for their surplus fish (Malinowski 1922). Then there is Wood's example of the Mandan-Cheyenne trade – the former grow crops, and grow a surplus to obtain meat and other animal products from the Cheyenne hunters. Each tribe has specialised, restricting its subsistence activities and restricting its area of settlement and direct exploitation of the land, and each therefore relies upon the other to provide a balance (Wood 1974). In a rather different situation, the inhabitants of the Amphlett Islands subsist by making pottery for sale, as their islands are rocky and grow poor and insufficient crops; in pre-contact days they seem to have held a virtual pottery monopoly which brought them in many baskets of food from their customers. Perversely, though, the clay for the pots was not Amphlettese but had to be imported (Lauer 1970). These examples of subsistence barter all have one thing in common, in that they bring together people of different communities, whether at village level as in the Trobriands, or at the tribal level of the Cheyenne and Mandan.

Within a small-scale community, there may be a great deal of food redistribution, the motivation for which is likely to be social, and the transaction takes place as a gift (as in Tikopia: Firth 1939). In the more complex societies, market economies may exist, and different sections of the community may either exchange produce and manufactures, or buy and sell for cash on a regular basis. (For description, see Bohannan and Dalton 1962, including contribution by Hodder on 'The Yoruba rural market'.)

Currencies

Currencies exist in a number of small-scale societies, and it is worthwhile exploring their nature here because they illustrate admirably the social role of exchange; also, currency is an artefact deliberately made for use in transactions, and as such it is of particular interest to the economic archaeologist. One community, that of the Kapauku Papuans, will serve as an example, as its members are particularly active in the sphere of exchange, and they have developed several types of currency (Pospisil 1972). Cowrie-shell money is the standard Kapauku currency, despite the lack of access to and ignorance of the sea. The shells are ground and polished, and given various values according to shape and size and source. Other small white shells threaded on to necklaces are also used as money, and come in two standard lengths. Then there are imported blue glass beads, of lesser value than the shells. These three currencies can be used to buy food, artefacts, houses, land, services, in fact an uncommon range of goods for a primitive society. However, some things can only be bought with special, or limited currencies: to obtain a wife, for example, a man must make two payments to his bride's family. The first or major payment must consist of old, precious cowries and pigs; other types of money to the same value cannot be substituted – e.g. many low-value cowries cannot be used in default of a few precious ones. The second and lesser payment should consist of low-value cowries, glass beads and necklaces, although in this instance iron axes and one or two other categories of artefact may be used instead. A similar use of special or restricted currencies for special or restricted purposes can be found in a wide range of societies, and often an artefact such as a particular type of axe or necklace may be used solely for exchange, and solely within a limited sphere of ceremonial transactions.

Gift and ceremonial exchange

The example of the Kapauku currencies has introduced the concept of different spheres of exchange, and it is largely the ceremonial sphere that we are now concerned with.

Tribute

Much of the redistribution of produce and goods in a primitive community represents the physical expression of social links in addition to any economic function. Thus a Polynesian chief may receive food from his dependents, and give back to them more or less what he got, or he may receive food and give a feast to everyone's enjoyment and benefit and the prestige of the whole community. Where hierarchies are more marked, and societies more complex, tribute to rulers is probably more varied, since part of the definition of a complex society lies in the specialisation of its sections. So the ruler receives a multiplicity of objects, perhaps of different tribal origins. Then, since it is so often his duty to give as well as to receive, the gifts are given out again. But not, it must be noted, back whence they came; that is an insult in any society. The Azande kings received much tribute in the form of food, which helped to feed the royal household and court, and also manufactured goods as tribute from the provinces. Many of these artefacts were made by subject peoples, or traded into the provinces from neighbouring tribes. Evans-Pritchard describes the arrival of this tribute: the foods and oils and pots and gourds, honey, slaves and guns from the east; from the south oils and oracle-poison, ceremonial axes, spears, iron, torches, hats and mats and dyes and barkcloth, and sabres and foreign knives. The tribute was brought to the royal court by caravans of porters, many of whom were foreigners, either war captives or members of a subject tribe. Some of this was given back to the king's subjects 'what goes to the prince along the path of duty is returned along the path of privilege' (Evans-Pritchard 1971). One result of kingship may, therefore, be a great redistribution of goods of different origin, and a certain amount of cultural mixing.

Gift-partnership

At a less exalted level than royal tribute, they may be considerable systematic exchange between communities based on gift-partnership. Some peoples regularly come into contact with each other, whether because the one group are pastoralists moving through the other's village, or both are hunters meeting at a public camp, or a fair is being held, or some other seasonal event. In such cases, a member of one group will often have a particular friend or partner in the other group with whom he or she exchanges gifts at each encounter. They may also trade their respective surpluses, but not in every case or at every meeting, and it is the gift-giving which is seen as the key relationship. The non-commercial nature of the exchange is clear when Esquimos give each other stone pipes (Balikci 1970), less so when Tibetan pastoralists give animal produce to farmers in return for silver jewelry (Ekvall 1968); yet in each case it is fair to interpret the exchange as a means of establishing a friendly relationship between two people, rather than a step towards profit. All the active members of the two communities are likely to have partners, and contact is firmly established through the many individual links – and over the years a number of artefacts will pass across the cultural boundaries.

If, and it does happen, either participant has a partner in yet another culture, indirect contacts may be far-flung and objects can be given across several exchanges. Here, perhaps, is the nucleus of the ceremonial exchange cycles, but before turning to these the archaeologist should note that simple gift-exchange between the ordinary members of different cultures can move artefacts further across the face of the earth than direct trading expeditions, pillaging or royal tribute. Peaceful exchange can move objects far beyond their original cultural context, the ultimate owners having knowledge neither of the place nor of the people whence their import came. New Guinea Highlanders received pearl-shells at many removes, and thought, it is said, that they grew on trees, for they knew nothing of the sea. The presence of foreign objects in an archaeological context is therefore proof neither of direct cultural contact nor even of any passage of cultural information. Even the presence of a number of imports from one culture found together does not have to imply direct contact, since the tendency to formalise exchange through partnerships, and the universal rule against returning a gift to the giver, creates channels of gift-giving which direct the flow of goods in a non-random manner.

Diplomatic exchanges

Some of the tribute which an Azande king received was used to cement relationships with neighbouring monarchs. The king Gbudwe, who ruled towards the end of the last century, sent beads, flywhisks, animals' teeth, gourds and honey, and children captured from foreign peoples, to his fellow kings as gifts (Evans-Pritchard 1971). This was diplomatic gift-giving on a par with the presents sent to and given by Elizabeth I of England, if not quite matching the sumptuousness of the Field of the Cloth of Gold. Not only kings, but leaders at all levels of personal authority are likely to exchange gifts of equal value with their peers, especially when they wish to establish or maintain friendly relations. Giving presents is an almost universal way of establishing contact, especially when strangers meet, or when a situation is potentially hostile (and it was, incidentally, much practised by European explorers). The way in which diplomatic exchange can work, and its repercussions on the aspects of culture, is analysed by Chagnon in his account of Yanomamo feasts and alliances (Chagnon 1968a).

The Yanomamo, it will be remembered, are farmers living in the forests of southern Venezuela and northern Brazil who practice shifting agriculture. Their villages are small, perhaps 60-200 people, and built as a continuous structure with only one entrance. The ethos of Yanomamo life is fierceness, expressed in raids on other villages and a chronic state of inter-village warfare. Few villages can survive alone, and it is necessary to form alliances with other groups for defence – alliances which begin with the exchange of food and gifts at feasts in the respective villages, which are strengthened by intermarriage and sealed by a joint raid on some third party. Choosing a potential ally and making the initial overtures of friendship is a delicate and dangerous business and the opening move may be to declare an interest in some product of the other village, such as hammocks or pottery. 'Trade', writes Chagnon, 'functions as the social catalyst, the "starting mechanism", through which mutually suspicious allies are repeatedly brought together in direct confrontation.'

The trade follows certain rules. At a feast, the hosts must make gifts to the visitors, and only later, when the visitors are hosts in turn, do they reciprocate. When they do so, it must be with a different kind of item. One side of the alliance is always indebted to the other, a situation which tends to favour continued meetings and promotes the stability of the alliances. Each village is expected to specialise in one or more items that it will provide for its allies: dogs and drugs and cotton and bows and arrows as well as the hammocks and pots mentioned above. And an ally will quite possibly create a deliberate shortage of whatever its partner has: the people of one village that Chagnon visited denied all knowledge of pot-making, said their local clay was not of the right sort, and explained that their allies provided all the pots they needed. 'Later in the year their alliance with the pot makers grew cool because of a war, and their source of pots was shut off. At the same time, Kaobawä's group began asking them for clay pots. [They] promptly responded by 'remembering' how pots were made and 'discovering' that the clay in their neighbourhood was indeed suitable for pot manufacturing. They had merely created a local shortage of the item in order to have to rely on an ally for it, giving sufficient cause to visit them' (Chagnon 1968a, 100-1).

Exchange-cycles

Gift-partnership, the deliberate creation of shortages and specialisation, and the development of rules of exchange between groups are all to be found in the ceremonial exchange cycles which, in various parts of the world, link together communities spread over vast distances and belonging to a range of cultures and subsistence modes. Malinowski's account of the *kula* exchange cycle is the classic of the anthropological literature on this subject (Malinowski 1922). Also to be considered are Thomson's study of exchange patterns in northern Australia (Thomson 1949), and Wood's of the aboriginal pan-American network (Wood 1973).

Kula exchanges take place between the islanders living to the east of New Guinea (Fig. 56). They are but one of a number of different types of exchange in the area, which interlock to a certain extent, but it is chiefly the *kula* that brings people from the scattered islands into contact with each other. Malinowski described the sequence of events from the standpoint of Sinaketa, one of the Trobriand Islands, where a number of the adult men had exchange partners in both clockwise and anti-clockwise directions, who in turn had similar partners thereby creating a ring of participants round the islands. A chief might have several hundred partners, an ordinary man perhaps only four or five, but in all cases these would be permanent and even inherited links. As with the Yanomamo diplomatic exchanges, and many other gift partnerships, a permanent state of indebtedness was created by expecting only one partner to give at a meeting, the receiver reciprocating and maybe adding a bit more on the next occasion. Other features common to many cultures and clearly displayed in the *kula* system are the

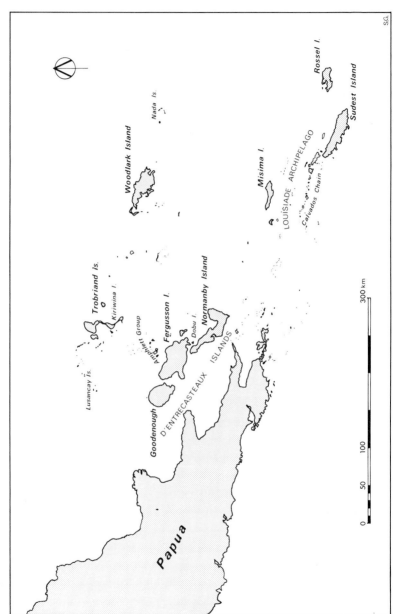

Figure 56. Map of the Kula region, Melanesia

limited number of goods held to be appropriate for exchange, the localised production of these goods, and the very strict rules governing the direction in which they travel (always away from source and away from the immediate giver). In this case, the chief items of exchange, the *kula* valuables, are red spondylus shell necklaces, which travel clockwise, and white shell armbands, which travel in the opposite direction. Finally, the valuables must not be hoarded, but always given away.

The exchange of valuables takes place when the men of a village decide to embark on a *kula* voyage to another island where they have partners. The voyage is attended with much ritual and magic, and the *kula* exchanges themselves are governed by a strict etiquette. At the same time, however, a good deal of subsidiary exchange takes place, some of which is of a minor ceremonial nature and some direct barter.

The *kula* exchange cycle therefore promotes the redistribution of articles around the Melanesian islands and to a certain extent encourages specialisation in a manner similar to the Yanomamo pot story: the Amphlett Islanders are participants in the exchange, and the trade in pots which helps them to subsist on their rocky islands is carried along the *kula* network. The cycle has other effects, some of which were noted by Malinowski: 'It welds together a considerable number of tribes, and it embraces a vast complex of activities, interconnected, and playing into one another, so as to form one organic whole' (p. 83). '... Though transacted between tribes differing in language, culture and probably even in race, it is based on a fixed and permanent status, on a partnership which binds into couples some thousands of individuals' (p. 85). In other words, the ceremonial exchange system is in some respects like a formalised game which brings together people who might otherwise be hostile, and this political outcome may be added to the economic effects noted above.

The archaeologist will already have noted that the distribution of *kula* goods is not random, but away from source in certain prescribed directions, and that the rules of the game encourage the perpetual movement of goods and discourage or prohibit hoarding. The valuables become more and more precious with each exchange, until they fall apart with old age when they become worthless. The main items, the necklaces and armbands, are ornaments, but they are *not* worn – this is a further rule of particular archaeological interest – and in some cases the armbands are too small to be worn even by children. The *kula* valuables are artefacts made solely for the purpose of ceremonial exchange, and there is some evidence that in pre-contact times the range of valuables was greater, including purely ceremonial pots and ceremonial polished stone axe-blades (Brookfield and Hart 1971).

Thomson's description of the ceremonial exchange cycle in aboriginal Arnhem Land displays some features similar to the *kula*, albeit taking place in an inland, hunter-gatherer context instead of an island farming one. The Arnhem Land aborigines had evolved a system of constant kinship obligations which involved giving presents – to relatives, to old men if one was an initiate, to a potential mother-in-law if one was a young man, and so forth. Most gifts would be reciprocated immediately or in the near future. The act of giving was held to be good, yielding prestige, friendship, enhanced social status and, most important, spiritual power (märr) and good luck. The desire to give therefore exerted a strong pressure to manufacture artefacts suitable as gifts, and people collected appropriate raw materials all the time. When gathering they would collect decorative feathers, wood for spears, fibres for string and nets, and pigments in addition to food. Any odd moment of leisure would see both men and women getting on with the preparation of gifts. The types of objects made were localised to particular groups and innovation was not encouraged; therefore most artefacts could be attributed to source, however far they eventually travelled.

Giving was not random, but organised through exchange partners. Each person would have a number of partners with whom he regularly exchanged goods; goods once received were not hoarded, but passed on, because it was the fact of giving that mattered, and they were passed on always away from source. A man's partners would live on all sides of him and he would be at the centre of a network bringing him goods perhaps as follows: from the east, iron spears and pounding stones and flint spearheads; from the north, where there were contacts with Indonesia, calico and blankets and belts, knives, pipes and glass; from the west and northwest, personal decorations and hooked spears and fighting clubs; from the southwest and south, boomerangs, belts, and spears; and from the southeast more boomerangs, dilly bags, fur coverings and flint spearheads. All these he would pass on, in any direction except whence they came. The resulting distribution pattern shows goods radiating out far from source and travelling far beyond the limits of direct human contact (Fig. 57). For example, almost every Arnhem

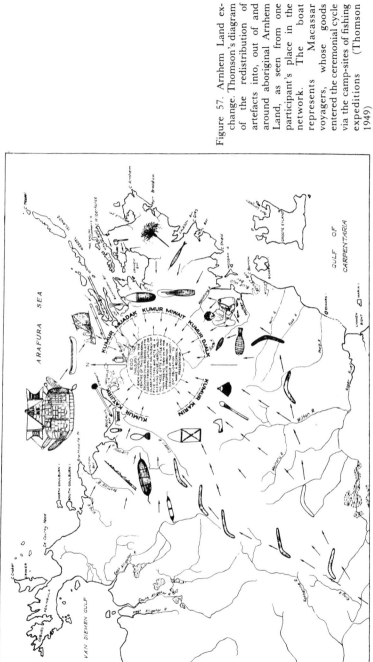

Figure 57. Arnhem Land exchange. Thomson's diagram of the redistribution of artefacts into, out of and around aboriginal Arnhem Land, as seen from one participant's place in the network. The boat represents Macassar voyagers, whose goods entered the ceremonial cycle via the camp-sites of fishing expeditions (Thomson 1949)

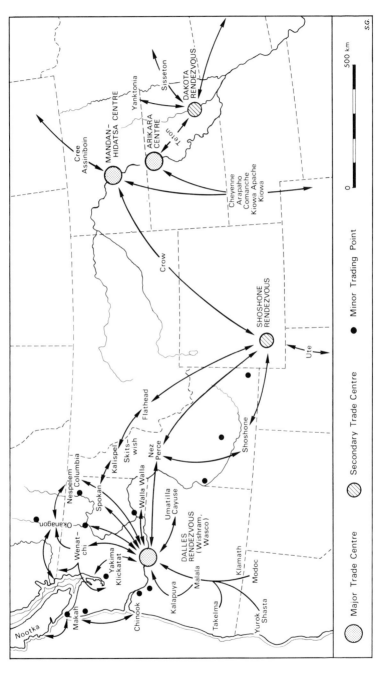

Figure 58. North American exchange. Based on Wood's map of the aboriginal redistribution network from major and secondary trade centres

Land spearhead was made of flint from a single quarry; yet certainly most spearhead owners (i.e. adult men) had not visited the quarry nor even come into contact with those who worked it. Likewise, an inland rock painting of an Indonesian knife reflects only the efficiency of the exchange cycle, and not the penetration of Indonesian traders deep into Arnhem Land.

Finally, the American network, which has already entered into several discussions. To appreciate the working of this exchange system, which is perhaps less ceremonial in function and more directly concerned with trade than those of Melanesia or Arnhem Land, it is necessary to examine two interlocking networks. Wood takes as his examples the Pacific-Plateau network (i.e. North West Coast) and that of the Middle Missouri (i.e. Great Plains). Fig. 58 gives an idea of location and distances involved.

The Pacific-Plateau network was based on a recognised trade centre at the Dalles on the Columbia river, a place where there was an abundance of salmon and where two groups of fishers had settled permanently. They acted as host-villages for an inter-tribal trade fair that was held every autumn, themselves trading some 500 tons of dried salmon annually. Exchange took place between host and visitors and also among the visitors. As well as the local salmon, other food was brought in to the fair, including fish-oil, edible roots, edible seeds and dried meats. Trade goods included furs and skins, clothing and buffalo robes, feathers and shells; after European contact, horses and guns were added, before any European traders themselves reached the Dalles. These goods were accumulated for exchange either through hunting, gathering and fishing beyond the requirements of daily subsistence or from previous trade at a secondary centre. The Dalles fair was a rendez-vous for many different tribes, of sufficiently diverse culture to have no common language, and each tribe was noted for specialisation in certain goods. The Nez Percé, for example, were expected to bring buffalo robes, as they were an inland tribe with access to the Plains.

The Middle Missouri network was based on the farming villages of the Mandan-Hidatsa, who exchanged the surplus from their crops of maize and beans for the dried meat, skins and buffalo robes of hunting peoples. As at the Dalles fair, many tribes congregated regularly each year at the villages, and to overcome language difficulties a sign language was evolved, and the visitors exchanged goods with each other as well as with their hosts.

So far, then, we have two discrete trade networks each with its own centre where an annual autumn fair was held. The link which turned these inter-tribal systems into a trans-continental one was provided by the secondary spring fairs. There were a number of centres for these, where people would trade to accumulate exotic goods for the big autumn fairs. One of the spring fairs attended by tribes who belonged to the Middle Missouri network was held at the Shoshone rendez-vous, and here too came some of the tribes from the Pacific-Plateau network. A Haida slate obtained at Dalles one autumn could be passed on in six months time at the Shoshone fair to a hunter who would trade it at a farming village the following autumn to some visitor from the far side (i.e. the east) of the Missouri network, who in turn might pass it on at a spring fair attended by eastern tribes. So, in a matter of years, goods travelled from Pacific to Atlantic coast, from Athapaskans to the tribes of Florida, and vice versa.

Trade in both networks was fostered by the establishment of regular partners. In the Pacific-Plateau system these were often a matter of family tradition, and reinforced by intermarriage despite tribal and cultural differences. In the middle Missouri, where the trading tribes were as often as not at war with each other, enemies adopted each other as fathers and sons in order to trade safely. These relationships, as well as the development of common languages, helped to disseminate rather more than mere objects along the networks. 'In addition to staples of the trade ... most anything could change hands at trade fairs: tools, trinkets, folk tales, songs, dances and brides, amongst other things. The dances and other forms of social intercourse led to active sexual recruitment, which contributed to gene flow along lines of trade. Gambling at the fairs was rampant, and provided an avenue of exchange for many goods other than those brought for the express purpose of trade. In other words, the flow of goods and ideas ... was a simple matter ... often a very rapid process' (Wood 1973, 164-5). Cultural contact *par excellence*?

Co-existence

Separate human cultures can and do co-exist within a single territory, maintaining their own separate identities, and living more or less peacefully together. Certain conditions promote co-existence, just as others make it impossible, and chief among both of these seems to be subsistence. If two cultures have different subsistence modes and occupy different ecological niches within a territory, if they make use of different resources or of different parts of the same resource, then it is unlikley that they will come into direct competition with each other. A cultural symbiosis can result, each side intensifying its particular subsistence efforts, and exchanging the resultant surplus with the other, as shown in Wood's analysis of the Cheyenne/Mandan-Hidatsa relationships. Enduring cultural co-existence, it can be argued, is dependent on the absence of direct competition. If, on the other hand, both groups want to exploit the same resources, either one side must conquer and drive out or enslave the other, or a state of permanent hostility ensues, as for the Nuer and the Dinka. Ecologists are familiar with similar states of competition and co-existence in the animal world, and it would not perhaps surprise them to find how closely human populations conform to their rules.

Temporary co-existence can often be seen as an extended form of trading contact or as one phase of an annual cycle of movement and it most frequently results from the passage of a nomadic tribe through settled lands. Many examples could be cited from pastoral contexts (see contributions to Cohen 1974, vol. 2, and Chapter 6 below). The Himalayan Tarali traders, whose journeys with their laden flocks of sheep and goats were described above, are away from their home base for many months at a time, and part of this time is spent camping in the fields of friendly villagers while the salt trade takes place. For perhaps two or three months the herds graze the farmers' fields, leaving their manure behind as payment.

Elsewhere, two cultures may live together for a short while with a lesser degree of economic intermeshing, or even indifference if the resources each uses are quite separate. The Indonesian fishermen who camped regularly on the coast of North Australia concentrated their attention on the *bêches-de-mer* in the ocean while the permanent inhabitants of the land continued their normal hunting and gathering activities. Contact was made for exchange purposes and a number of trade goods passed into the Australian network, but the two economies were not interdependent.

Many instances of permanent co-existence have already been noted, in the contexts of settlement and social organisation. There are the Mbuti hunter-gatherers who live in the forests around the villages of Bira and Lese cultivators. There are the Fulani pastoralists who dwell in the same lands as Hausa farmers. There are the Kede, whose river expertise has spread their settlements along the banks of the Niger among other Nupe tribes. Subject peoples who maintain their own separate identities can also be said to co-exist with their conquerors. Some would say this is the state of the Hausa, and certainly the subject tribes of both the Swazi and the Azande live with their overlords and still maintain their own cultural identities to a greater or lesser extent. In contrast to the above situations, the Iban, in the course of their aggressive colonisation of the interior of Sarawak, came across two groups of hunter-gatherers who were living off the forest much as the newcomers intended to do. One group resisted the invaders and was wiped out; the second group co-operated, acted as guides and was rapidly absorbed into the lowest echelons of Iban society. Both hunter-gatherer cultures were lost in the process (Freeman 1970). This example highlights the degree to which all the previously mentioned groups do perpetuate their own distinct cultural identities, despite decades or centuries of contact and borrowing.

One instance will now be examined in more detail, that of the Hausa and Fulani in northern Nigeria (Smith, M.G. 1965). The Hausa are farmers and craftsmen, living in towns, villages and hamlets that are organised into states or emirates. Farming is dominated by cereal cultivation, especially Guinea corn,, millet, maize and rice: root crops are also grown, and a range of vegetables such as onions and peppers. Some animals are kept: donkeys for transport, horses for prestige, various poultry and sheep and goats. The Hausa own very few cattle and the main farming emphasis is on plant foods.

Most farmers also practice some craft, of which there is a very wide range. Smith notes that 'Hausa classify men as hunters, fishers, builders, thatchers, butchers, tanners, leatherworkers, saddlers, weavers, dyers, woodworkers, blacksmiths, brass and silversmiths, calabash-workers, potmakers, drummers, musicians of various types, praise-singers, barber-surgeons, tailors, embroiderers, washermen, porters, commission agents, traders of various kinds, including *fatauci* (specialists in long-distance overland trade), makers of sweetmeats, makers of baskets or mats, tobacco grinders, specialists in herbal medicines, clerics, rulers, officials, and their agents' (Smith, M.G. 1965, 124-5). Women also practice a range of crafts and occupations.

The products of all this activity are brought to the markets, which are an important feature of Hausa economy and held at regular intervals in the towns and villages; all important towns have at least one daily market. The markets are one of the institutions that bring the Hausa into regular contact with the Fulani.

The Fulani are pastoralists, and nomadic, and consist of several groups which cover a very much greater territory than just Hausa-land; however this is one of the areas where their numbers are considerable. The Fulani economy is animal-oriented, concentrated upon large herds of cattle which are tended with devotion, and taken from pasture to pasture according to seasonal variation in the availability of grass. The pastoral Fulani contrast with the Hausa in their singlemindedness. For them, there is none of the diversity of crafts, for nothing can compare with cattle. Their specialisation in animal foods and products brings them to the markets where they sell milk and butter, and buy cereal foods and some of the many Hausa offerings. They also sell their cattle for meat, on the hoof because it is the Hausa who butcher the animals and sell the meat. Given the very efficient and widespread market system, the agricultural Hausa and the pastoral Fulani are able to exchange (or buy and sell) their surpluses with relative ease, and this has no doubt helped to perpetuate them in their separate cultures.

There are, in addition, groups of Fulani who farm as well as herd, and Fulani who are town-dwellers. The latter live in the Hausa towns, and are most commonly the rulers and nobility of the total community. For an explanation of this situation, we need to look to the history of the two communities, in particular that of the Fulani. They appear to have come originally from Senegal (W. coast), and to have spread, partly as pastoralists and partly as holy warriors of Islam, for some 3,000 miles across West Africa in the course of 800 years. In the early nineteenth century they generated a series of Holy Wars in northern Nigeria to purify the lax Hausa Muslim states, and the conquered farmers were thenceforward administered by Fulani emirs.

There are therefore two levels of Fulani: Hausa contact and co-existence. At the subsistence level, the two cultures have kept and perhaps exaggerated their native and contrasting activities, and they have achieved a degree of mutual benefit. At the ruling level, the settled town Fulani have become imbued with Hausa culture, and even with Hausa blood, and their main concern is the government of the settled peoples of the Emirates. It is they, for example, who see to the law and order of markets and who promote Islamic religion in the Hausa states. Yet despite much cultural confusion and borrowing at the ruling level, the two peoples still see themselves as distinct, and the Fulani are typical pastoralists in thinking their own cultural ethos far superior.

The separateness of the resources used by the two cultures for their subsistence is clear in this instance, although naturally in practice there are occasions when herds graze the wrong fields and destroy crops, or farmers are unwilling to allow access to the pastoralists. Overall, however, a subsistence symbiosis is achieved and the division of people on economic grounds no doubt helps to maintain the cultural division. The division is reflected in the different types of housing and the different style of dress of the two peoples, but there are blurrings. The pastoral Fulani buy many of their artefacts from the Hausa craftsmen, and the town Fulani have adopted the house-styles of their subjects.

It has been suggested that the economies of the two cultures serve to keep them functioning together as distinct groups. They are kept together also by a common religion, Islam, and by common rule to a certain extent. Except that the Fulani also live outside Hausa territory, one would be hard put in some cases to distinguish the two cultures as a genuinely separate, and not merely specialised facets of a complex supra-culture. In terms of the material culture, there is a degree of mixing which might blur any distinction in the subsequent archaeological record. And, without a doubt, the 'subject' Hausa culture produces far more that will leave an archaeological record than their overlords the Fulani: more and more durable housing, more and bigger settlements, more disturbance of the land for subsistence and many, many more artefacts. Co-existence in this instance is unlikely to be a state of affairs that declares itself openly to the archaeologist, but it should at least be a possibility that lurks in his mind, as well as in the evidence. The first intimations of the presence of two cultures will probably not be artefactual but economic, and confirmation can only come from an examination of the whole range of archaeological evidence.

Warfare

Warfare in pre-industrial contexts covers a wide spectrum of hostilities from raiding to conquest, all of which bring people into contact with others. Various definitions of primitive warfare have been given (e.g. Bohannan 1967), and the simplest of them all is probably of most use to us here: warfare is fighting between any two distinct groups of people, whether between two state armies led by their respective warlords, or between two small villages of farmers. Perhaps to the surprise of the archaeologist, a state of war is relatively common wherever enough people are gathered together for fighting to be practicable. Perhaps also surprisingly, it is not always a totally awful state of affairs for the participants, and we shall see that in some cases warfare is a community prestige game rather than a fight to the point of annihilation. Endemic or chronic fighting between two groups is different in some important respects from expansive or conquering warfare, and the two will be examined separately.

Endemic warfare

Endemic or chronic warfare best describes the state of affairs when fighting each other is an established part of life for two communities, although open hostilities are not necessarily continuous. Fighting may take the form of raiding, or of set battles, sometimes both in sequence. The oft-cited people the Nuer can be used to illustrate both the integration of endemic warfare into a culture and its expression in the form of raiding.

The Nuer's enemy are the Dinka, a very similar people in many respects, and equally oriented to hostilities. 'As far as history and tradition go back, and in the vistas of myth beyond their furthest reach, there has been enmity between the two peoples. Almost always the Nuer have been the aggressors, and raiding of the Dinka is conceived by them to be a normal state of affairs and a duty, for they have a myth, like that of Esau and Jacob, which explains and justifies it. Nuer and Dinka are represented in this myth as two sons of God who promised his old cow to Dinka and its young calf to Nuer. Dinka came by night to God's byre and, imitating the voice of Nuer, obtained the calf. When God found that he had been tricked he was angry and charged Nuer to avenge the injury by raiding Dinka's cattle to the end of time' (Evans-Pritchard 1940, 125).

Fighting the Dinka for cattle was the Nuer's second great love, cattle being the first. Young men were expected to go on raids to prove their adulthood, and the warriors would usually set off at the end of the rainy season, travelling for two or three days until they reached a Dinka settlement. Here, at dawn, they would drive out the enemy and then seize his cattle and perhaps settle down in the camp for several weeks, as a base for raids further into Dinka territory. The warriors lived off the milk and meat of the captured cattle and off Dinka grain, and before returning home they shared the booty among themselves. Useful captives were taken home and soon absorbed into Nuer society, but dependent old women and babies were killed.

Sometimes the Dinka would retaliate and come back to fight the raiders who had taken over their homes. Then a set battle would develop between the warriors of the two sides. Battles seem however to have been relatively few, and raiding of the Dinka by the Nuer was the most common feature of the warfare; Dinka culture did not lay stress on defence and retaliation, but accepted that the Nuer would always be the aggressors, a situation explained by the same myth as that of the Nuer quoted above (Southall 1976). The intensity of Nuer operations was quite high, with some part of Dinka territory being raided each year, and most Nuer men taking part in an expedition every two or three years.

Evans-Pritchard notes that Nuer endemic warfare was directed against the neighbouring people most like themselves, that the captured Dinka were easily assimilated into Nuer society and even visited by their own relatives, and that from time to time in the past Nuer and Dinka had united against the Egyptian government, as well as Nuer taking in Dinka refugees in times of famine. Thus the fighting cannot be seen solely as an expression of implacable hostility: neither side was intent on wiping out the other, despite the killings. On one level, though, it can be seen as a means of keeping the amorphous Nuer groups united, for in defining the enemy they defined themselves, and in outwitting or defeating the enemy they proved their own valour and superiority. If they had defeated the Dinka they would have defeated their own objective: Nuer without Dinka to fight would be Nuer disoriented indeed.

The integration of warfare into the functioning of a society, as seen in the case of Nuer, can be discerned in many other cultures. Bands of young Cheyenne warriors customarily made night raids on the camps of their enemies, intent on winning scalps and horses and the chance to prove their own worth in Cheyenne eyes (Hoebel 1960). Maori chiefs led their warriors into a series of battles against fellow Maori, where the weapons and the fighting and the outcome were all closely bound up with the chief's spiritual power and the ritual (as well as the physical) wellbeing of the community (Best 1927). The Dugum Dani of New Guinea fight to appease the ghosts of their ancestors in a sequence of engagements that seem more like an over-enthusiastic football match than warfare. However, the

Dani also engage in mass slaughter, and so it is to Heider's analysis
of their hostilities that we now turn, to examine both the nature of
ritual warfare and to contrast this with the sporadic eruptions of
great violence (Heider 1970).

The Dani, whose settlement pattern is fairly diffuse (see Chapter
2), form confederacies of neighbouring compounds which in turn
form alliances. War frontiers are set up between alliances, with
watchtowers and battleground (Fig. 59), and the adult men of each
group spend the greater part of their waking hours manning the
watchtowers. Each side makes sporadic surprise raids on the other,

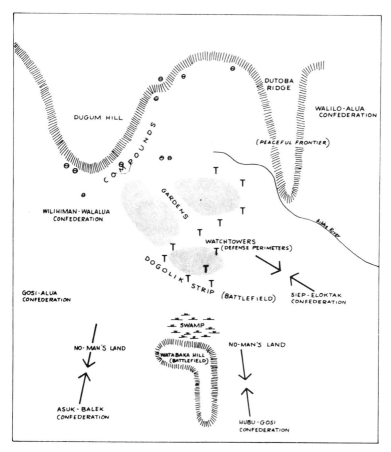

Figure 59. Dani territory showing location of confederations (groups of allies),
watchtowers, frontiers and battlefields (Heider 1970)

with the intent of ambushing and killing any man, woman or child of the enemy. A death placates the ghosts of the aggressors' side, death left unavenged aggravates the ghosts of the dead person's side; thus there is always cause for further raiding. Amid these raids, a bigman from either side may decide to call a battle.

Preparations for battle start with a pig feast for the prospective warriors, and ritual observances. The next day, the younger warriors go to the frontier and shout a challenge to the enemy. The two sides arrange a battleground, and both go home to dress for war. All the men decorate themselves with feathers and bits of fur, with the intention of making themselves obvious, and they collect their weapons and move off to the battleground. Here they fight all day long, until the light fades or until it starts to rain. If it is very hot, they stop and rest, or perhaps hurl insults instead of arrows at each other. Though a number of arrow wounds are likely, the actual fighting is not intense and not only rain, poor light, or excessive heat stop the action: 'Once, during a particularly slow battle, a large cuckoo dove flew back and forth over the lines. All fighting stopped as the warriors, boisterously laughing, threw sticks and stones at the bird' (Heider 1970, 111).

People are more likely to be killed in a raid than a battle. Their death is celebrated by the enemy with two days of dancing to inform the ghosts of their success, and also to notify them that a new and dangerous enemy ghost is at large. Yet, despite ghost involvement in the hostilities and despite the eternal threat of raids, the Dani do not seem perturbed at living in a state of war. They enjoy manning the watchtowers as a precaution against raids, they enjoy the battles, and while the men fight the women carry on quite normally with their gardening.

The raids and set battles Heider calls the ritual phase of war, dominated 'by the arranged battles fought in elegant attire and the emphasis on supernatural, rather than economic, effects' (p. 118). In contrast, non-ritual war is short, violent and bloody, and causes major economic upheaval. In one dawn attack on a group of compounds in the 1960s, well over 100 people were killed, pigs were plundered and buildings were destroyed by fire. The attack was made by warriors on a section of their own alliance, not on the ritual enemy. After some days of fighting, the local confederacies and alliances were thoroughly shaken up and rearranged, and so too were the local territories with many people moving to live in new areas. Such eruptions may have taken place every decade or so in the past, re-aligning the players for the long-drawn out ritual fighting.

The present context is hardly the place to attempt an explanation of Dani warfare, but we may note some possible causes suggested by Heider, all of which turn on the role of fighting in Dani culture as a whole. Ritual warfare is seen as the means of bringing together the greatest number of men, partly for a game which all enjoy and partly as a testing-ground for emergent leaders. Violent warfare seems mostly to result from simple aggression between allies (*not* enemies), in a culture which has little personal authority and few mechanisms for regulating relationships between people. In discussing social organisation, it was noted that group size and permanence was closely related to the degree of personal authority, and that mechanisms to avoid aggression included group fluidity, group fission or the investment of authority in a chief or arbitrator. Dani violence appears to erupt when the tensions *within* a group are not resolved by any of these means, and its eruption may be delayed by the distraction and enjoyment of ritualised fighting. For our present purposes, we can note also that formalised warfare provides a framework for social contact, and as for the Cheyenne or the Maori, an avenue to personal aggrandisement. Therefore it is not surprising to find that in so many instances of endemic warfare there is a definite emphasis on display.

The effects of endemic warfare are various, and some will already be apparent from the accounts of Nuer and Dani fighting. People are killed or captured, land and animals change owners, and the monotony of ordinary life is gloriously broken. In several instances the repercussions of one phase of hostilities seem designed to promote future clashes, and this is well demonstrated in the Yanomamo cycle of events.

Each Yanomamo village, it will be remembered, lives in expectation of raids from enemy Yanomamo villages and in the hope of making such raids themselves. The diplomacy of alliance-making has already been discussed, and we can now turn to the fighting that results from these manoeuvres. The Yanomamo fight because fierceness is an essential quality of manhood, to avenge raids from hostile villages, to prove to their allies that they are acting in good faith, and to capture women. Because the fierce warrior is the only proper Yanomamo, they practice female infanticide and raise a disproportionate number of male children. The consequent shortage of women when they reach adulthood is a permanent source of aggression, and raids to capture women from other villages provide an outlet and a solution at one and the same time. Raids and the defence of one's own women requires warriors, and so female infanticide continues ...

One effect of this situation is to disperse Yanomamo villages far and wide through the forest, as movement away from enemies is a common defensive strategy. (Fig. 22 shows the moves of a single village.) However, it is only the peripheral villages that react in this way; those in the interior of Yanomamo territory cannot escape, and they tend to fight less and to build up more balanced and enduring alliances, with the village headmen playing a slightly more prominent role in diplomacy and maintaining law and order (Chagnon 1968b). This suggests that the peripheral warfare is, like that of the Dani, in some respects a means of regulating social relationships and reducing internal aggression in the absence of, or as an alternative to, personal authority.

More constructive results of endemic warfare may be seen in the development of permanent leagues and alliances between different communities. One of the best known of these is the League of the Five Nations, which emerged from the Iroquois tribes of eastern North America and which fought and ultimately defeated the lesser-known league of four nations or tribes which included the Huron. These leagues were set up against a background of perpetual warfare similar to those described above (Trigger 1969). The leagues may have emerged under the influence of particularly strong chiefs in the seventeenth century, when the tribes were no doubt already affected by European trade goods and guns and the repercussion of European politics. They represent the germs of political units larger than the individual tribes, units that might have achieved permanence had the Indians survived the European onslaught.

Historically, we know that leagues of allies did in some circumstances stabilise as larger political units, as in the case of the Bushongo of West Africa. Here, in yet another state of endemic warfare, five tribes united for defence under the leadership of one man, and this union evolved into the Kingdom of the Bushongo which effectively secured peace within its bounds and improved the prospects for defence against outsiders.

The contact which warfare engenders can stimulate the development of larger political units through, or with, a parallel increase in personal authority, and without the conquest of one group by another. This is a plausible theory, but it must be remembered that warfare rarely has such an outcome, and for the few examples of unification cited above there remain many communities who abide happily in their separate and aggressive groupings.

Conquest

The one mode of warfare which has many times led to permanent contact and co-existence between different cultures is conquest.

Whereas endemic warfare occurs where there is a balance between two opposing groups, expansive warfare is waged by one strong group intent on gaining land, slaves, plunder and power from other cultures. Greed, therefore, is one motivation for this form of hostile contact; other possible causes are the desire for personal aggrandisement of a ruler, and the need of states to keep their armies occupied and remunerated. Religious zeal can be an equally effective driving force, and one we have already met in the Fulani domination of Hausa states. Shortage of land does not appear to be an important reason for a career of conquest in many cases. The Iban, perhaps, ate up the territories of other people in their rapid use of virgin forest for shifting agriculture, but even here expansion was encouraged by the head-hunting ethos of their culture.

Zulu expansive warfare in South Africa has been relatively well-documented, having culminated in a disastrous clash with European settlers. The Zulus' immediate forebears were Bantu pastoralists, who moved into south-eastern Africa around 1450 A.D., displacing Bushmen hunter-gatherers. For three centuries they lived much as the Nuer do, herding and cultivating and fighting each other, and their social organisation was similarly diffuse and flexible. Then, for reasons unknown but possibly linked to population growth, the nature of warfare changed from endemic local hostilities to conquest, and by the late eighteenth century the small disparate tribal units had been welded into several kingdoms bent on subduing each other. Gluckman describes the next development: 'In this struggle Shaka, head of the Zulu tribe, was victorious; by his personal character and military strategy, he made himself, in ten years, master of what is now Zululand and Natal [*c.* 80,000 sq. miles], and his troops were campaigning far beyond his boundaries. He organised a nation out of all the tribes he had subdued' (Gluckman 1940, 26).

Shaka was assassinated in 1828 and the expansion of the previous

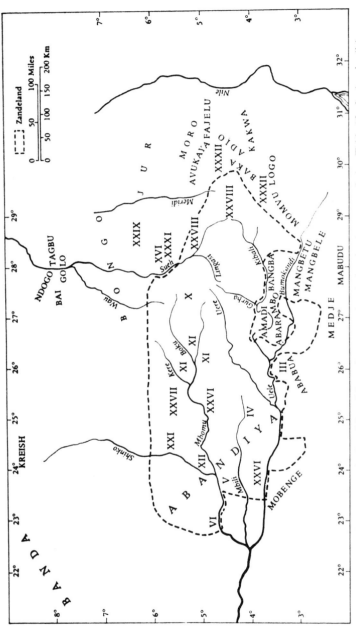

Figure 60. Azande territory and tribes. Map of the major groups absorbed under Avongara rule (see Table 4 for further details). The territory now includes parts of the Sudan, the Central African Empire and Zaire (Evans Pritchard 1971).

decades was replaced by internal plottings and conflicts amongst his successors. By the end of the nineteenth century, the situation had been drastically altered, with the imposition of white rule. The phase of Zulu expansion, conquest and assimilation of other tribes was therefore relatively brief, but nevertheless effective in terms of creating an enduring national identity.

Another African land united by conquest was that of the Azande, and the following notes will give an idea of the possible complexity of such states. In the early eighteenth century the Ambomu of the Mbomu valley began to spread out from their homeland east towards the Nile and north into the Sudan (Fig. 60); they were led by the aristocratic Avongara clan, which may have been originally of a different culture, or perhaps only the foremost of the Ambomu clans, but certainly they were the rulers. The expansion continued for nearly 200 years until checked by Arabs and Europeans, and in those two centuries a multitude of peoples were brought under Avongara rule and welded into the Zande nation. Table 4 indicates the major cultures involved.

The degree of integration of the different peoples into Zande culture has differed. Some have merged almost completely with their conquerors, contributing elements of their own culture to the national pool and retaining their separate identity perhaps only in a clan name. The process which led to such amalgamations is described by Evans-Pritchard: '... it was the traditional Zande policy to encourage submitted peoples to accept Avongara rule voluntarily, to stay in their homes, and to become Azande ... We are told time and again by our authorities that once a people submitted they were left with their own chiefs ... All that was asked of the subject peoples was recognition of Avongara suzerainty, that they should keep the peace, and a payment of tribute in labour and kind to their rulers which was no more than Azande commoners contributed towards the upkeep of the courts. Bit by bit Azande infiltrated among them and married with them. Commoners of standing settled among them and encouraged them to adopt Zande habits and to speak the Zande tongue by offering them hospitality – it is through food, Azande say, that men are subjugated, and by justice ... "Azande subject themselves to princes on account of the gifts they receive from them". Finally some princeling was sent by his father to rule them ...' (p. 33). And the greater the percentage of foreigners the more autocratic that rule was: among their own kin the Avongara were relatively democratic, but in ruling subject

Table 4: Peoples Contributing to the Zande Complex (from Evans-Pritchard 1971)

Almost assimilated culturally		*Still speaking own languages*		*Minor contributors to Azande*	
SUDANIC					
I	Abandiya	X	Apambia	XXXII	Mundu
II	Adio	XI	Basiri	XXXII	Avukaya
III	Abwameli	XII	Biri	XXXIV	Jur peoples
IV	Angada	XIII	Medje	XXXV	Moro peoples
V	Nzakara	XIV	Momvu	XXXVI	Logo
VI	Nzakara	XV	Mangbele		
VII	Abarambo	XVI	Mbegumba		
VIII	Amadi	XVII	Bongo		
IX	Bangba	XVIII	Golo		
		XIX	Tabbu		
		XX	Bai		
		XXI	Gobu		
		XXII	Kreish		
		XXIII	Banda		
		XXIV	Ndogo		
		XXV	Baka		
BANTU					
		XXVI	Ambili	XXXVII	Mabudu
		XXVII	Akare	XXXVIII	Ababua
		XXVIII	Abuguru	XXXIX	Mobenge
		XXIX	Huma		
		XXX	Abangbinda		
NILOTIC					
		XXXI	Mberidi		
NILO-HAMITIC					
				XL	Fajelu
				XLI	Kakwa

peoples the hierarchy expanded, a phenomenon to be discussed below.

The material culture of the Azande is a patchwork of contributions from the different peoples belonging to that nation, and the crops that they cultivate reflect the same mixture. The staple cereals grown were of Abarambo origin, and these people probably also introduced American maize to the region. The groundnut is another American import, introduced relatively late to the Zande perhaps via one of their Sudanese conquests. The banana was introduced via the Mangbetu, as was the fig tree that yields bark to make clothing, and many other plants. (Incidentally, it is astonishing how many of the Zande crops are of American origin.)

Various shapes of house are built; a mud-walled one of Mbomu origin, a temporary wall-less shelter and a clay and stake walled house from the Amiangba, huts for circumcision and secret societies from the Amadi (together with these institutions), and Ambomu huts with roofs reaching almost to the ground. Granaries come from the Amiangba.

Iron-working comes chiefly from the Basiri, though some of the artefacts which they make originate from other subject peoples: arrows and harpoons from the Amadi, the Belanda and the Abuguru. Straw hats are made, the crown being Ambomu in origin, the decorative patterning Mangbetu and the brim a European influence.

And so the list continues, through pottery, woodcarving, basketry, mats, musical instruments and dances.

Likewise customs ranging from circumcision to cannibalism, via witchcraft and burial practices, are thought to have been adopted by the Azande from among the subject cultures, and thereby spread to the whole nation.

Evans-Pritchard sums up the quite remarkable account of Zande conquest and cultural assimilation with the following four points: 1. The Zande evidence illustrates the need to distinguish between relatively static primitive societies and those like the Azande who undergo considerable cultural and social change (cf. Piggott 1965: innovating and conserving societies?) 2. The developments and changes occurred in a purely African setting, without influence from Arabs or Europeans except towards the very end: '… our evidences show how a people right in the centre of Africa have taken over, used, and developed, long before any contact with higher civilisations, what has appeared to them most valuable in the habits of the people they have come into contact with' (p. 119). 3. The evidence indicates that the Zande migrations and conquests caused much cultural change and development, with greater complexity of social relations and political institutions. Zande oral tradition supports this interpretation: 'Azande think of their present way of life … as being the result of a long process of development which started when the Avongara consolidated the Mbomu clans and the Avongara-Ambomu began their migrations and conquests, a process shaped by wars, movements into new ecological zones, colonisation, ethnic admixture, and cultural borrowings in each new

area of dispersal. As they see it, their political system with its ruling
class, court etiquette, a regimental organisation, an administrative
establishment, political control of judicial procedure, and inequality
of wealth started from humble beginnings and slowly developed'
(p. 120). 4. The Avongara-Ambomu supremacy resulted not from
technological superiority, which they did not have anyhow, but from
the possession of a more sophisticated *political* organisation than the
peoples they subjected (Chapters 8 and 9).

There is a final point to note, one that many archaeologists will
find the most striking, namely that the available evidence suggests
that the original conquering Avongara-Ambomu were hunters and
not farmers. The Azande have no domestic animals except for dogs
and chickens, all their major crops definitely come from subjected
peoples or neighbours, and ninteenth-century travellers' reports
describe the Avongara-Ambomu as dressed in skins, the men being
hunters and only the women cultivating. It is hard to accept that
such a situation could arise, that a hunting and gathering
subsistence base could support more sophisticated political
institutions than adjacent farming cultures, for such a notion is
contrary to all our ingrained evolutionary schemes of subsistence
and social development. Nevertheless, Evans-Pritchard lays out
ample evidence to support his case, and whether or not the Azande
were conquering hunters, the possibility of such a phenomenon is
brought before us.

The Azande and the other great African conquering nations that
we have come across, the Fulani, the Swazi and the Zulu, have all
achieved a new level of cultural complexity as one outcome of their
wars. The complete annihilation of a people is rare though not
unknown, but co-existence and the merging and absorption of
cultures commonly occur. The culture of the conquerors is likely to
be altered as much as that of their new subjects, particularly where
invaders have had to adapt to a new physical environment. The
economies of the different peoples are likely to function together as a
more complex system than either side possessed previously, though
whether this will be through specialisation as with the Hausa and
Fulani, or through a pooling of resources and techniques as for the
Azande, it is hard to say. Political and social hierarchies are
emphasised and extended to cope with the incorporation of new and
more people into one unit, and in all the instances quoted kingship
(or its Fulani equivalent the emirate) has become established as the
government of the new state.

The artefacts of war

Here we shall look only briefly at a few examples of specialised artefacts from the warring cultures discussed above. The presence and form of defensive structures is variable. The Dani build watchtowers, but otherwise do not take account of the endemic fighting in their architecture, and compound fences are built to control pigs rather than people. The Yanomamo *shabano* is defensive, it would seem, and so is the Maori *pa* with its ramparts and fighting

Figure 61. Weapons from Polynesia, made of wood, tooth and skin (S. Goddard, Exeter City Museum)

Figure 62. Warriors' dress.
(a) Blackfoot soldier.
(b) Blackfoot finery
(Curtis photographs and
captions)

platforms (Bellwood 1971, Fox 1976; and see figs. 42 and 43). Those who raid and those who are raided make less provision for defence specifically against their human enemies, but as these people often possess large numbers of animals they may build stockades, corrals or cow byres to keep out intruders of all sorts (Rowlands 1972 for further examples).

Weapons are best illustrated, not described. Fig. 61 shows a range of fighting implements, and it is interesting to note that in most instances the objects are specialised forms used only in warfare, and their shape may be quite distinctive when compared with similar hunting artefacts. There are cultures where this specialisation is taken a step further, and weapons are invested with power – a power that is often linked with the power of a leader as we have already seen for the *Meru* of Maori chiefs. The use of weapons as insignia of power and authority probably derives from circumstances such as these, and then the spear or battle-axe can be a purely symbolic and ceremonial artefact, no longer functional.

Similarly, battledress can give rise to items which are no longer functional in their original context. We have seen that most warriors indulge in personal display, and many dress up in conspicuous and gorgeous clothes and ornamentation before fighting; even practical items such as shields can be elaborated for display purposes. Beyond a certain point, elaboration will impair fighting efficiency but the conflict of roles can be solved by having two sets of battledress: an extravagant showy ceremonial set for display purposes and a sober, strong and practical set for the actual fighting. Fig. 62 illustrates some of these alternatives.

Contact: some implications for archaeology

The aspects of contact described above have many implications for the interpretation of archaeological evidence, and readers will no doubt have ideas in mind beyond the few to be discussed here. In studying small-scale and pre-industrial societies, the overwhelming impression is one of manifold direct and indirect contacts between communities. This is so in all types of environment, with examples to be found among all the major modes of subsistence and from a wide spectrum of social structures. In the past, once mankind had achieved a certain minimum population density, we may suppose that communities had a similar desire for contact with other groups, and that they were familiar with a similar range of mechanisms for achieving their goal, whether through exchange or through warfare. This supposition is not based merely on vague inferences drawn from the ethnographic record but supported by ample archaeological evidence for the movement of raw materials, manufactured objects and groups of people from one region to another, in every part of the inhabited world.

Exchange

The enthnographic literature on exchange provides various possible models for the interpretation of archaeological distribution patterns, most of which are already well-known if not well-tested: gift-exchange, barter, war-booty, tribute and diplomacy have reached the archaeological literature. Whichever model one favours for particular contexts, there is one common aspect of distribution that is consistently relevant, which is that artefacts travel further than people. This applies whatever the means of contact. Time and again, one reads of people who obtain goods and do not keep them but pass them on, and frequently there are rules which prohibit passing things back to their source and encourage their ever-wider dispersal. Gift-exchange cycles and trade-fair networks are immediately understandable as efficient dispersal mechanisms; war booty and tribute may be less obviously so, but they too can serve to spread material things beyond their original cultural context as when an Azande king used choice items of tribute for a diplomatic gift to a fellow monarch. The aboriginal North American trade networks similarly carried objects far beyond their home-land, and although *kula* valuables were exchanged within a single cultural area, they too travelled further than any individual inhabitant of the region.

Long-distance indirect contact may be postulated from prehistory, with the more confidence in that we know it flourished in many proto- and early historic contexts. Models depending on indirect contact are especially useful where objects are found at several cultural removes from their source, that is where they have travelled across one or more culture-areas before coming to rest. Evidence of this sort is to be found in the distribution of jade axes in the British Isles. Jade does not occur naturally in these islands, and the probable source of raw material for the axes lies at some distance, in the Upper Rhine region, the Jura or the Alps. The 100 or so axes known from Britain are therefore unlikely to have arrived through a single transfer from source to final owner, as this would have meant leap-frogging the Neolithic cultures of the Low Countries and Northern France to reach the Channel, and perhaps several more cultures within Britain before reaching a resting-spot in the vicinity of Stonehenge, in the Somerset Levels or in Scotland (Coles, Orme, Bishop and Woolley 1974). But if we suggest that these jade axes travelled through many contacts along a network motivated by ceremonial exchange or by a system of trade-partnership and fairs, then their presence in the archaeological record may be explained simultaneously with several other categories of evidence for redistribution. By the late fourth millennium b.c. there existed in the British Isles a redistribution mechanism that was moving flint and pottery and a bewildering variety of stone axes around the country. We do not know for sure that the jade axes moved along the same lines of contact, but it is likely since all these categories of artefact may be found in the same context, for example, beside the Sweet Track, a late fourth-millennium plank-built pathway that crossed the Somerset Levels (Coles and Orme 1976, 1979). Grahame Clark has already investigated the possibility that the stone axes were redistributed by means of exchange cycles, and he relied extensively on ethnographic accounts to support his case (Clark 1966). The other possibility, a mechanism more akin to the pan-American trade-fair network, has yet to be considered in detail.

A further point to note from the study of distribution networks is that the objects passed around are not necessarily functional. We saw this with the *kula* armbands that were too small to be worn even by children, and other items peculiar to ceremonial exchange may be similarly useless in terms of their original function. In non-ceremonial networks certain categories of artefact may evolve into primitive currencies and they too are no longer functional in their original sense. Non-utilitarian objects discovered by the archaeologist may also be items for ceremonial exchange or a form of currency, or possibly both. The former is more likely when objects are found singly, as with the jade axes or some of the more outstanding decorated axes of the Scandinavian Bronze Age (Fig. 63). The latter interpretation, objects as currency, may apply where collections or hoards are known. These occur from periods as remote as the Upper Palaeolithic when quite useless spearheads of very fine flint were manufactured by the Solutreans, and they are quite common by the Neolithic and Bronze Age when stone and metal axes were collected together in great numbers (e.g. Danish flint axe

Figure 63. Non-utilitarian axes? (a) Early Neolithic jadeite axe found beside the Sweet Track, Somerset, England; length 20cm (Somerset Levels Project). (b) bronze axe from Galstad Tumberg parish, Vastergotland, Sweden; made of thin bronze over a clay core (still preserved), and found with six neck rings (Jan Eric Sjoberg, Goteborgs Arkeologiska Museum)

hoards and Breton socketed axeheads; see also Ottaway and Strahm 1975).

The exchange cycles recorded and discussed at length by anthropologists are found in small-scale societies, in both farming and in hunter-gatherer contexts. They are not, apparently, a phenomenon of more complex societies. This should be borne in mind when interpreting the prehistoric evidence, for it implies that while such models are relevant to the earlier phases of European prehistory, they may no longer be applicable once there is evidence for complex, stratified societies like those of the first millennium b.c. It may be that something like the *kula* achieves for small groups of people like the villagers of the Trobriand and Amphlett Islands what the Avongara conquests wrought for the peoples who became the Azande nation, in that both bring about contact between otherwise separate communities and both make available to the participants a wider range of goods that is produced by any one culture in the system. The one model works where social and political hierarchies are minimally developed, the other depends on and fosters the growth of political power and social complexity.

Contact and cultural development

The importance of trade as a stimulus to cultural development has been well-advocated by prehistorians (e.g. Childe 1925; Renfrew 1969), and where anthropologists have considered the societies they study through time, they have been in broad agreement on the significance of trade. However, we should note that this is not the only stimulus. Any form of peaceful contact that encourages the redistribution of goods, be it the barter systems of the North American networks, the markets of West Africa or the gift-exchanges of Arnhem Land, also encourages specialisation. Most systems of redistribution operate on the basis of localised specialisation, and we have seen how in the Yanomamo case it is created at need and how for the Cheyenne and Mandan-Hidatsa it promoted economic diversity and a more successful *overall* exploitation of the environment. In the British Isles, the same archaeological evidence which indicated the presence of redistribution networks also shows specialisation – axe production based on localised sources of suitable stone, be it flint from Grimes Graves in the east or Tievebulliagh igneous rock from off the north coast of Ireland, and the production of fine pottery based on the gabbroic clays of the Lizard peninsula in

Cornwall. The making and distribution of these objects was not prompted solely by need, as they were often sought out by people who could have relied on closer sources of supply; for example, the people who used the causewayed enclosure on Windmill Hill were using some pottery from distant Cornwall in addition to locally-produced wares. This suggests that the possession of exotics was desirable, possibly because it demonstrated successful participation in the exchange network, and so the demands of participants from all over the British Isles would eventually give flint-miners and potters a market far more extensive than their immediate neighbourhood. This would encourage their increased specialisation, and a corresponding increase in production by their neighbours to supply them with food and other types of goods. The time-scale and extent of such developments are unknown, but we can postulate that the long-term effects of the Neolithic redistribution networks would be to encourage local diversity of economy and of artefacts within an overall common culture.

Cultural complexity also results from conquests, particularly when the economy of the conquered differs from that of the invaders. In such cases, the two subsistence bases can be welded together to the advantage of both, whereas little new will be gained from merging two similar systems. Hausa farming and Fulani pastoralism add up to something more than the sum of the two parts, and Zande hunting could be a successful addition to local systems of agriculture in a way that invading Zande farmers could never have achieved. Hunting and farming economies can work alongside each other, and pastoralism and farming likewise, and both co-exist in contexts apart from conquest. However, pastoral and hunting economies are likely to clash, as did the Zulu and the Bushmen and, at much the same time, the European cowherder and the North American Indian hunter-farmer. Where there is a clash of interests, conquest depends on the subjugation or abolition of one economy, and no greater diversity ensues.

The diversity consequent on invasion has been discussed in these pages chiefly in the light of the Zande example. The successful control of a mixture of peoples was achieved through the development of social and political hierarchies to their ultimate expression in the Zande Kingdoms, and it was noted that other African conquerors like the Swazi and the Zulu had developed similar traits. Indeed, it is something of an anthropological naiveté to state that conquest leads to complexity, for the point was made long ago. Yet it is none the less relevant to note that ethnohistory from the Zande to the Zulu bears out this statement, and so does the early history of Europe. The gradual emergence of the English nation in the early mediaeval period has its similarities to that of the Swazi, and Charlemagne would no doubt have recognised a worthy rival in Shaka.

In archaeological contexts, where there is apparent evidence for the intrusion of one culture into the territory of another, and for the continuity of traits belonging to both groups, one possible interpretation of events would be that of conquest and cultural continuity based on a diversity of economies. If the above speculations hold true, this should lead to the subsequent development of economy and of political and social organisation to a degree of complexity achieved by neither side before. Simple co-existence, on the other hand, is unlikely to demand the same degree of political control: Fulani pastoralists have developed Emirates to rule the Hausa, but the Tarali have no such control over the villagers of the Himalayas with whom they co-exist on a relatively egalitarian basis. Where, in such schemes, does evidence fit like that for the expansion of Beaker traits across Europe? Diversity of economy, co-existence and cultural continuity seem likely, but evidence is lacking for the immediate emergence of European political hierarchies that one should expect to ensue from a conquest.

While on the topic of invasions, there is one point to note briefly. Conquerors may well leave a simpler and less profuse archaeological record than those they conquer. The Fulani make less and own less variety of things than the Hausa, putting their capital into herds instead of material culture. The majority of them live in small and temporary camps, as befits nomadic pastoralists, in contrast to the permanent towns of the Hausa. The Avongara seem to have retained very little in the way of material culture that was distinctively theirs, before the adoptions of so many traits from their subjects. So conquest may not greatly alter the material culture of a region, and hence it may have no marked direct impact on the archaeological record – a point that has been demonstrated historically with the Norman Conquest of England. Indirect evidence may be more significant in the long run, for example evidence such as the emergence of kingdoms.

Contact, competition and display

It was argued at the beginning of this chapter that exchange and warfare could both be seen as means of contact and socialisation.

This is clearly so in the case of exchange fairs and expeditions, but perhaps less evident when people are fighting. We saw, however, that battles were the major social occasions in the life of Dani men, and that Nuer-Dinka hostilities led to intermarriage as well as to killings, and we have already discussed the co-existence of cultures that can ensue from conquest. Likewise, exchange and warfare both promote rivalry between members of a group, and provide a context for competition between the players. *Kula* participants are vying with members of their own community to see who will achieve the best exchanges and hence the most prestige. Dani and Cheyenne warleaders alike are out to win renown amongst their peers as well as to beat the enemy, and a Maori chief increases his power over his followers and not his opponents by killing the latter. The competition in all cases is for standing within the group, and for the prestige that may bring leadership. This would not have any direct bearing on the interpretation of archaeological evidence but for the display element involved. Part of the competition for prestige emerges as display, and people may go to great lengths to decorate themselves, to show off as warriors, and to demonstrate their generosity, creating and using many otherwise redundant artefacts in the process.

An element of competitive display may lie behind the production of a number of prehistoric artefacts. The accumulation of fine stone axes, of green jadeite armrings and bright blue callaïs pendants and necklaces in Breton megalithic burial chambers points to a certain ostentation. The glorious and sometimes quite impractical trappings of the European Bronze Age warrior, especially the beautiful but ineffective bronze shields, indicate a more martial context for competitive display. And the collections of exotic and highly specialised artefacts in the luxurious waggon and chariot burials of a small element of first millennium society suggests competitive acquisition and gift-giving between peers who were princes and kings. The contexts of these instances of competitive display help us to gain some insight into the cultural values of past societies, and into the nature of the organisation systems that some men were so eager to dominate.

Endemic warfare and the competitive display of warriors may give rise to a situation where the display becomes equally or more important than the fighting, and this is borne out by the instances where some other form of competition has displaced fighting like the cricket matches which now take the place of battles in the Trobriand

Islands. In situations like this, there may be a lot more show than actual fighting, and therefore a mass of evidence for a martial society need not mean that every community was in a permanent state of siege. The Celts of Britain immediately before the Roman Conquest had a multitude of defended settlements, many of them striking and impressive to this day. They had a well-developed range of weapons, including some highly ornamented ones and including the chariot which was surely designed for prestigious display as well as for battle. Literary references add information about the personal ornamentation of warriors, including tatoos, and about practices such as head-hunting, and suggest an ambience full of martial boasting and bravado (see Fig. 3). But the evidence for rural prosperity, like that achieved at Gussage All Saints in Dorset (Wainwright 1977), suggests that there was a good deal more talk than action.

Warfare, alliances, diplomatic gifts and ceremonial exchange cycles: all bring peoples into contact with each other, and so we come back once more to the main theme of this chapter, the multiplicity of contacts between primitive communities: contacts, moreover, which impinge on all aspects of culture – on subsistence and manufacture, on social organisation, on political systems, on prestige, and on religion – to such an extent that these may be welded together and interchanged and substituted so that trade becomes diplomacy and diplomacy is gift-giving which brings an alternative prestige to that of the warrior. Contact, therefore, should leave its traces woven through the fabric of archaeology, and we should be prepared to unravel the patterns in the evidence until those traces are found.

5. Ritual and Religion

Ritual and religion are taboo subjects in archaeological circles, denounced by the brave and avoided by the sensible; only a perverse few continue their studies in this dangerous field. Is it then perversity that devotes a whole chapter to the subject, when many other worthwhile fields of study have been omitted? I prefer to think that it is an example of one of the purposes of this book at work, with ethnography correcting the biases of fashion and providing the archaeologist with a balanced view of his central subject, namely man. By the end of this chapter, readers who have previously avoided the topics of ritual and religion may agree that they are proper subjects for archaeological study, and should not be left to the lunatic fringe.

The present dearth of archaeological studies in this field has been aggravated by the way in which the word 'ritual' has been used, to cope with evidence that was not immediately explicable in commonsense terms. This is generally held to be a misuse of the term, in the sense of it being overworked, whereas the real abuse has been to employ the word without exploring its meanings, to use it as a final explanation of the data when it should have been no more than an initial classification. Therefore, instead of perpetuating the avoidance brought in to counteract over-use, we should be doing the opposite – we should explore the fields of human behaviour classified as religious or ritual in order to achieve some measure of understanding. The pages that follow will be devoted largely to the validation of this argument, that the proper archaeological study of man should include his religious and ritual life.

At this stage, some definition of the subject is needed. The minimal definition of religion favoured by many anthropologists was given by Tylor as 'a belief in Spiritual Beings' (Tylor 1871). This coupled with magic, made up the realm of the supernatural, and these two categories of magic and religion remain dominant in the anthropologists' studies. To them we should add myth, totemism, witchcraft and sorcery, all of which belong to the ritual world of man. Other topics though not exclusively ritual should still be included, and foremost of these are politics and the organisation of society in their ceremonial and symbolic aspects. Ritual and religion in the broadest sense comprise the symbolic content of life, and it is thus that they should be understood here, though much of the focus of discussion will be on narrower aspects.

There are problems, clearly, with the definition of ritual and religion, problems of quite a different order from those which arose in dealing with settlement or the food quest. This is due partly, one suspects, to the current schizophrenia of western culture concerning its own ritual life, and also to one of the dominant characteristics of both ritual and religion, namely that they mirror very closely one or more aspects of their parent culture and these aspects can differ widely from one culture to the next. This leads to considerable problems of cultural bias, and marked cultural variation in what is understood to be ritual or religious behaviour. An example may help to illustrate this. The birth of twins is a normal and natural, if not very common event, in most western cultures (at least, it was before the advent of fertility drugs), but for many other cultures twins are abnormal and supernatural. Moreover, in some of the cultures which see them as abnormal, twins are welcome as good omens, whereas in others they are abhorred as signs of great wrong. Thus what the observer takes to be natural may be supernatural for the participants, or vice versa.

There are other traps: if a giant monster fish lives in a lake and stops all fishing by humans, is it natural or not? (Burch 1971). Is the fisherman's avoidance of the lake ritual? Do his actions fall more, or less, into the realm of religion than the actions of those who pursue the Loch Ness Monster? Secondly, does a Christian ethnographer, believing in miracles but disbelieving the existence of tribal gods, study the religion of a society more, or less, objectively than an atheist? It is apparent that there can be no consistent division of sacred from profane, natural from supernatural, normal from abnormal, which can be applied to all cultures. The field of ritual and religion is wide, and its boundaries must necessarily remain imprecise.

If this leaves the reader more uncertain of the subject than he was at the beginning, that is all to the good, for we as archaeologists have been all too certain that the nature of ritual and religion is such that we cannot study them as we do technology or economy (Clark 1957). A little questioning and exploration of the subject would be healthy.

The anthropologists' exploration of religion began almost before the birth of the discipline. Tylor's *Primitive Culture* (1871) is generally taken as the first classic study of primitive religion, and it is remembered chiefly for the distinctions made between magic, science and religion, and for the minimal definition of religion quoted above. Tylor's work was probably much influenced by the late eighteenth-century enquiries into the nature of religion, so well-described by Manuel (Manuel 1959), and also, undoubtedly, by the evolutionary mode of thought crystallised in Darwin's *Origin of Species* (1859). Similar influences were at work on Tylor's contemporaries, and we find that nineteenth-century enquiries are devoted primarily to a search for the most primitive and therefore most ancient species of religion. This was accompanied by the collection and classification of religion, rituals and their variations, a process which culminated in Frazer's voluminous *Golden Bough* (1907-36). Tylor's categories of magic, science and religion were turned by Frazer into an evolutionary sequence of modes of thought, that began with magic, developed into religion as man became more sophisticated, and finally emerged as science in modern advanced cultures.

There is much more to Frazer's work than this, but in the present context it is what we should note, since much of the earlier ethnography of religion was cast in a similar evolutionary mode of thought, and some of this seeped through and influenced archaeology. Frazer and his peers used the Australian Aborigines as examples of a people whose religion was of the most primitive, at the same time as Sollas and others were equating the technology, economy and organisation of the Australians with earliest man (Sollas 1911). Totemism was singled out as a key feature of Australian ritual, and for many decades was seen as an early and primitive version of religion, a view that strongly influenced some interpretations of Palaeolithic art (Ucko and Rosenfeld 1967).

Durkheim, albeit more sociologist than anthropologist, was the next major contributor to the anthropological study of religion; he also took Australian totemism as one of his main areas of study, but his approach was new in that he was concerned not with the development of religion, but with its place in contemporary society (Durkheim 1912). He argued that the form a religion took was dictated by society, in that religion was the supernatural reflection of its parent culture: man created god in his own image, and organised his religion along the same lines as his society. We shall return to this argument and its developments in subsequent pages, for its implications have considerable relevance for the archaeologist.

Due to the influence of Durkheim, the decades from the 1920s onwards were dominated by a functionalist approach to the study of ritual and religion, with almost all interest in history and development gone. Malinowski, Radcliffe-Brown and Evans-Pritchard made considerable contributions in the inter-war years, largely through studying some aspect of the field such as magic or witchcraft, and then analysing its role in maintaining the functioning culture (e.g. Malinowski 1922, Radcliffe-Brown 1922, Evans-Pritchard 1950).

Other aspects, such as sorcery, shamanism and myth now had their scholars, and the subject became much fragmented and specialised. This may account for contradictory claims such as those of Bohannan that 'there is probably no single subject with which anthropology concerns itself today on which the literature is larger than on tribal religion' (Bohannan 1969, 310), and of Middleton that since Malinowski and Radcliffe-Brown 'the study of the religion of non-literate peoples has, with some monumental exceptions, met with a curious lack of interest by ethnographers' (Middleton 1967, ix). What is happening here is that myth, for example, which is one scholar's study of religion is another's study of social order, and the field of ritual and religion, as we noted earlier, is very hard to define to the satisfaction of all concerned. However, it is possible to see in recent years a resurgence of interest in the study of religious beliefs and practises *per se*, and a decline in the mechanical functionalist approach, and here one may point to the works of Levi-Strauss, Leach and Mary Douglas (Levi-Strauss 1964, Leach 1969, Douglas 1970).

Although the limits of the field are hard to define, we can adopt as a framework for discussion the more evident needs of the archaeologist. These are a general awareness of what ritual and religion can encompass in cultures other than his own, and a more detailed consideration of those aspects which appear to be amenable to archaeological study; in this case, three have been selected: feasts, funerals and symbolic dualities. We shall concentrate more on ritual aspects than on religious beliefs, to the extent that people's actions are more within the realm of archaeology than is the detailed reconstruction of the beliefs that motivated the actions. Inevitably, such a treatment is open to criticism as being both superficial and selective, superficial from the anthropologists' point of view and selective on all counts. But if this chapter can go some way to counteracting the devaluation of ritual and religion in the archaeological world, then it will be justified.

The individual: rites de passage

For the purposes of description, it will be useful to divide ritual and religious behaviour into two broad categories, one focussed on the individual and the other on the community. In many cultures, the stages of a person's life are marked by prescribed ceremonies which have become known as *rites de passage*. The stages of birth, initiation, marriage and death do not pass unnoticed in western cultures, which accord varying degrees of importance to baptism, weddings and funerals and which increasingly treat examinations as a series of initiation ordeals. The *rites de passage* of the Tiwi of North Australia will now be described briefly, to show how these are performed in one particular culture (sources: Hart and Pilling 1960, Goodale 1971). The intermingling by the Tiwi of apparently practical actions with apparent superstition provides a good example of the difficulty referred to above of observing and interpreting the ritual of a culture without imposing one's own values.

During pregnancy, a Tiwi woman should not have intercourse, or she may conceive a second child and give birth to twins, which is bad. She should neither bathe in the sea nor in any other big expanse of water, as this would offend the rainbow spirits. She should not eat yams, as this would cause the baby to die, and some other foods are forbidden. She should not cook, as this would cause the children to turn in the womb and hurt. Birth takes place at a campsite adjacent to the main family camp; the father is forbidden to come near, as he would become too fearful, but no one else is excluded and all women may give active practical help. The mother is not allowed to eat until the day after the baby is born, and for five days she and her infant stay in the camp apart. Then their bodies are decorated with paint and they are taken back to the main camp. A few months later, the baby's father gives it a name, which will be possessed by no one else; the infant, with this naming, becomes a recognised member of the community.

Owing to the complexities of Tiwi custom, women are born married, promised to a man perhaps as early as the time of their own mother's puberty ceremonies. Thus for women, the next major ritual occurs at puberty, after they have started living with their husbands. During a girl's first period, she is taken with other women to an isolated camp for five to ten days, and she is forbidden to gather food or cook it, or to make a fire or to touch water, and her husband may not see her. Afterwards, she is painted and taken back to her husband's camp, which is also her father's, and there follows various ceremonies which would amount to a wedding in other cultures, since the father ceremonially hands over his daughter to his son-in-law. He may also designate *her* future son-in-law during these ceremonies.

Initiation occurs for both men and women over a period of about six years, apparently beginning when they are about thirty years old. The initiation ceremonies take place each year during the communal yam festival. Each initiate has a sponsor, and for a while will live apart from the rest of the community, but with both sponsor and spouse. There are food restrictions for the initiates while they are isolated, and a number of customs, ornaments and body-paint designs appropriate to each of the six grades or stages of initiation. After a person has gone through all the stages, he or she is recognised as a full adult member of the community.

Finally, there is the *rite de passage* which looms largest in Tiwi culture, the funeral. When someone dies, they are buried immediately and with a certain amount of ceremony. The mourners are the people who happen to have been in the same camp as the deceased, and those among them who are close relatives paint their bodies and wear arm rings and come under a range of restrictions which they will observe until the end of the funerary ceremonies. A few months after burial a second ceremony, known as *pukamani*, is held, and this is the dominant occasion. It is organised by a close male relative of the deceased, who sends out messengers to inform and invite all other Tiwi connected to the dead person. He commissions some of those who are not closely related to make carved wooden grave posts, and his wives organise food for the forthcoming occasion. The first stage of the *pukamani* begins with each group of mourners performing songs appropriate to their status vis-à-vis the deceased and the company as a whole. There is ritual fighting between groups of spouses and between grave-post carvers and others, and ritualised tree-climbing and jumping over fires. In the second stage of the *pukamani*, which may last up to thirty six hours, everyone collects together to paint and decorate their bodies. This done, they move en masse to the graveyard, stopping to sing and dance on the way and also when they get there. The next day, songs and dances continue and the gravepost-makers are paid for their work with other artefacts and the posts are carried to the grave and set up. Now the mourners wail and cut themselves until the end of the ceremonies is reached; then they wash the paint off their bodies, gather together again and return to camp.

This final *rite de passage*, although caused by and focused on one individual, serves to bring together an otherwise scattered community, a point that Goodale emphasises with regard to the first phase of the *pukamani*: 'Through this medium Tiwi legends are kept alive, news is distributed, new theatrical productions are staged and reviewed, all kinship ties between the performers are strengthened ... many of whom would not be in daily contact' (Goodale 1971, 306). Tiwi funerals may therefore be seen both as rituals focused on the individual and as rituals whose function is supra-individual, designed for the community as a whole.

Community rituals

Whereas the *rites de passage* are linked to the biological framework of the human life, and therefore remains surprisingly constant in occurrence cross-culturally (though not necessarily similar in performance), other types of ritual vary in both focus and performance, and in so far as cultures differ so do the events for which rites are developed. The similarities to our own cultural backgrounds are less obvious than with the ceremonies for birth, marriage and death and the spectrum of activities studied by anthropologists as aspects of ritual and religion may seem surprisingly wide, and perhaps even inappropriate when events such as warfare and football violence are included. Yet institutionalised conflict in New Guinea and institutionalised conflict in the football stadium have both been interpreted as rituals that underline matters of import to the cultures which produced them.

Some of the aspects of culture which more commonly have their ritual side have inevitably been touched on in earlier chapters, and rightly so for one cannot entirely divorce secular from ritual even for the purposes of description, let alone analysis. These aspects include production, in terms of hunting, agriculture and crafts, power, especially the power of hereditary chiefs and kings, and contact both through exchange and through war. Other important aspects that should be noted, although space forbids discussion, include healing, witchcraft and sorcery, and justice; the references given above will provide an introduction to these.

The section below on the rituals and beliefs of the Naskapi and the Dogon will attempt to show how the various aspects interrelate with the overall culture, and only a very brief general discussion will be given here. Indeed, 'general' is hardly the right word, for the more one looks at any aspect of ritual or religion, the more clearly the relationships to individual cultures emerge, and the more difficult it becomes to look at any one side in isolation. Thus one may cite the Mbuti practice of lighting a fire for the forest as an example of a hunting ritual, but it means very little without an understanding of the general context of the Mbuti's relationship to the forest (Turnbull 1965). Mary Douglas touches on the same point in her account of the Lele of Kasai when she writes: 'It is useless to discuss any aspect of Lele religion without first summarising the material conditions of their life. This is not because these seem to have determined the bias of their religious thinking. On the contrary, the manner in which they have chosen to exploit their environment may well be due to the ritual categories through which they apprehend it' (Douglas 1954, 1). Lele culture emphasises the differences between men and women and likewise the differences between forest foods and grassland resources, the former being by far the most important and largely the preserve of men. Hunting is closely linked to religion and accompanied by much ritual, which is also part and parcel of the male-female divisions. Lele hunting ritual is therefore not only an essential action designed to promote success in the chase, but also, together with the actual hunt, something which serves to reinforce group solidarity and the cohesion of the culture. The same interpretation may be made of Iban farming rituals (Freeman 1970) or the rites of Shai pottery production in Ghana (Quarcoo and Johnson 1968), in that each has a relevance to its culture beyond the growth of cereals or the making of pots.

Behind the individuality of these rituals, there are some elements that recur repeatedly in other cultures, also in a ritual context. Such is the Mbuti use of fire as a ritual agent, and the Lele ritual opposition of pairs (male and female: forest and grassland).

However, it would be premature to claim any regularity about the occurrence of such elements, any cross-cultural laws at work, and it would be dangerous in the present state of studies to *assume* any common meaning for recurring features.

Anthropological ideas about religion have been strongly influenced by the work of Durkheim referred to above (p. 218), particularly where he drew attention to the close relationship between the structure of a society and the structure of its religious beliefs: man created his gods as a mirror to his own culture. This idea lies behind comments concerning the interlinking of secular and ritual aspects of culture, and it is carried a stage further by those who see ritual and religion as a means of reinforcing a culture and contributing to group solidarity. Although there are many ifs and buts and complications to this hypothesis, and the anthropologists of religion have developed it in some directions and rejected it in others, the central idea is a useful one for the archaeologist to work with because it may help him to a greater understanding of past cultures. If rituals, albeit unconsciously, mirror some part of the society that performs them, and if the archaeologist has evidence of a ritual nature to study, then this will best be done in the light of all that is known of the past culture.

But before we turn to the archaeological possibilities, it would be advisable to explore a little more fully the integration of religion and culture, and this will be done by a brief examination of two societies, the Naskapi of North America and the Dogon of Africa.

The Naskapi (source: Henriksen 1973)

The Naskapi Indians live in Labrador, fishing and sealing on the coast in summer and hunting caribou inland in winter. Summer life is now largely spent in a Europeanised context, but winter hunting remains surprisingly unaffected by contact, and it was here that Henriksen studied the traditional life and values of the Naskapi. Their hunting territory covers some 15,000 square miles, for a population of about 150 of whom about 30 are adult male hunters. The main source of food in the winter is caribou, and the main producers are therefore the hunters, who tend to work in pairs or small groups although it is possible to work alone. A good hunter will build up a following and gain prestige but he does not become leader of a permanent group as the nature of the society is very mobile, and a man who is nothing but a follower in one camp is likely to strike off on his own, or join another group where he may have more standing.

The good hunter's position is based partly on his role as provider, for *all* food must be shared with everyone in camp. This is one of the essential values of Naskapi culture, the common sharing of all produce of the land, of which Henriksen says: 'By common sharing, I refer to the rules which obligate any individual who is the holder of certain goods to share them equally with any other individual, regardless of the relationship between the giver and the receiver, and regardless of whether the receiver reciprocates. However, he is obligated to share with the original giver *just as he is obligated to share with everyone else* when he has anything to share' (p. 40). Sharing contributes to the survival of the whole community in the Barrens, for caribou are widely scattered and all the hunters in a camp are unlikley to be successful on every expedition, but as long as one man kills his quarry everyone will eat.

The importance of sharing is embodied in the central ritual of the Naskapi, the *mokoshan*. This is held regularly throughout the winter months, about every seven to ten days on a day when there is no hunting, and it is held to please the caribou spirit and to bring good luck in hunting. The long bones of all caribou brought back to camp are always saved and collected together, and on the day of the *mokoshan* they are taken into a tent where all the hunters gather. The bones are shared around and then, with great care to observe the proper procedures, the men cook and eat the meat on the bones, and the crushed and fatty bone ends, and they extract and eat the marrow which is the most important part of all, and their families are called in from time to time to eat too. Any part of the bones which is inedible is burnt on the stove within the tent, for the food is sacred and must not be treated like ordinary food (pp. 35-9).

Henriksen summarises the importance of this ritual feast as follows: 'The caribou, the caribou hunt, and the sharing of its produce lie at the heart of Naskapi culture. The sacred marrow from the long bones of the caribou is eaten raw by all the hunters in a ritual context where crucial cultural values are communicated and confirmed. Inside one tent, they sit in a circle for a whole day, partaking in this communal meal through which their relationship to the natural and supernatural worlds is expressed. Also communicated in the ritual are some of the dominant characteristics of their social life, notably that of the fundamental interdependence of one Naskapi upon the other, and the importance of sharing the fruits of the hunt' (p. x). One would not understand the Naskapi without knowing about the *mokoshan*, nor the *mokoshan* without having studied the rest of Naskapi culture.

The Dogon (source: Griaule and Dieterlen 1954, 83-110)

The Dogon, living in villages in the Sudan, are cereal cultivators who have a very elaborate system of beliefs concerning the Universe and its creation and man's place within it. These beliefs influence, among other things, the layout of their houses and villages and fields, and it is on this aspect that we shall concentrate.

Dogon creation myths are complex and overlapping, as clear in their main theme and as difficult to sort out in details as those of the Old Testament. Life originated with a seed. The seed vibrated, causing a spiral of growth from its centre that at the seventh vibration burst out of the seed and spiralled onwards to reach the outer edges of the Universe (Fig. 64). Each vibration represents a cultivated seed, and the first one contains signs which represent the twenty-two categories of the Universe, divided between the four elements of the earth, air, fire and water. These signs were flung out as the seed came to life, and each in turn brought life to the things it symbolises.

The first seed was contained within an enormous egg, the Universe, which was divided into two twin placenta, each of which contained a pair of twin sons of God, or *Nommo*, who in turn each possessed a male and a female principle. A twin from one placenta emerged prematurely from the egg, and a bit of the placenta came with him and became the earth. The world he created was incomplete and the real world was created and peopled by the

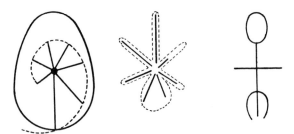

Figure 64. Symbols of the Dogon world. Left to right: the first seven vibrations of the egg of the world; the pre-figuring of man in the egg of the world; the life of the world – the heavenly and earthly placentas (Griaule and Dieterlen 1959)

Nommo of the other half of the egg, who gave rise to eight and then twenty-two mythical ancestors. Creation of the real world took twenty-two years, beginning with four years of sowing millet seed so that from the fifth its annual growth would be perpetual.

The first seven vibrations of the first seed also represent a man, two for his head, two for his arms, two for his legs and one for his sex organs. Moreover, the seven seeds plus the original seed are lodged between a man's shoulder blades, and they are paired, and their ordering influences a man's position in life. Man is likewise an image of the Universe, his head the egg of the world and his body and limbs the germinating cells which emerge from it. The Dogon diagram to show this also follows the principle of twinness, for it can also be seen as a heavenly placenta and an earthly one formed by the two rounded shapes, and the four original twins in the divided egg formed by the cross in the middle.

The figures reproduced (Fig. 64) here are all based on Dogon representations, and this symbolic visualisation of the creation myths affects the layout of their field systems and of their settlements. Field systems ought to be based on a spiral, like the

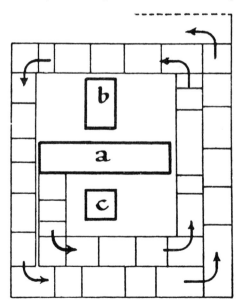

Figure 65. Dogon field-systems. Idealised plan of the spiral lay-out of fields around the three original fields (a), (b) & (c), imitating the spiral of creation (Griaule and Dieterlen 1954)

spiral of creation, which starts from three central ritual fields; along this spiral every family should have four pairs of fields, one facing north, one south, one east and one west, and each individual field should be linked with one of the eight original seeds (Fig. 65). Within a field the ground should be cultivated in a continuous weaving or oscillating line from east to west and back to east, moving from the north edge to the south, a movement based on the vibrations that started the first creative spiral. Eight rows of millet are planted, each row eight steps long, making blocks within the field that again symbolise the eight original seeds and also the first eight ancestors.

At the core of the field system lies the village. This is oriented north-south, with the blacksmith's forge at the head and shrines at the feet. Homesteads form the chest, and out on the eastern and western edges of the village are the hands, huts that women live in during their periods. A cone-shaped shrine and a hollow stone represent the male and the female sex-organs, and the village as a whole is a person. Villages are built in pairs, as twins, and one is the Upper village or heaven and the other is the Lower village or earth.

Just as the village is a person, so is the homestead (Fig. 66). It fits into an oval shape, the original egg or placenta, and the rooms form the various parts of the body: kitchen as the head, main room as the body and workroom as the stomach, stores along the sides as the arms, towers and stable as the legs, and the entrance passage which leads to the workroom as the penis, a layout which symbolises a man lying on his right side which is the correct position both for intercourse and for the grave.

This symbolism is carried further in the house and the clothing of a Hogon, or district chief. A Hogon's tunic and trousers are striped with dark blue, light blue, red and white, colours which represent earth, air, fire and water and also north, south, east and west, which is appropriate as the Hogon himself personifies the Universe. The headdress of the supreme Hogon is woven by eight other chiefs from the stalks of seven sacred plants that grew from the original seeds.

The house of a Hogon has a room with a platform where he sits, and this platform is built of mud and the chopped stalks of eight strains of millet. The wall behind it is divided into two vertically by a row of four bosses. On the left hand side are painted the northern stars, and on the right hand side the southern stars. The bosses are decorated with spirals and divided into quadrants, and the quadrants of the three lower bosses add up to twelve lunar months,

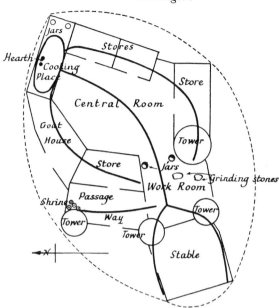

Figure 66. Dogon homestead. The oval outline of the complex represents the original egg, whilst the plan represents a man lying on his right side, individual rooms forming parts of the body. The plan also represents *NOMMO*, or the son of God in human form, and the kitchen and the stable are the heavenly and earthly placentas (Griaule and Dieterlen 1954)

with the top boss making the thirteenth. The four bosses also represent the four seasons. Between two doors on the eastern wall is an egg-shaped sun, painted red, with twenty-two rays, and on either side of the doors are two smaller bumps to represent the solstices.

Eight steps lead up to the house, for the first eight chiefs, and a further eight steps lead to the left into the Hogon's own individual hut, by which there are eight stones, also for the eight past chiefs. To the right is a hearth, and eight stones for future chiefs. Eight storerooms, on the other hand, are not for chiefs but for the eight original plants.

Thus the chief and his house and his clothes and the houses and villages and fields of every Dogon are all embued with some relationship to the creation myth, and they are purposefully made by man, and man purposefully acts, to fit the patterns of creation.

Many of these representations, layouts or actions have a dual or multiple significance and many themes recur, for instance pairing or twins, or the numbers eight and twenty-two. The complexity of the system is evident even from this brief account, and yet it has touched on only one or two aspects of Dogon beliefs and their material consequences. One is reminded of the point made by Mary Douglas with regard to the Lele, that a society's beliefs may influence subsistence strategies as much as vice versa and the impossibility of totally separating out the different aspects or systems of a culture is yet again evident.

Feasts, funerals and symbolic dualities

The feasts of the Naskapi and the houses of the Dogon might both leave archaeological evidence, but the beliefs that lie behind them could not be recovered by contemporary archaeological techniques. So why examine them? Certainly not to suggest that any such beliefs operated in a similar society in the past: to imply that there were Hamburgian *mokoshans* or Eggs of the Universe at New Grange and Knowth would be courting disaster, and if any reader is thinking along such lines then I have failed to convey one of the fundamental purposes of ethnography for archaeologists, a purpose particularly evident in this context of ritual and religion. The ethnographic accounts are *not* to provide parallels for any given archaeological situation, but they are intended to demonstrate through their detail some of the general influences which bear on the life of small-scale societies. In this instance, the Naskapi and Dogon descriptions reveal the interdependence of beliefs and actions at different levels of society, and religion is seen to be as important an influence on action as climate or terrain. The integration of different aspects of culture is clear, and the Durkheimian view that systems of belief function to maintain the validity and solidarity of a culture is applicable in both the American and the African context. In addition to the simple recognition of the presence and influence of systems of belief, the relevance for the archaeologist lies in an appreciation of the way in which that system relates to or reflects the totality of a culture.

   Furthermore, each society examined here emphasises one particular aspect of culture in relation to religion. The Tiwis' greatest ceremony is the funeral, whereas the Naskapis' central ritual is a feast, and the Dogon accord ritual significance to the number and placing of things. In other societies, too, these aspects of culture play a ritual or ceremonial role, and they are aspects which may be within the grasp of archaeological study. If so, they may add a little detail to the very general point made above, that the archaeologist should admit the place of ritual and religion in past communities.

Feasts

Communal eating, or feasting, has been discussed in the present context with the Naskapi *mokoshan*, and mentioned frequently in previous chapters. Examining the food quest, we saw that an important factor in the settlement pattern of hunter-gatherers was the public phase or large gathering, often based on an abundance of food. Power politics may be a matter of feasting one's followers or rivals, whether in New Guinea or on the North West Coast, and feasting was used as a means of contact both diplomatic as for the Yanomamo and for exchange as in the *Kula*. Feasting is also a frequent element of funerals, as we have noted for the Tiwi. In all cases, eating together has a significance beyond the mere satisfaction of hunger, and it becomes evident that the feast has a widespread and great symbolic importance for people of all sorts.

The precise symbolism of the feast will vary from culture to culture, just as the immediate motivation for a feast is different in different contexts. The Naskapi *mokoshan* is held as a hunting ritual, to please the caribou spirit and bring good luck to the hunter. A New Guinea pig feast is given by a man who wishes to demonstrate his skill as a public organiser and orator, and he hopes that those who take part will be his supporters. In the Potlatch, North West Coast Indians vie with each other for power and position through a ritualised escalation of feasting and exchange. The Yanomamo feast is motivated by a need for allies and it is used as a means of bringing together two wary villages for long enough to begin negotiations. Those who attend a Tiwi funeral need food, but the lavishness of supply is connected with the extra-funerary aspects of occasion, both political and social.

Food has often been accorded symbolic value by man, and it is a common ritual or symbolic agent that has provided anthropologists with much to ponder (e.g. Douglas 1966, or Levi-Strauss 1964). It is usually interpreted as a means of communication as well as something to appease hunger, and in this light food-sharing or feasting becomes a communion in several senses of the word. Underlying all feasts whatever their motivation, is the importance of sharing food as a demonstration of unity, of group solidarity and dependence, such as Henriksen brought out for the Naskapi *mokoshan*. If eating together binds people to one another, it is possible that feasting assumes prominence at times when there is a need to do this, in other words on those occasions when groups are disrupted, as by death, or when they are coming into being, as with a political faction or an alliance. Feasting is also prominent when an otherwise scattered group collects together, and in more complex societies the members of a subgroup may eat together ceremonially, thereby underlining their group identity within the larger culture. Traces of a feast are therefore likely to be more than traces of an abundance of food. They signify the past existence of active social processes, the presence of a group whose unity and identity was being proclaimed, affirmed or attempted. Overt religious beliefs or ritual elements pertaining to the feast need not detain the archaeologist in this connection, for their presence or absence does not alter the basic assertion of unity and solidarity which prevails in both secular and sacred contexts.

Funerals

A decade has passed since the publication of Ucko's paper on 'Ethnography and archaeological interpretation of funerary remains' (Ucko 1969). Ucko was concerned mainly with the rituals associated with death: disposal of the body, type of tomb or grave, grave goods, different rites for different sections of a community, etc., and he argued that an ethnographic awareness could prevent the archaeologist from making oversimple interpretations of the evidence before him. This paper remains the best available survey of funerary customs for archaeologists, and it has been put to good use by some among them, though many appear to have been deterred by the impossibility of unravelling situations such as the following Ashanti practice: 'In Ashanti, there is a general rule that the body should *not* face the village; however, there are some Ashanti who say that immediately after burial the body turns itself round to face the village. Some, but not all, Ashanti therefore bury the dead *facing* the village knowing that the body will turn itself round and will therefore eventually conform to the rule of facing the forest' (Ucko 1969, 273).

But there is value in the ethnography of funerals beyond the details of ritual practice. Discussions following Ucko's work have established that, while grave goods may not relate directly to the wealth or occupation of the deceased, they do have significance for the living community that performs the burial rites. Following from this, it appears that the *overall* funerary strategy of a culture can be very informative, and its study may yield hypotheses about the nature of the parent society (e.g. Shennan 1975, for the application of this idea).

These points are valid for Tiwi funerals, which we have seen to be ostensibly focussed on the dead and in practice equally concerned with the living and with their relationships to each other. The scale of a funeral relates not only to the age and standing of the deceased but also to the position and ambition of the man who is organising it, who will in all likelihood be the senior close male relative of the deceased. Tiwi culture accords increasing power and prestige with age and most of all to old men, and this is reflected in the funerary practices: infants may have no funeral at all, children just a small one, women and young men a medium one, and the biggest ceremonies are reserved for men who die old. But a man might engineer a bigger-than-normal funeral for one of his children, if he wanted to increase his own prestige (Hart and Pilling 1960). Prestige also accrues from the number of grave posts set up, and here it is the ability and willingness of the chief mourner to feed and pay the post-carvers which counts. Payment is made with other artefacts – traditionally stone axes, spears, baskets, ornaments and paint – so the funeral acquires another aspect as promoter of manufacture and exchange (Goodale 1971).

The social and political aspects of the funeral may also be seen in the songs and dances and ritual battles that are a major part of the ceremonies, during which the people who are present and who perhaps meet only rarely in the normal course of events, sort out their relationships with each other as well as with the bereaved and therefore changed family. The funeral, in these senses, is very much a ceremony for the living, designed to support and perpetuate contemporary cultural values.

The scale of Tiwi funerals reflects their male gerontocracy, and in other cultures the criteria used to distinguish people in life may also determine their treatment in death. Age, sex and wealth are common dividers, though occupation, clan, totem, caste or any other feature that matters to the living society may be used (see Ucko 1969). If archaeologists can recognise any such distinctions in funerary evidence, then it would be worth considering their operation in the once-living culture: interpretation along these lines has already been attempted in some contexts and we shall explore the possibilities further below.

Symbolic positioning

The account of the Dogon illustrated the influence which beliefs have on the layout of settlement and structures, and it was noted several times that positioning to left or to right was significant, for example house layout represented a man lying on his *right* side. Distinction between left and right is made significant in a very wide range of cultures, and values are assigned to the two positions. We should recognise this readily enough in aspects of our own culture, linguistically for instance with gauche, sinister, politics of the Left or Right, right-hand man, etc., where things of the left are generally derogatory or dangerous and things of the right correct and pro-establishment (see Hertz for an early and fascinating exploration of this theme). Other pairs of opposites may be invested with a similar symbolic significance, most commonly male and female, light and dark, red and white and hot and cold. The Mapuche Indians of Chile have an elaborate series of such pairings which includes the following:

left	*right*
evil	good
death	life
night	day
sickness	health
evil spirits	ancestral spirits
sorcerer	shaman
underworld	afterworld
poverty	abundance
hunger	fullness

(from Faron 1967).

In this system, things on the left are generally evil or undesirable and those on the right are good. The same values recur in other contexts, for instance a bird singing on the right is a good omen, but if the song comes from the left it is bad. In a dream or a story, the person who turns left at a fork in the road is headed for disaster, but he who turns right will meet with success. Natural elements and social categories are also paired and attributed to left or right, and in general the more beneficial or powerful items or those with a stronger positive ritual value are associated with the right:

left	*right*
winter	summer
cold	warm
north	south
moon	sun
blue/black	yellow/white
layman	priest
junior	senior
incest	marriage
woman/child	man

Other cultures might well be expected to view things in a totally different manner from the Mapuche, but many of these groups of opposites recur in other cultural contexts, especially the association of male with right and female with left, and the attribution of the positive element in a pair to the right, and the negative or neutral element to the left. The Dogon man, it will be remembered, should lie on his *right* side, in bed and in the grave – and left-wing politics are naturally sinister to a right-minded establishment.

The archaeologist has evidence at his disposal which allows for a search for recurrent significant positionings of a similar nature, especially for the distinction of left and right and male and female. The exact meaning of the distinction will not emerge, but to recognise that there *is* such a symbolic distinction in the evidence would in itself contribute to a greater understanding of the past culture, whether one is looking at art or burials or settlement layout. Here, as with funerals, the study of ethnography can provide an understanding of the sorts of things which can be accorded ritual – and hence cultural – significance. It can therefore focus the attention of the archaeologist on new aspects of the evidence.

The archaeological study of ritual and religion

The preceding pages have explored the pervasiveness of ritual and religion, and examined the close relationship that these have to their parent culture, with the implication for archaeologists that they should *expect* all past cultures to have engaged in ritual, religious and ceremonial activities. Some of these activities in some of the cultures will have left behind material evidence; although this evidence will not proclaim its full inner meaning to the archaeologist, it is more likely to be understood if it is studied in the overall cultural context than in isolation.

Both ritual and religion tend to be tied very closely into some other aspect of life, and we have seen that cultures differ in their views as to what is secular and what is sacred. For these two reasons, it would be unwise to suggest any direct comparative approach to the study of these subjects, as one might perhaps have done for subjects like the use of wood in primitive societies. Instead, it is hoped to demonstrate through three archaeological studies, that an ethnographic awareness and background knowledge of the subject is in itself of value, and can contribute at several levels of interpretation. The first two studies are of evidence from cemeteries, dealing in the first case with a specific anomaly in the data, and in the second with the broader possibilities of interpretation of the site. The third study concerns the interpretation of two groups of British Neolithic sites whose function is not obvious, and it leads to an exploration of the possible contributions of ethnography in more general terms, drawing on most of the aspects of ritual and religion discussed above, as well as material from several other chapters.

Branč

The Early Bronze Age cemetery at Branč in Slovakia has been studied by Shennan with a view to determining the social organisation of the community from which the dead came (Shennan 1975). Age, sex, position and orientation of the body, and type and number of grave goods were all considered for 274 burials, yielding a range of suggestions about male and female statuses and possible marriage practices. One result of the study raises an interesting possibility. Shennan noted that most females were buried on their left side (81 per cent) and oriented E-W or NE-SW, whereas most males were buried on their right side (69 per cent) and oriented W-E or SW-NE. However 20 per cent of the skeletons identified as male were found lying on their *left* side and oriented for the most part like the females. Shennan suggested that this anomaly might be due to a systematic bias towards sexing skeletons as males (Shennan 1975, 282).

We can suggest other possibilities, one of which relates to the association of male with right and female with left discussed above.

Let us suppose that a similar association was made by the Branč community, and that this was why they buried men lying on their right and women on their left sides. If so, why were some men deliberately buried like women? Maybe they were expected to flip over once the mourners' backs were turned, like the Ashanti. Or perhaps they were treated like women in death because they had acted a female role in life. Faron reports that Mapuche male shamans were not considered fully masculine, and dressed in women's clothes for their performances, and were sometimes suspected of being homosexual (Faron 1967, 177-8). There are numerous other North American instances of shamans adopting female attributes (e.g. the Cheyenne: Hoebel 1960). Ethnographers have also reported examples of homosexual marriages, where men adopt a permanent female role, and examples of men living as women as an accepted role within the community (Brain 1978). It could therefore be suggested that the Branč males lying on their left side like women were buried in this manner because they had lived as women, and that male homosexuals formed a recognised section of the community.

In this brief example, an awareness of the possibilities of symbolic positioning has provided a hypothesis, which remains to be tested against the archaeological evidence. Are these men accompanied by female grave goods? Or by grave goods suggesting an exclusive occupational group? If the latter, is there any possibility that they were shamans or sorcerers? Maybe the hypothesis would have to be dismissed on closer examination of the evidence, untenable or unproven. But it is only by asking new questions and searching for an answer that archaeologists can come closer to understanding the past, and it is one of the roles of ethnography to prompt the question.

Vedbaek

The excavation and publication of the Mesolithic cemetery at Vedbaek in Denmark provides further material for analysis in the present context (Albrethsen and Brinch Petersen 1976). The cemetery was discovered adjacent to a mesolithic settlement site, beside an inlet on the Zealand coast. Altogether twenty-two flat graves have been found, apparently deliberately laid out in parallel rows. The bodies were placed flat on their backs in the graves, and were in the majority of cases covered with red ochre and accompanied by grave goods. The details of the burials are summarised in Table 5.

Albrethsen and Brinch Petersen make a number of inferences on the basis of these details. They suggest that, although the correlation is not perfect, burial was with either tools or ornaments and that tools are normally found with males and ornaments with females. Therefore, it is thought likely that the unsexed infant in grave 8 was a boy as it was buried with a flint blade, a tool found with several definitely male burials (e.g. 5, 6 and 10). Bodies 4 and 19c, likewise unsexed, have both 'male' and 'female' grave goods and therefore present problems. The authors argue that 4 was male, having a flint blade by the pelvis like all definite males, and a bone dagger which is also interpreted as a male artefact, which together outweigh the 'female' pig's teeth lying by the pelvis and right arm. Body 19c, when examined together with the other unsexed adult (19a) and the baby (19b) in the same grave (Fig. 67), is thought on balance to be female. The 'male' flint blade is in a unique position under the chin, and the body possessed an elaborate chest ornament made up from the teeth of red deer, humans, pig and aurochs. The only other body with ornamentation made from a variety of animal species was definitely female (8b), and a similarly ornamented burial found at Dragsholm was also female, suggesting that this was a regional female style of dress. Bodies 19a and 19b had no grave goods, but 19a had been killed by a bone point that pierced its throat. The authors suggest that this group was a family, the husband being 19a and the wife 19c and that 'the wife and child have had to follow the husband in the grave, and the blade-knife below the woman's chin might symbolise the weapon with which they were slain' (Albrethsen and Brinch Petersen 1976, 22).

Age as well as sex is noted to affect the distribution of grave goods. Two old people, a male and a female, rest on antlers (10 and 22) but no body under 40 years old does so. Women appear to be buried with ornaments when aged between 18 and 35 but not when they are older (22), whereas men in the 40-60 age range are buried with their tools (the authors quote grave 12 here, but the skeleton was unsexed and graves 5 and 6 would be better examples). Age also affects the burial rite itself: none of the skeletons whose age at death could be determined were over one year old and under eighteen, and the cemetery seems to have been only for infants and adults.

Some additional speculation is possible, based on a general ethnographic awareness of ritual and religious practices, which may

Grave	Sex	Age	head orientation	disturbed?	flint blades	tooth pendants	antlers	other
Table 5. The Vedbaek Burials								
1	F	18-20		Disturbed				
2	M	50		Disturbed				
3	F	40-50		Disturbed				
4	-	-	N		1, R of pelvis	Pig— 5 by pelvis, 1 by R arm		bone dagger L of pelvis
5	M	40-60	NE		1 centre pelvis 3			
6	M	40-60						antler axe by R arm
7	-	18-20			Undisturbed but no grave goods			
8a	-	o	E		one at pelvis			swan's wing
8b	F	18	E			c. 190— at head (deer & pig) & at pelvis (deer, seal, elk) 1, by head —pig		hammerstone L of head; shell deco; stones below heels
9	M	20-60						
10	M	50	W		2, R of pelvis		under shoulder & pelvis	pebble by L elbow; 5 stones over legs bone awl & core axe
11	-	-	No Skel				one	bone spatula across pelvis core axe by right shoulder
12	-	40-60	E		2, L & R of pelvis			
14	M	-			1, on pelvis			
15	F	-			Very disturbed by grave six			
15	-	o						
18	-	o						
19a	-	25-30	W		no grave goods but killed by bone point in neck			
19b	-	1	W		no grave goods			
19c	-	35-40	W		by & below lower jaw	chest ornament- deer, pig, man, aurochs		roedeer bone & pebbles
20	F	-						
21	-	6 months			no grave goods			
22	F	40-50						2-head & shoulders

help to suggest certain patternings of the evidence. Taking only the burials where both age and sex have been determined, the definitely male skeletons are found all to be in the 40-60 age range, whereas the females are 18-50 years old. Age affects goods also, in that no

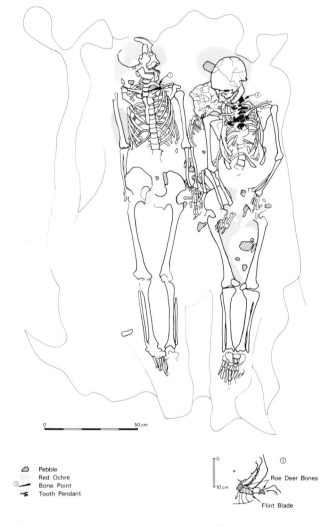

0   50 cm

⌀ Pebble
   Red Ochre
①— Bone Point
↶ Tooth Pendant

②   Roe Deer Bones
10 cm
Flint Blade

Figure 67. Vedbaek triple burial. Grave from the Mesolithic cemetery, containing two adults and a baby. Note the flint blade under the jaw of the skeleton to the right, and the bone point in the neck of the left-hand skeleton (Albrethsen and Brinch Petersen 1976)

skeleton aged under 40 was found with antlers, and no skeleton aged over 40 was buried with tooth-ornaments and none of the skeletons whose age was not determined had both types of grave goods; here, age seems to exert a greater influence than sex for both a male and a female over-40 have antlers, and female under-40s and possible male under-40s have animal teeth.

Other evidence from Vedbaek suggests that the Mesolithic community regarded age as an important distinguishing factor, probably in life as well as death. The burial of babies with adult females is probably because mother and child died in childbirth (e.g. 8 and possibly 15), but the independent burial of a six month old baby (21) and the inclusion of the one year old in grave 19 may imply that babies were regarded as individual members of the community, and this would accord with the baby in grave 8 being given a flint blade.

From the time they began to be mobile until about 18 years old, no individual was buried in this cemetery, which could suggest that people became adult members of the community in their late teens and until that time, if they died, their funerary rites were performed elsewhere. Moreover, no definitely-male young adults were present, and the possibly-male 19a comes from an abnormal grave, so it may be that only the older men were buried here, those who had reached the senior age-grade of 40 and over. However, young females were definitely present and two had died at about 18 years old, one with a newborn baby (8), which suggests marriage for females at about 16-17 years old. It would be hasty to assume that initiation for men occurred at about the same age, given that there are no definitely male skeletons under 40. However, skeleton 19a which the authors thought was male and which falls into the male height range was between 25 and 30 years old at death, and it had no grave goods despite the profusion given to 19c. Skeleton 7, unsexed, also had no grave goods and was 18-20 years old, an age at which females were particularly at risk, but if 7 was female then this burial was unusual in the total absence of grave goods. If 7 was male, and if 19a is also accepted as male, then it might be that males in the 18-40 age grade *were* receiving burial but without any non-perishable grave goods. In this case, sex would have been a greater differentiating factor for young adults than for the old, which would be a fairly normal situation.

Grave 19 remains problematical. The skeleton on the left, 19a, has already been noted as probably male on the basis of height (165cm;

male av. ht. 170.8cm), and the one on the right, 19c, as possibly female on the basis of chest ornament. Height also suggests 19c could be female (154cm; female av. ht. 154cm), and the positioning of the individuals in the grave might confirm the sexing. In grave 8, the female adult was buried with a (male?) baby by her right shoulder. If 19c is female, then she too has an infant lying by her right shoulder and the other adult, supposedly male, is also on her right, all of which is consonant with the ideas discussed above concerning the association of males with right and females with left, and therefore also with the interpretation of 19a as male.

Grave 11 contained no skeleton, just red ochre and one deer antler and a bone awl and a flint axe. For some reason or other, the body was not available for burial, but the grave goods suggest that the person whose funerary rites were carried out was an adult, probably belonging to the senior age grade because of the antler, and possibly male because of the axe.

The problem remains as to why no children were buried in this cemetery. With a sharper focus on age as a significant distinguishing factor, one possible explanation may be offered for this, based on a closer examination of the ages of people who *did* receive burial in the Vedbaek cemetery. Basing the analysis only on the definitely aged and sexed skeletons, we find old men and women (40-60 years old), young women (18-20 years old) and young babies 0-1 year old) present. There are no 20-40-year-olds, either male or female, except for the anomalous pair in grave 19. Now let us suppose that the pair in grave 19 belonged in this cemetery precisely because they were anomalous. Then the cemetery as a whole may be interpreted as a burial ground for those who were different: for the very young and the very old, whom Ucko notes as frequent cases for special funerary treatment because of their tenuous hold on life (Ucko 1969), and for women who died giving birth to their first child, which might have been recognised as a particularly dangerous event. The pair in grave 19 would tend to confirm the interpretation of the whole cemetery as a burial ground for those who were different, for they received the same sort of funerary rites as the rest of the people who were buried here, which would suggest that they belonged in the cemetery. If therefore, they were anomalous, but not outcasts in death, then one might assume that they received burial with their peers.

The Vedbaek sample is too small to be dogmatic about any of these interpretations, but they do all suggest a culture where a person's role was determined primarily by age and that the three major age grades were the under 18s, the 18-40 year olds and the over-40s. Although one line of argument does suggest that the young adult males and females were differentiated, sex appears to be a less-important overall distinction than age, for there are cross-cutting 'sexed' grave goods, but the age distinctions are more closely adhered to. In a late Mesolithic hunting, fishing and gathering context with an abundance of food, we might therefore see the Vedbaek people belonging to a culture where both men and women were food-producers, and the lack of a sharp distinction between male and female burials suggests that perhaps the women's contribution to the food quest was recognised, and their status in life similar to that of the men, as it might be if they took part in one of the more prestigious aspects of the food-quest such as fishing.

As with Branč, nothing is proven, and one must come back time and again to re-examine the archaeological evidence in the context of each fresh hypothesis, and as with Branč the main role of ethnography is to help the archaeologist to know what sorts of question to ask.

Neolithic enclosures: ritual or secular?

In lowland Britain there are two groups of Neolithic sites which have received a considerable amount of attention in recent years. These are the causewayed enclosures, dated for the most part to the earlier Neolithic, and the henges, which are generally attributed to the later Neolithic. There would appear to be some overlap in the period of use of the two types of sites. The function of neither group is clear, and much of the debate has been concerned with their ritual or ceremonial status. Hence it seems appropriate to examine them here, to see whether an awareness of the nature of ritual and religion in small-scale societies has anything to contribute to solving a specific archaeological problem, and if so, how.

Several full accounts have been given recently of both types of site (e.g. Wilson 1975, Palmer 1976, Drewett 1977 and Whittle 1977 for causewayed enclosures, and Wainwright 1971 and 1975 and Catheral 1976 for henges). These provide sufficient information to give a general description for each type. The causewayed enclosures are defined by one or more rings of banks and interrupted ditches, situated both on prominent hilltops (e.g. Knap Hill) or in a low-lying situation (e.g. Great Wilbraham). The ditches are normally external to the banks, and it was the recognition of frequent causeways across them (e.g. Windmill Hill) that gave the sites their name. Henges are normally defined by a single bank and ditch broken by one or more obvious entrances (up to four, as at Avebury); the ditch is usually, but not always, internal to the bank, and the majority of henges are more massive and have a larger central arena than the causewayed enclosures (fig. 68 for comparative plans).

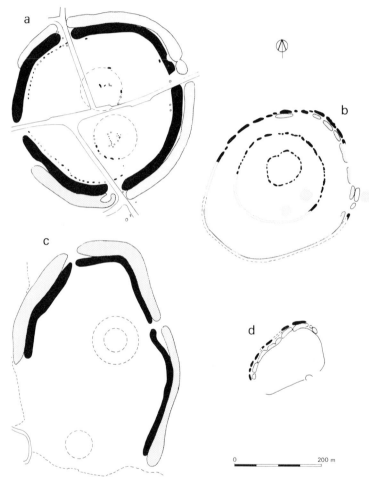

Figure 68. Causewayed enclosures and henges. Plans drawn to scale for comparison of site area and size of banks and ditches. (a) Avebury, Wilts (henge); (b) Windmill Hill, Wilts (c. camp); (c) Marden, Wilts (henge); (d) Knap Hill, Wilts (c. camp) (Wainwright 1979)

Despite their differences, the sites have been discussed together by some prehistorians in view of the possible continuity from the one to the other. Isobel Smith (1971), Renfrew (1973c) and Wainwright (1975) have all discussed the replacement of the earlier causewayed enclosures by the later henges within particular territories, citing as examples the sequence from Maiden Castle to Mount Pleasant in Dorset, or from Knap Hill to Marden in Wiltshire. As well as common territory, the sites present similar enigmatic evidence for interpretation such as the presence on some of them of large quantities of domestic rubbish including animal bones (e.g. Windmill Hill and Marden) and a variety of imported artefacts, especially pottery (e.g. Maiden Castle and Mount Pleasant), and a number of human bones, both deliberately buried (e.g. Hambledon Hill and Stonehenge) and casually lost (e.g. Offham and Durrington Walls). It should be noted, however, that some sites have produced very little non-perishable rubbish, notably the large henge at Avebury.

It has generally been assumed that henges had a ceremonial or ritual function, but the causewayed enclosures have undergone many re-interpretations. They were first seen as settlements (and called causewayed camps), and then variously as defended sites, cattle compounds, fair grounds, communal meeting places and ritual sites (a brief summary of the interpretations is given in Drewett 1977). The consensus of opinion over the last decade has been that both types of site are ceremonial, providing evidence for hypotheses such as Renfrew's that they served as tribal foci and witness the rise of chiefdoms in the course of the third millennium b.c. (Renfrew 1973b).

Recent and ongoing excavations (e.g. Offham, Hambledon Hill, Marden and Mount Pleasant), together with the discovery of the previously unrecognised low-lying causewayed enclosures through the use of aerial photography (Wilson 1975), have added considerably to the body of knowledge about both types of site, and new interpretations have been suggested. Drewett (1977) has advocated a primary funerary function for the causewayed enclosures, seeing them as a ritual area where the dead were exposed before or instead of burial. In contrast, Whittle (1977) has reverted to settlement as the primary function, with overtones of ritual. Wainwright, having excavated and published three major henges as ceremonial sites, has since written that he 'would not now regard the late Neolithic earthworks as anything other than secular'

(Wainwright 1975). This drastic change of mind stemmed from the similarity between the evidence from the henges and that from the Iron Age farm (Gussage All Saints) that Wainwright subsequently excavated (Wainwright 1977): both were enclosures with banks and ditches and rather isolated big round buildings and quantities of animal bone and discarded artefacts, and if the later site was a domestic settlement, then why not the earlier ones?

Numerous possible functions have therefore been suggested for these sites, many of them involving some element of ritual or ceremonial, but recently with a trend to secularisation. The problem before us, therefore, is to decide which if any of these possible functions are plausible, and to see how the ethnographic study of ritual and religion can contribute to reaching a solution.

Indeed ethnography has already been used to substantiate some of the arguments summarised above. In discussing Durrington Walls, and in particular the function of the large circular structure by the entrance, Wainwright turned to an account by Bartram, a traveller in eighteenth-century America. This described the round council chambers of the Creek Indians, a description that fitted a site excavated at Irene in Georgia in the late 1930s: 'The remarkable similarities between the eye-witness accounts and the excavated remains of the Creek council chambers and certain timber buildings of the early second millennium B.C. in southern England are very clear. Structures in both groups are closely comparable in overall diameter, their roofs were supported on six concentric rings of timber uprights, they had a hypothetical open court in the centre and possessed one entrance. Furthermore, the midden outside the wall of the rotunda at Irene parallels in a remarkable way the midden or repository outside the Southern Circle at Durrington Walls. *The temptation to transfer the known function of the Indian structures to those in Britain must however be resisted on account of the disparities in cultural background, geography and time between the two groups.* Nevertheless, Bartram's descriptions of the Creek council chambers in the eighteenth century could be transferred to the "Woodhenge" structures with no anomalies regarding the latter. The combination of excavation and documentary evidence at Irene does demonstrate one area in which the function of the British structures may be sought, as well as providing an ethnographic parallel for the breakage of pots and their deposition in a special repository outside the building [pots used for sacred drink]. *The evidence tends to confirm the special nature of these structures and to deny a purely domestic function*'

(Wainwright and Longworth 1971, 233; my italics).

Remembering that Wainwright has since refuted a ritual interpretation of this site, we should nevertheless note that the authors quite rightly point out a danger to be resisted (first italics), but they point it out so carefully and in such detail that many readers will easily succumb to the temptation, an event more or less assumed in the final sentence (second italics).

I have quoted this paragraph in full, while acknowledging Wainwright's more recent secular interpretation of the site, because it does illustrate very neatly how *not* to use ethnography as an aid to archaeological interpretation. A single parallel is worse than useless. The better it seems to fit the archaeological evidence, the less one looks for other possibilities, and presented with one good idea and no other information to balance it, the mind readily accepts the suggested equation without asking why the ethnographic example should have any bearing on the archaeological evidence at all.

Drewett uses ethnography in his discussion of the hypothetical functions of causewayed camps, to show the sorts of things which are possible in pre-literate societies. For example, he takes the problem of whether or not these sites were fortified settlements, and demonstrates that the objections to their being fortified stem largely from an ethnocentric view of warfare: 'In many pre-literate societies warfare has a strong ritual function with a formal mode of behaviour recognised as correct. A strong physical barrier need not necessarily be equated with an effectively strong barrier. One has only to think of the invisible but immensely powerful barriers around cult houses in Melanesia. The ritual aspects of warfare may lead to the development of war specialists like *gwan muot* among the Nuer, whose duty is to shake a spear in the face of the enemy and deliver an invocation against them (Evans-Pritchard 1965, 177). The ritual aspects of the battle may be so pronounced that it may become little more than a 'mock-battle' in which more insults than arrows are traded (Kopytoff in Gibbs (ed.) 1965, 464). A simple equation of pure physical strength in terms of ditches, banks and the like, with effective strength *is surely to ignore a whole range of other elements so frequently found ethnographically and yet impossible to isolate from material culture alone left to the archaeologist'* (Drewett 1977, 223; my italics).

Ethnography has been used in this instance to open up the range of interpretations, but not to choose between them, and it is not being used for direct parallels so much as for a background of piecemeal parallels. Use in this manner has been criticised,

especially when culture after culture is quoted to show that things
are different elsewhere (the 'among the ...' syndrome); the
cumulative examples can have a thoroughly depressing and negative
effect, as with Shennan's reaction to Ucko's 'nihilistic' paper on
funerary customs (Shennan 1975). Drewett himself touches on this
in the last phrase of the paragraph (italicised), when he states the
impossibility of recognising archaeologically the sorts of 'elements'
he has just been quoting. This manner of using ethnography has
become fairly common and acceptable in recent years, and
doubtless occurs often enough in the present work. It is indeed
useful if we want to avoid ethnocentricity, but it does tend to
promote an even greater indecisiveness among archaeologists than
they are normally prone to, for it is rare for every single example to
point in the same direction.

What, then, can be done to achieve a more positive approach to
the problem? One way may be to tackle it from the ethnographic
side, to change the question from the archaeological 'Were
causewayed enclosures and henges sacred or secular sites?' to the
anthropological 'Do ritual and religion affect culture in ways that
could have any bearing on the problem?' Some of the topics
discussed in the first part of this chapter appear to be relevant, and
while they do not give a conclusive answer, they should contribute to
a more coherent and positive argument than Drewett's collection of
examples, without falling into the trap of the single parallel (cf.
Chapter 6 for a similar exercise).

The main theme of the ethnographic survey of ritual and religion
was the integration of these with their parent culture, both in the
sense of religion being a reflection of facets of its parent culture, and
in the sense that they might impinge on any aspect of 'secular' life.
The Naskapi *mokoshan* illustrated the former point, and the account
of the Dogon showed the latter at work. Moreover, the difficulty
was discussed of distinguishing ritual from secular, supernatural
from natural according to consistent cross-cultural rules, for such
rules simply do not exist. So we find that ritual and secular are
relative terms, and that even in their own sense of the terms, other
cultures are likely to merge the two categories to a degree that we do
not recognise or expect in our own culture. A site, since it is sites
that we are concerned with, is as likely to be both ritual and secular
as exclusively one or the other, and we have noted elsewhere that
many sites are multi-functional (e.g. Chapter 2). One hypothesis to

examine, therefore, is that the Neolithic enclosures were both ritual and secular.

A second relevant theme to emerge from the ethnographic survey is the use of both feasts and funerals in rituals and ceremonial contexts, which might be predominantly religious, or predominantly secular even for burials, but which were both associated with large gatherings of people. Burials could be used to prompt a gathering, and feasts to keep it together, and both contributed to the promotion of group solidarity and helped to foster networks of indebtedness that would maintain relationships within a group or between groups. The indebtedness arose partly from the exchanges that took place at such gatherings, whether funeral gifts or obligations as illustrated by the Tiwi case, or diplomatic exchanges such as those of the Yanomamo. On the whole, attendance at burials is limited to members of the deceased's immediate community or network of relationships, whereas feasts can be either for a closed group or for two or more sets of people who recognise their own distinct group identities but wish for some contact across the boundaries.

Turning back now to the archaeological context, the evidence for straightforward burial is not very common from causewayed enclosures, but there is evidence for the deliberate burial of bits of bodies and of groups of disarticulated bones, notably from the current excavations at Hambledon Hill (R. Mercer, pers. com.). Henges provide more evidence for deliberate, formal disposal of bodies or bones, as for example at Dorchester (Oxon) and at Stonehenge. If there is continuity between the two types of site, this represents a development of one aspect of use. Another development is the invasion of some henges by stone settings at some time during the first half of the second millennium b.c. Stonehenge is undoubtedly the best-known example of this 'lithicisation', to use Wainwright's term, and it occurred on a smaller scale at sites like the Sanctuary, near Avebury. Thirdly, and again supposing continuity, there is the morphological development from camp to henge. All these developments reflect a formalisation of certain aspects of site use.

Therefore one might suggest that the enclosures provided a setting for gatherings of people from one or more groups, who were establishing and asserting their common cause through feasting and exchange, and who also buried some but not all of their dead within these places. There may well have been political overtones to the

NEOLITHIC SUSSEX

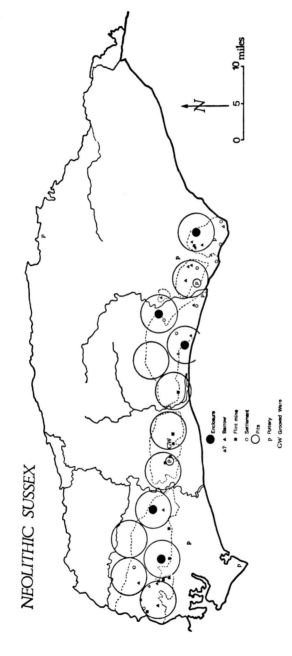

Figure 69. Map of Neolithic sites in Sussex, with circles indicative of possible group territories, five of them having causewayed enclosures at their centre (Drewett 1977)

gatherings, even if they were called for the joint performance of a ritual, in the manner of a carefully-managed Tiwi funeral or New Guinea pigfeast, or along the lines of the competitive Potlatch. In all these cases, men are vying with each other for prestige and recognition as leaders, or they are looking for confirmation of an established position.

Feasting on site is suggested by the animal bone evidence, particularly such details as the joints of meat from Durrington Walls. The quantities of broken pottery may also be the relics of abundant eating and drinking. Evidence for exchange was summarised by Smith (1971) who detailed the range of foreign imports found at Windmill Hill in particular, and it continues to accumulate with jadeite axes found at Hambledon Hill, and at Offham evidence that flint cores were being prepared for use elsewhere (Drewett 1977, 217).

Elements of prestige and display are present in the actual building of the sites, massive and conspicuous and with lots of 'redundant' features such as rings of banks and multiple entrances, or the shafts in the ditch at Maumbury Rings (Dorset). And, so obvious as to be easily ignored, both types of site enclose an arena of sorts, not very good at Windmill Hill perhaps, but so excellent at Maumbury that the Romans resurrected it (Bradley 1976). Occasional finds, like the huge wild aurochs at Durrington Walls, also hint at an element of boasting and conspicuous display. Finally, the burial element may be due to an interest in ancestors, whose presence could well have been used to add to the power and effectiveness of the sites, and perhaps to validate the claims of anyone seeking or confirming his personal power.

These ritualised elements could not take place in a vacuum, and people must live somewhere even if it is only for the duration of a feast, so domestic occupation within or very close to the sites is likely. Given the multiplicity of possible functions, long occupation seems likely, or at least repeated occupation throughout the year, and if so this would be by a single closed group of people to whom the site would belong. In this context, the evidence for exchange can be interpreted as the result of periodic meetings between two or more groups on the home ground of one of them.

Two sorts of evidence from outside the immediate enclosure context may be relevant next. First, in parts of southern England it has been suggested that the enclosures were fairly regularly spaced, indicating group territories with a focal point, an argument illustrated by Drewett's map reproduced here (Fig. 69 and cf. Renfrew 1973c). Secondly, we have already noted that there was an extensive Neolithic exchange network that involved the redistribution of axes (Clark 1966) and pottery (Peacock 1969) in a manner that was not entirely utilitarian, and which has been likened to the ceremonial exchange cycles known from ethnographic studies (see Chapter 4). So we may see the enclosures as centres for a territory (as Renfrew argued), possibly as settlements (as Whittle suggested for the camps) and certainly both secular and ritual (incorporating both Wainwright's interpretations), frequently used by the inhabitants of the territory and sometimes used by visitors as well, invited for purposes of trade or gift-exchange, for feasting and perhaps for making alliances.

Throughout all the functions runs a common possibility of power-seeking, and its success could account for some of the developments towards a more formal situation that we noted above. The later henges are in general bigger than the earlier causewayed enclosures, and would have taken more labour to build, and their territories appear to have been larger (Renfrew 1973c). Moreover, we noted in discussing social organisation that as chiefs became more powerful and their position more hereditary, so their ritual role increased, and in discussing contact we noted that ceremonial exchange networks belong in relatively egalitarian contexts (e.g. bigmen and village chiefs) and not in the more complex or more hierarchical societies. Now on the one hand the postulated development from camp to henge is based on the acknowledgement of an increase in the formal, ritual aspects of the sites, and on the other hand the bulk of the evidence for exchange is to be found on the causewayed sites. Therefore both the nature of the sites and the nature of the evidence to be found within them is consonant with successful power-seeking that led to the emergence of a more hierarchical society, where power was concentrated in fewer hands than before.

This brings us a long way from asking how ritual and religion may affect culture, but perhaps that is only to be expected when the emphasis has been on their integration with other activities. Indeed, given the frequency with which this particular argument has led from ritual to power-politics, perhaps this was the aspect of his culture that Neolithic man mirrored in his religion.

6. Pastoralism

Pastoralism has been chosen to provide a detailed example of the application of ethnography to archaeological studies since it is a subject which draws together much of the material already surveyed, and at the same time the mode of life is one that prehistorians are not familiar with, but which they tend to romanticise. In the study of British prehistory, pastoralism has frequently been evoked to explain an awkward lack of settlement evidence, and one suspects that authors have enjoyed the idea of fierce and independent groups of herdsmen sweeping over the downlands, driving their cattle from pasture to pasture and occasionally meeting together at some otherwise enigmatic site, to trade and to hold ceremonies. Windmill Hill rodeos are not far over the horizon.

A few examples from the recent literature will illustrate the persistence of this yearning for early British pastoralism. In her contribution to *British Prehistory* (ed. Renfrew) Isobel Smith (Smith 1974) suggests, in the course of a masterly survey of neolithic pottery styles, that 'by the late third millennium b.c. the subsistence economy may have been essentially pastoral' (p. 123). Andrew Fleming, in an article on the Wessex Bronze Age, declares that 'the Wessex Culture was largely pastoral in nature' and suggests that herdsmen made use of the Wiltshire and Dorset uplands on a seasonal basis, as pasture and burial grounds (Fleming 1971). Barry Cunliffe, in his survey of the British Iron Age, sees the south and east as largely agrarian and the north and west dominated by pastoralists (Cunliffe 1974). Most recently of all, Paul Mellars has argued that the Mesolithic inhabitants of Britain deliberately fired the forests to aid hunting, a practice that could have led to the depletion of wild herds and hence the development of a degree of human control over animals in order to conserve them. The Mesolithic is therefore put forward as a possible context for the rise of herding and pastoral economies, as Jarman suggested not so long ago for the Italian Postglacial and as Bahn has recently postulated for the Upper Palaeolithic of Western Europe (Mellars 1976; Jarman 1971; Bahn 1978).

Are any of these bids for pastoralism at all realistic? Did prehistoric Britain provide the physical and social environment conducive to such a way of life? To answer these questions, it is necessary to have some knowledge of pastoral societies, to be aware of their main characteristics and to know what range of environments they exploit. It is here that the ethnographic studies become essential, to provide the archaeologist, through both recent and modern accounts of such societies, with the information and the understanding that he needs. (The following survey is based mainly on Gulliver 1965, Lewis 1965, Stenning 1965, Leeds 1965, von Fürer-Haimendorf 1975, Evans-Pritchard 1940, Forde 1934, Ekvall 1968 and Weir 1976.)

Everyone knows that pastoralists keep animals, but there is rather more to it than that. Unlike mixed farming, in pastoral economies the animals far outnumber the people, with herds and flocks running into the hundreds or thousands. Normally there is one species that predominates, such as the cattle of the Fulani or the reindeer of the Chukchi, but other animals are also kept and it would not be uncommon to find people tending cattle, sheep, goats, donkeys and other herd animals, with chickens too in a number of cases. The Himalayans, for example, keep yak and cattle and yak-cattle crossbreeds, and sheep and goats (Fig. 70).

The herd animals of pastoralists yield food, and other contributions to subsistence, in the living state as well as when they are killed. Food includes milk from cattle, sheep, goats, camels and horses, and milk products such as butter and cheese, and also blood taken from the living animal. We have noted earlier the extensive Nuer use of byproducts which includes the use of dung for fuel and as floor and wall plaster, and urine for washing and tanning. Living animals also provide, year after year, hair and wool to be woven or felted into cloth and many pastoral societies are renowned for their textiles. And they provide transport, whether carrying people and young animals and goods on their backs, or pulling a sledge or waggon. Almost any species of herd animal can be used as a beast of burden, from the reindeer of northern Eurasia to the horses and camels of Arabian deserts (Fig. 71), including the sheep of the Himalayas who transport packs of salt across the high mountain

Figure 70. Himalayan herds. (a) sheep and goats. (b) yak, with pack-animal in the foreground (Royal Geographical Society)

passes. Often, different sections of the herds will be kept for different purposes and perhaps even bred to these ends, so that a milk camel may never be trained for riding nor a pack-ox bled for food. Farmers, with their fewer animals, cannot always afford and

Figure 71. Transport for pastoralists. Load-carrying Bedouin camel (Royal Geographical Society). See also figures 51, 52 and 70

may not require such specialisation. The pig, incidentally, is the one common species of domestic animal which is of little economic use when alive: it is not practicable to milk it, its coat does not lend itself to transformation into cloth, it does not provide transport. It is not easy to herd, and it is an omnivorous forest dweller rather than a grazing or browsing inhabitant of the plains. Pastoralists do not keep pigs.

Animals once dead are used by pastoralists in ways that would do credit to an Esquimo for resourcefulness; in this respect, pastoralists are more akin to hunters than farmers. The Nuer cattle provide a sacrifice in their dying, and meat as soon as they are dead. Their skin makes leather, and rawhide bindings, their bones and horns and hooves make artefacts, and fuel if necessary. No part of the beast is wasted. Lapps and Chukchi are equally economical in their use of the reindeer, in ways even closer to the Esquimo's disposal of the caribou.

Pastoralism therefore entails a heavy economic dependence on animals, both living and dead. This is quite unlike the situation found in mixed farming societies where animals are so often kept primarily for prestige and ceremonial purposes, and not as a source of food.

The pastoralist's economic interest in his herds is complemented by a very marked cultural orientation towards them. Much time may be spent tending favourite animals, cosseting them, grooming and decorating them, talking to them and talking about them to anyone ready to listen. The obsession of pastoralists for their animals is nowhere better revealed than in Evans-Pritchard's exasperation at the Nuer: 'I used sometimes to despair that I never discussed anything with the young men but livestock and girls, and even the subject of girls led inevitably to that of cattle' (Evans-Pritchard 1940, 19). 'Cherchez la vache', he said, 'is the best advice that can be given to those who desire to understand Nuer behaviour' (p. 16). Likewise the horse dominates the culture of the Kazak, and the reindeer that of the Chukchi.

The near-complete orientation of a culture to animals naturally affects many aspects of life. In practical terms, care for the animals yields a range of special buildings to shelter and protect them, possibly rather better structures than those that house their owners. Interest in the animals nearly always leads to the development of an extensive vocabulary to describe and discuss them, such as the vast numbers of terms used to describe Nuer cattle colours. It is also likely that animals will be used as a standard of comparison and will come to symbolise other things, so entering into music and art. Nuer cattle songs may be ephemeral, but Siberian designs epitomise the pastoral arts in concrete terms (Fig. 72). It is only to be expected that much skill should be lavished on decorating the animals themselves, thus Bedouin camels decked for riding and Lapp reindeer harnessed to a sleigh show off the best of their owners' arts (see also horse in Fig. 52).

Given the great cultural importance of animals to all pastoral societies, it is not suprising to find them playing a central role in ritual and ceremonial affairs. The Chukchi sacrifice reindeer, and the Nuer's scale of offerings accords directly with his cultural values, vegetables being very lowly, goats mediocre, and cattle the supreme sacrifice in times of severe illness or natural disasters. The myths of both Nuer and Dinka draw heavily on cattle-imagery, and the chief shrine of the Dinka is called the Cattle Byre of God. Marriage settlements among pastoralists centre on the herds, on husbands providing the bride's family with a sufficient number of beasts, and there may be an extended system of animal exchanges through all the phases of a marriage from betrothal to the burial of the partners.

Figure 72. Pastoralists' art. Animal themes are widespread in the art of pastoral societies, and have been for millennia. This representation of tiger attacking elk comes from prehistoric Siberia

So the herds become the currency of the pastoralist's life.

True pastoralists are mobile, in response to the needs of their herds. The animals are moved from one pasture to another in a perpetual search for grass, and the people follow after. The pattern of such movements varies greatly from one society to another, but it is rarely random and usually the migration conforms to an annual pattern designed to exploit each ecological niche of the total environment when it is at its most valuable in terms of water and grass. Distances covered range from a few miles to several hundred, depending on how far-flung are the resources which make up the annual intake of the herds. The Jie cattle herders of Uganda move within a compact area 65 by 25 miles, according to seasonal changes in the rainfall pattern which affect the local availability of both grazing and water. The Kazak of the Asian steppes, by contrast, move perhaps 200 miles from winter to summer grazing grounds, and back again.

The mobility of pastoralists is one characteristic of their mode of life that most archaeologists acknowledge. It should not be allowed to mask the fact that the permanence of most groups' pattern of movement allows them to establish a home base, and some nomadic herders have a positive superfluity of settlements. The long-distance moves of the Kazak bring each family and its herds back to the same sheltered valley for over-wintering, where they sometimes build stone walls to protect the animals, and occasionally stone dwellings for people too.

Whether or not there are permanent buildings, occupation sites are frequently permanent, albeit not permanently inhabited, and one sees here another close resemblance between hunters and pastoralists. This similarity is continued in the use of tents, and in the adherence to a fixed annual cycle of movement. The hunter-farmer cultures of North America exhibit similar traits, perhaps because their subsistence is likewise *closely* bound up with animals. This point should be borne in mind when considering the archaeological record, as it suggests a possible confusion of the evidence for pastoralists with that for hunter-farmers.

The Jie, who exploit a relatively small territory, have centrally-placed permanent villages; these are occupied by some sections of the population all the year round, and the people who look after the herds pass through on their seasonal migrations. In the Himalayas, where rapid changes in altitude yield considerable ecological variation within a few kilometres, a single community may have a main permanent village of solid, stone-built houses, and a lower and equally permanent village where the weather is slightly milder, and perhaps several smaller and higher homes for exploiting the summer pastures, with tents and stone walls for protection at the highest altitudes of all. These different settlements could well be taken each to represent a different community and the high-altitude bases could even suggest a different economy. There are pastoralists, it is true, such as the Lapps and the Bedouin who live chiefly in tents, but clearly permanent settlement sites do not exclude a pastoral economy any more than the absence of such sites indicates one.

The pastoralists overriding interest in their animals was noted above, and the importance of the herds in terms of food briefly explored. Yet meat and milk and blood are rarely, if ever, the sole source of food. Few pastoralists talk much about it, and few ethnographers waste many words on the matter, but most pastoralists grow crops. The lack of emphasis on the agrarian activities of pastoralists is no doubt a reflection of the inferior status according to work of this nature. The Kazak and the Fulani assign the care of their fields to poor relations who are too feeble to have herds of their own, while the Tuareg have slaves to farm for them and the Jie see crop-raising as women's work. In all these cases, crop-production forms an important element of the subsistence-base, but it is regarded as low-status work to be performed by second-class citizens, and this is why it is largely ignored.

If terrain and culture forbid any attempt at agriculture, or if, as in many cases, the pastoralists cannot grow sufficient for their requirements, trade supplies the deficiencies. Normally surplus animal products are exchanged for the cereal surpluses of settled farmers, each side thereby benefitting from the specialisations of the other. The Fulani trade meat and cheese for Hausa crops, while the Chukchi took reindeer furs to the Russians in exchange for flour, sugar, salt and tea.

Trade encompasses the exchange of many objects in addition to food, and no pastoral society is without some trading contact with outsiders. Pastoralism may be an independent way of life, but it is definitely not one of total isolation and self-sufficiency. When one comes to appreciate it as a sophisticated specialisation of animal husbandry, and remembering the ease with which pastoralists move around, then the pastoral emphasis on trade is understandable: they have the animal products that farmers lack, they have transport, and their way of life takes them through varied regions and diverse cultures. Metal objects are particularly favoured among the manufactured goods obtained by trade, in the form of bowls and pots and cups or as weapons and especially as jewelry. Frequently, such trade takes place in an urban context, or at least with people from an urban and metal-using society, as the Hausa or the Russians. It is relevant to note here that Chukchi reindeer-herding began to flourish only when trade links were established with the urbanised Russians, and I would suggest that the pastoralist, who is so like the hunter in many ways, has one crucial difference in that he can only develop his economy successfully as a complement to a complex and probably urban society. Indeed, in this light, pastoralism is not independent but a part of some complex economy made up of a number of specialisations and probably several cultures. The World of Islam exhibition, 'Nomad and City', has clearly illustrated this symbiosis (Fig. 73) and its reality can be further substantiated by the many references in the ethnographies to links between pastoralists and farmers or pastoralists and townsmen. (Even people with the slightest degree of dependence on outsiders, such as the Nuer, import some essential goods.)

The trade objects mentioned above are typical of the pastoralists' durable artefacts. Metal pots and cups and jugs are lighter and more durable than pottery, more prestigious than skins and gourds. Weapons are essential to the men for warfare, for protection of their herds and for prestige, and a quantity of silver jewelry can emphasise the wealth of both men and women, and yet it is relatively easy to carry around. Clothing and tents and sleeping rugs and milk gourds and so forth are likely to be home-made, and many pastoralists produce a wealth of textiles. The relevance of this to the archaeologist lies in the differential chances of preservation of the artefacts: the home-made goods are manufactured from animal products and normally perish, whereas the imported metal objects have a much higher chance of survival. Therefore a pastoral society could leave an archaeological record that was dominated by the artefacts of another culture (Fig. 74).

One characteristic traditionally ascribed to pastoralists, which most of them do indeed possess, is a proud and independent outlook on the world. It is reasonable to speak of a pastoralist mentality, for whether Kazak, Chukchi or Nuer, Jie or Fulani the herdsmen has a firm belief in his own superiority and the feeble character and moral laxity of others. Pastoral societies are often at war, raiding other mens' herds and conquering other peoples' lands until, in some cases, they absorb a variety of other cultures into their own. This the Fulani have achieved in West Africa, and the Swazi in the south east, while the people of the Eurasian plains were swept up in the conquests of the Mongol hordes.

Finally, in this survey of the common characteristics of pastoralism, we come to the environment. Some would say it should have been examined first, but that would have been at the risk of discussing all the cultural features in terms of environmental determinism, whereas the balance of the pastoral mode of life is more complex than that. Yet, undoubtedly, the physical background is relevant and a recital of the pastoral regions of the world gives some indication why: they inhabit places like the Sahara and the Sudan, the Zagros, the Steppes, Siberia, and the slopes of the Himalayas. All these provide open grassland or park-tundra environments, with sufficient variety to guarantee pasture throughout the year. There may be some scrubby bush and patches of woodland in sheltered valleys, but forest cover is not present. Herd animals, after all, belong to the open spaces; that is their natural environment and likewise the environment in which man best exploits them. Space is another common feature, best illustrated by the remark that a Chukchi pasture 'was sometimes so

NOMAD & CITY

The Bedouin

MUSEUM OF MANKIND

The Ethnography Department of the British Museum Burlington Gardens London W1
Weekdays 10-5 Sundays 2.30-6

World of Islam Festival

Figure 73. Nomad and City. Posters for the Museum of Mankind exhibition mounted for the World of Islam Festival, emphasising the contrast and complementarity of pastoral and urban life (British Museum)

Figure 74. Turkana chief wearing a mixture of indigenous and imported clothes and
   ornamentation. The least perishable elements, the shells and metal ornaments, are
   imports, but the way in which they are put together and worn is typically
   Turkana (Royal Anthropological Institute)

crowded in summer that one could even see the tents of others in the distance' (Leeds 1965, 100).

There may seem to be an element of contradiction in this with the stress placed earlier on the symbiosis of pastoralism with other modes of life. But for a part at least of their annual cycle of movement, all pastoralists exploit an environment which is marginal or impossible for farmers. The Scandinavian Lapps, for example, herd their animals to the north where the growing season is too short to raise cereal crops, but they and the southern farmers meet and trade in the intermediate region. The Fulani, who live in and among the Hausa and rule them, spend a part of their year taking the herds to distant pastures; they could not keep so many animals if they did not move away from the farming areas, and the pastures they go to are not suited to agriculture. In this light, pastoralism may be seen as a refinement or specialisation of mixed farming, in order to exploit territory that is otherwise open only to the hunter. It extends the range of human settlement into new and marginal areas. It also raises the population level within an already settled area by exploiting enclaves of marginal land within the region that farming does not or cannot use.

Now that the main characteristics of pastoralism have been described, we shall return to the question of whether or not such a mode of subsistence could have flourished in prehistoric Britain. The survey has been brief, and certainly incomplete, but it gives an idea of the range of features to be sought in the archaeological record. One need not expect all pastoral societies to possess every characteristic discussed above, but the majority should be present and some will be crucial. These vital characteristics are pre-conditions for pastoralism; and they are, first, the availability of a suitable type of herd animal, secondly, a physical environment dominated by open spaces, and thirdly, the presence of a complementary farming culture. The third precondition is the most debatable, but the overriding impression gained from ethnographic reports is that pastoralism arises from and is dependent on settled mixed or arable farming, or even on farming with attendant urban settlements.

Mellars' suggestion that the Mesolithic witnessed the rise of pastoral economies must be ruled out on two counts, though not on all three. Suitable animals were available in the British Isles. Red deer were present in quantity, but although this species has become a fashionable 'potential domesticate' it should be noted that its modern exploitation is dependent on modern techniques of control, especially fencing. Cattle were also present, their numbers the subject of some discussion (P. Evans 1975), and they could have been herded. The environment, however, was becoming increasingly one of forest cover in the Postglacial period (Pennington 1974), and there was no complementary farming culture until late in the period when the first Neolithic settlers arrived. Moreover, there is no incontrovertible archaeological evidence for pastoralism to support the argument, and the Mesolithic is probably best seen as a period of increasingly sophisticated hunting economies, similar to those of the North American forests.

By the late Neolithic, there is evidence for the presence of domestic herd animals in Britain, with cattle and sheep bones being quite common on archaeological sites. Cereal pollen and cereal grains attest an established tradition of cultivation, and pollen evidence indicates the existence of open grassland. There is therefore a more promising outlook for pastoralism than in the Mesolithic, and it is worth examining both the physical and the cultural environment more closely.

The open grassland indicated by pollen is confirmed by the quantities of turf used to build barrows, and other sites such as Silbury Hill; turf is a sign of permanent open grassland, and the environmental evidence from some henges suggests the existence of open spaces for up to 500 years before the building of the monuments (Evans 1975). Equally, though, there is evidence from extensive forest cover, both in the form of pollen and from such sites as the Mount Pleasant henge, where quantities of heavy oak timber were used in the building (Wainwright 1975). We should therefore probably allow for a patchwork of forest cover and open ground, in varying proportions according to local conditions. Animal herding would be feasible under such circumstances, and certainly animals were grazing; otherwise there would have been no open grassland that persisted for centuries. However, it was noted above that pastoralists specialise in the exploitation of impoverished areas marginal to farming, and the Neolithic pasture that has been studied was not poor land, for the pollen record shows time and again the regeneration of forest cover (Dimbleby 1967, Evans 1975, Beckett and Hibbert 1978).

In terms of agricultural environment, the late Neolithic was a time of settled and prosperous farming communities, and we have already noted the ample evidence for exchange. Two important features of the pastoral background were therefore present. Other indications are not so promising. There is plentiful evidence for pottery, which is alien to a nomadic way of life. There are signs of increased pig-rearing, and the pig is the one animal not beloved by pastoralists. And there is no metal in Britain at this time. These three items, marginal in themselves, together argue against the presence of pastoralists. All extant pastoral societies, to take the last point first, make use of metal tools; the significance of this is not clear, but probably related to the invariable contact with sophisticated farming and urban communities. The pigs and the pots could belong to the settled farmers that pastoralists trade with. But their presence, coupled with the sporadic nature of the open grassland, implies a flourishing mixed farming subsistence with no separate pastoral specialisation, and the absence of metal confirms such an interpretation of the evidence. There is no need to introduce pastoralism to explain the late Neolithic archaeological record, and the changes from the early Neolithic are best interpreted as the results of the development from shifting agriculture to settled mixed farming.

Archaeological evidence from the earlier part of the second millennium b.c. has been interpreted in terms of the rise of the Wessex Culture, a prosperous community, whose wealth Fleming suggested was based on pastoralism. The pollen evidence for open space in this period is supported by information from snail studies, and by the siting of many barrows in a manner to exploit intervisibility over long distances. Authorities are agreed that the earlier part of the millennium saw a decrease in forest cover compared to that of the Neolithic (Evans 1975, Pennington 1974). The open ground was exploited partly through an increase in the number of sheep kept, and the first good archaeological evidence from the British Isles for spinning and weaving wool dates to this period (Henshall 1950); the sheep provided the necessary raw materials and were therefore an asset alive as well as a source of meat when dead. The pattern of animal exploitation is in this respect more akin to what is known of pastoralism than anything noted for earlier periods.

The Wessex phase provides evidence for the use of metal: metal weapons, mainly in the form of daggers, and metal for jewelry. The famous Bush Barrow burial contained both daggers and jewels, and ornaments made from a wide range of materials, and the richness and display of the Wessex graves is suggestive of the pride and personal display typical of so many pastoralists. The metal and the wide range of other artefacts indicate flourishing trade.

The context is therefore altogether more appropriate to pastoralism than anything known from earlier periods, but there are still certain reservations to be made. This was an era of expansive mixed farming with permanent fields that would have benefitted from manure; but no large stretch of land was as yet marginal to crop-raising in so far as we can tell from the environmental evidence. Recently discovered evidence on Dartmoor, for example, includes ard-marks and other traces of cereal cultivation (Fleming, pers. com.), and the combined settlement, artefact and environmental evidence from this upland land-mass, later to be so suitable to pastoral exploitation, is indicative of mixed farming with regional variations in the relative importance of plant and of animal husbandry. Pottery is present throughout the British Isles, though its rarity in the Wessex graves is certainly evidence in keeping with the pastoral case. There is, too, no suggestion of an urbanised community; and as with the metal, although one cannot argue that towns are an essential and direct precondition of pastoralism, there does seem to be some causal connection between the two.

The evidence is not decisive either way. But it is all appropriate to the context of mixed farming, and there is nothing that cannot be explained except by assuming the presence of pastoralism. Therefore mixed farming, with regional variations in emphasis on plants or animals, should be taken as the subsistence basis of the earlier second millennium b.c.

To deduce pastoralism from the Iron Age evidence is hardly an innovation, since it is described in the literary sources from the end of the pre-Roman period (Caesar 1951). However, it is worth examining the archaeological evidence in the same manner as for the preceding periods, if only to see how it varies. The greater the difference in the archaeological case for Iron Age pastoralism, the greater the validity of the arguments against its presence at an earlier stage.

By the first millennium b.c., the natural environment had been greatly altered by man; his farming activities over the centuries had greatly reduced the forest cover and created vast impoverished tracts of land in regions such as the Pennines, the Yorkshire Moors, Dartmoor and Exmoor. These areas had been rendered unsuitable for cereal cultivation, and likewise unsuitable for the regeneration of forest cover (Dimbleby 1967). Their best potential for man would have been as grazing land, and this is doubtless how the marginal uplands were exploited.

Iron Age settlement evidence varies greatly from region to region. Among the many different types of site are some which look to have been designed for animal protection on a large scale. In the south of England, both the south-western 'hillforts' on slopes, with widely spaced ramparts (e.g. Clovelly Dykes), and the banjo enclosures (e.g. Woodham Farm), have been claimed as pastoral. The settlement evidence also implies the co-existence of very large communities alongside small farms, communities that lived at Cadbury or Crickley Hill or Maiden Castle with farmers scattered over their hinterland. Extensive excavations within some of the large hillforts, notably Cadbury, Danebury and Crickley Hill, have revealed numerous houses within the ramparts, and possibly some specialisation of occupation among the inmates (Alcock 1972, Cunliffe 1976a, Dixon 1973). Many prehistorians have suggested the urbanisation of Iron Age Europe, and several have now done the same for Britain, given this evidence from the hillfort interiors together with that from lowland 'oppida' such as Camulodunum (Alexander 1972, Cunliffe 1976; Collis 1976). One cannot argue for a totally urbanised society, but one can point with some confidence to proto-urban centres, to the sites which might have become Celtic towns in the fullness of time, but for the disruption of the Roman conquest – and to those which did rapidly become towns under Roman rule.

As in the previous millennia, there is ample evidence for trade, and in this period a definitely commercial element is indicated, first by the currency bars, and later by the use of coinage (Collis 1974). However slight the impact of these, they show that the later first millennium had moved into a more sophisticated sphere of exchange. Agriculture, too, had undoubtedly developed beyond mere subsistence, and farmers in the south of England were producing large grain surpluses which were probably sold (Reynolds 1974). Potential buyers would be specialist craftsmen, and perhaps some of the inhabitants of the larger hillforts, and pastoralists. The farm at Gussage All Saints has produced evidence of specialisation in animal-raising, in that all the horse bones from the site are from mature animals of three years old or more in contrast to the bones of other species which come from animals of all ages. The excavator interprets this as capture of adult wild ponies, but it is as likely to indicate trade with specialist horse-breeders (Wainwright 1977).

For the first time, the evidence for the use of metal is abundant, in the form of weapons, tools, knives and containers. All these are things that pastoralists possess. So too is the jewelry, flamboyant torcs and twisted bracelets, and luxurious metal objects such as the polished bronze mirrors. The discovery of one mirror in an otherwise impoverished domestic site at Holcombe in Devon (Pollard 1974) may be indicative of a herder's presence, acting in typical fashion by putting all his wealth into animals and prestigious metal ornaments, and not bothering much about the housing provided for people.

The animal element in Celtic art is well-known (e.g. Megaw 1970); it indicates a cultural orientation towards animals, which we know from the later Irish literature to be true of the post-Roman Celts. Equally appropriate to pastoralism are the various references in contemporary literature to Celtic pride and ferocity.

Iron Age Britain was certainly not overrun by pastoralists. Large tracts of forest remained, and many farmers practised mixed husbandry in addition to those which specialised in grain. Many sites have produced a wealth of pottery, and evidence for a wide range of craft specialisations. Yet all these elements which prove that pastoralism was not the only subsistence base, at the same time add up to a total environment far more conducive to such a mode of life than anything known previously. The ambience of the late first millennium b.c. is one of complexity, with complementary farming and pastoral cultures – two peoples intermixed in a symbiosis that exploited the varied environment to the full. Such a reconstruction, based on the archaeological evidence, would not be at variance with the general picture of pastoralism, known through ethnographic studies.

7. Anomalies

The reader who has persevered this far will need no final exhortation to make use of ethnography. The arguments for and against its use and the various methodologies for its application have been discussed in the first chapter, and they have been applied or ignored in all that follows, according to their value. Therefore, this final chapter will not take the form of a resumé, but will conclude with a tentative examination of some anomalies of western European prehistory – anomalies that have become evident in the course of earlier discussions, where ethnographic studies have suggested the presence of features at odds with their traditionally-assigned background. (N.B. all dates based on radiocarbon assay are uncalibrated.)

For example, the settlement of western Europe by farmers is generally assumed to have been achieved via shifting agriculture, a system that can rapidly and effectively colonise new land. Clark was the first to use radio-carbon dates to demonstrate the spread of farming from southeast Europe to the northwest, and Ammerman and Cavalli-Sforza refined the model once further dates were available (Clark 1965, Ammerman and Cavalli-Sforza 1971 and 1973). Their work was based on the assumption that the earliest-dated farming sites were also the first farming sites in a region, and it has been generally accepted on this basis (e.g. by contributors to de Laet (ed.) 1976), and reinforced by pollen analyses that indicate contemporary short-term forest clearance. But the farmers whose activities created the data for this model not only cleared fields and grew cereals, they also kept domestic food animals: sheep, cattle and pigs. The anomaly here is that ethnographic studies of shifting agriculture, and particularly those of pioneering shifting agriculture, show that animal husbandry does not feature in this way of life, except perhaps where a few animals are kept for prestige, ritual and ceremonial purposes. Pioneer farmers are hunters not herdsmen.

The second discrepancy in the traditional model of European prehistory is the presence of the plough. We must be careful here to distinguish between the relatively elaborate wheeled plough with a mould-board that turns the soil and sod over, and the relatively simple ard that scratched furrows through turf and topsoil. It is the latter which is known from the European prehistoric contexts, dating from the fourth millenium b.c. Modern farmers who practise shifting agriculture use spades and hoes and axes and digging sticks, but they do not use ploughs as their clearings rarely have a turf cover to be broken up. Indeed, shifting agriculture is sometimes distinguished by the term 'hoe agriculture' as a contrast to 'plough agriculture' which is generally a feature of more complex societies. Therefore, ploughing in fourth-millennium western Europe requires explanation, both in terms of the farming methods adopted and in terms of social organisation. Even the later prehistoric evidence for the use of ploughs, which increases considerably from the mid-second millennium, does not fit well with notions of small-scale, settled farming groups – recently envisaged by Cunliffe as 'a simple egalitarian society in a state of equilibrium' (Cunliffe 1976b). Plough agriculture as we know it from recent and contemporary contexts is advanced agriculture, a technique practised by farmers who belong to societies that are neither simple nor egalitarian in their organisation.

Next we turn to the earlier Bronze Age of central and western Europe, where the social organisation has in recent years been interpreted in terms of emerging chiefdoms, a development linked with the introduction of metallurgy (e.g. Sherratt 1976, Renfrew 1973 and 1978). The period is one when settled and mixed agriculture is well-attested in a number of regions, and the scale and permanence of agricultural operations is demonstrated in the discovery of many extensive field systems. These indicate a settled and apportioned landscape and a network of social relationships and social control more advanced than one might expect if the role of chieftain was only emergent. The fields, like the ploughs, are indicative of a more complex prehistoric society than we generally assume.

A third category of evidence which does not fit the model of small-scale prehistoric societies is that for wheels and waggons. These are known sporadically from the fourth millennium b.c., and from the later second millennium there is evidence of quite widespread use of both carts and waggons, pulled by horses and oxen. Once again, ethnographic studies suggest that features of this nature do not belong in simple and egalitarian societies.

Ploughs and fields and waggons were given scant treatment in earlier chapters, partly because they were taken to be features of more advanced agriculture and more complex societies than we have in general been discussing. Their presence in western Europe, in contexts where comparative studies indicate a certain discrepancy in the interpretations, therefore needs explaining. There are at least two possible lines of reinterpretation: were the societies of prehistoric western Europe basically different in their development from all others? or have we got the wrong ideas about prehistoric social organisation?

Alternative Europe?

What grounds are there for the first line of reinterpretation, for accepting the anomalies as signs of the essential difference of western Europe? Historically, we know that the course of development was different in this region to that in, for example, China, and we know that both differed from North America. In other words, no two regions or continents follow the same historical path. Therefore, it would be unwise to assume that prehistoric western Europe followed a pattern of development deduced from that of other regions.

Allied to this argument is the point made by Freeman in the context of comparisons between present-day peoples and those of the Pleistocene; having argued that modern man is biologically different to man of the Early and Middle Pleistocene, Freeman adds that the range of hunter-gatherer situations in the past must have been much greater than the few relics known in the present (Freeman 1968). The same could be said of later periods, and the range of variations on pioneering agriculture, or the range of contexts favourable to the adoption of pastoralism, could have been significantly greater than those which exist today.

This need not invalidate comparative studies and the use of ethnography. On the contrary, as much can be learnt from investigating the differences between two sets of data as from comparing their similarities. This is demonstrated on a broad scale by, for example, Goody's study of *Production and Reproduction* (Goody 1976), which is based on the contrasts between African and Eurasian agriculture and domestic economy. Goody suggests there may be significant correlations between the use of the plough and the customs of male agricultural labour and monogamy, which predominate in Eurasia, and between the use of hoes, female agricultural labour and polygamy, which predominate in Africa. It is the repeated groups of contrasting features that suggest a causal link between agricultural practices and marriage rules, a link that might not have been noticed in a study of similarities. An example of comparative studies on a smaller scale and in an archaeological context is Flannery's paper on village origins in the Near East and Mesoamerica (Flannery 1972), which clearly shows the insights to be gained through a study of differences.

We could therefore accept that western Europe was essentially different, and still approach the interpretation of its prehistory by making comparisons with other societies from other times and in other parts of the world. We could attribute the differences in the course of European history to the different prehistoric background. Then the anomalies noted above become simply differences, and we allow that the first, pioneering farmers in the land did practise animal husbandry and that the agricultural system which they initiated was relatively advanced, relative to the level of social organisation. Cunliffe's 'simple egalitarian society *c*. 1000 B.C.' could be the correct interpretation, and if not this, then at least the emerging chiefdoms of a millennium earlier could be accepted. In a different Europe, we might even consider the pre-Neolithic development of animal domestication, whether Mesolithic red deer or Palaeolithic horses (Jarman 1971; Bahn 1978) – a situation that would otherwise be thought highly unlikely on the grounds that specialisation in domestic animals entails pastoralism, which is a development from mixed farming, and an adjunct of complex societies.

These ideas will not be elaborated further here, nor examined in the light of the archaeological evidence, but this brief and perhaps summary treatment *vis-à*-vis the next section is not intended as a dismissal. The possibility that prehistoric western Europe was different to the rest of the world in a number of important respects must remain with us.

Alternative prehistory?

'Alternative prehistory' suggests the lunatic fringe of archaeology, where Stonehenge and Carnac are seen as power points of the western world and one-time centres of knowledge and civilisation now generally lost to materialistic mankind. Unfortunately, nonsense of this sort has detracted from serious suggestions of a different sort of past, and particularly from those based on the study of monuments like Stonehenge or Carnac. Most prehistorians will admit that Thom has shown there is more to these sites than a collection of stones set in the earth by man, but few will seriously consider changing their ideas about the nature of the communities that produced these works.

Renfrew is one of the few to have argued the need for archaeologists to examine social organisation, and to insist that the evidence is available in the archaeological record if one knows what to look for (e.g. Renfrew 1973d). He has demonstrated the possibilities in a number of papers, advocating for example the presence of simple, segmentary (i.e. acephalous) societies in the early Neolithic of western Europe (Renfrew 1976), followed by the emergence in favoured areas of chiefdoms in the later Neolithic and earlier Bronze Age (Renfrew 1973c). The latter argument is one that we have already touched on as being perhaps too cautious, but it is probably best appreciated when contrasted with Cunliffe's much more summary, and simple, interpretation of social organisation in the same period.

Recently, Bender has put forward the more radical argument that chieftain-led tribal organisation should be considered for the Upper Palaeolithic: '... the substantial nature of the sites ... suggests a considerable degree of leadership, which may often have been associated with ceremonial roles' (Bender 1978, 216). This organisation was not necessarily lost in the succeeding Mesolithic, and Bender argues that it was a necessary adjunct of sedentism and that together with sedentism it favoured the development of food production.

Bender's paper is concerned with the conditions that led to farming, but it has implications on a much wider scale, namely that we have grossly underrated the complexities of prehistoric societies, and also that we have neglected the study of social organisation to the detriment of our understanding of the past. Like Renfrew, she attributes the neglect to 'the assumed difficulty of finding evidence of social processes for past societies ... much evidence has been missed or dismissed because of the techno-environmental bias of past theories' (214). Perhaps some of this evidence consists of the anomalies that we began with – the fields and ploughs and waggons for example. We shall now return to these to see if they could be indicative of a much more complex social organisation in prehistoric western Europe than is normally allowed, possibly more complex and varied than Renfrew suggests and perhaps as well-organised and led from an early stage as Bender advocates.

The first anomaly that we noted, the presence of domestic animals on the earliest-known farming sites, is not directly connected with social organisation, but it is relevant to the understanding of succeeding periods. If we accept the evidence of ethnographic and historical records that pioneering farmers do not keep domestic animals, then it follows that these sites are not representative of the earliest Neolithic in their regions, but of a later stage of settlement. There is little evidence in Europe which has been interpreted as Neolithic before that which is associated with domestic animals – but would such evidence be recognised?

We noted earlier that shifting agriculture might leave minimal archaeological traces, both in the pollen record and in terms of settlements. It was also noted that forest-farmers are frequently hunters and sometimes gatherers, i.e. they exploit the wild resources of their environment, and their equipment is often no more elaborate than that of hunters. The archaeological evidence left by pioneer farmers might therefore be very similar to that left by hunter-gatherers. In this light, we should also ask whether the forest clearances now attributed in growing numbers to the Mesolithic (e.g. Simmons 1969 and 1975, Mellars 1976, Roux and Leroi-Gourhan 1964), are not sometimes signs of early cultivation.

There are prehistorians who have argued from other starting points that the evidence labelled 'Early Neolithic' is not characteristic of pioneers. Case, for example, has taken the monuments of the period as evidence of a long-settled and organised society (Case 1969), and in similar vein one can point to the evidence retrieved from 'early' sites like the Sweet Track of the Somerset Levels as indicative of communities settled in a well-known, carefully manipulated and successfully exploited environment (Coles and Orme 1976 and 1979). Much of the 'first-farming' evidence from the British Isles dates to the second half of the fourth millennium b.c. (e.g. Sweet Track *c.* 3200 b.c.). In Northern Ireland, the site of Ballynagilly has yielded a Neolithic house, artefacts and traces of cultivation belonging to that period, and also a hearth and two pits containing Neolithic pottery and yielding an earlier date of *c.* 3700 b.c. a possible pioneer settlement

(Ap Simon 1976)? In Britain and Ireland, it seems likely that the first colonisation by farmers should be dated to the beginning of the fourth millennium, and the evidence from the second half of that millennium reassessed in terms of established farming communities, not pioneers.

The back-dating of Neolithic colonisation allows a longer history of farming before the appearance of the next set of anomalies, the ploughs, fields and waggons. In southern Britain there is Neolithic evidence for tilling from Hambledon Hill in Dorset, and from below South Street long barrow in Wiltshire. In both cases, scratches in the subsoil suggest that an ard was being used to break up the soil. Pollen evidence shows that parts of the generally-forested landscape were becoming covered with turf (i.e. grass), and combined pollen, mollusc and soil studies have shown the use of turves to build long barrows (e.g. Dalladies, E. Scotland) and to make the inner core of Silbury Hill in Wiltshire. The sort of implement used to break up turf for cultivation, which would leave traces similar to those excavated at South Street, etc., is known from later representations in European rock art, for example from a very fine carving at Haga nr. Tossene on the west coast of Sweden (Fig. 75). Wooden ards based on this pattern have been made and tested at Lejre in Denmark, and do indeed leave evidence similar to that recovered

Figure 75. Ploughing. Bronze Age rock-art showing what appears to be a man ploughing with an ard drawn by two animals; Haga, near Tossene, Bohuslan, Sweden (B.J. Orme)

archaeologically (Hanson 1969). The wooden digging implement discovered in a late Neolithic context in the Somerset Levels may be an earlier and fairly heavy form of 'plough', possibly used withouit animal traction (Coles and Orme 1980; for the use of prehistoric ards and digging implements see Steensberg 1973 and Fenton 1974). The evidence from all these sources points clearly to plough-agriculture, as opposed to shifting or hoe-agriculture, in western Europe. In some regions it is known from the late fourth millennium b.c., and it was undoubtedly widespread from the later second millennium onwards (cf. Fowler 1971).

Turf replaces forest cover when animals graze and prevent the regeneration of shrubs and trees, and so the presence of turf is in itself indirect evidence for mixed farming. Even without it, the ample numbers of bones of domestic animals from sites of all sorts and dates is indicative of animal husbandry, and the careful and detailed study of the bones has sometimes indicated how the livestock were fitted into the overall economy. For example, the bone evidence from Neolithic and Early Bronze Age settlements beside the Swiss lakes has been interpreted in terms of rearing for meat in the earlier period, with developments later that may have included keeping sheep for wool and oxen for traction (Higham 1967). The Haga engraving, and numerous others from the rock-carvings of both Sweden and Northern Italy show that the use of animals for ploughing was known over a wide region by the later prehistoric period. We have already discussed the reasons for the probably late introduction of pastoralism, and these, taken with the direct evidence for the use of animals in farming operations, imply that communities were engaged in both plant and animal husbandry.

Domestic animals, turf and ploughs form part of a single farming complex to which we can add the fields. Field systems are now thought to date from the Neolithic in some parts of Europe, from western Ireland and southeast England for example (Caulfield 1978, Drewett 1978). Bradley has recently summarised the European evidence (Bradley 1978), and discoveries in the British Isles are summarised in Bowen and Fowler 1978. From these surveys we can see that much of the landscape of the British Isles, and probably large tracts of Europe, were covered with a patchwork of fields long before the introduction of sophisticated Roman agricultural techniques and laws of property. We do not have to argue for the simultaneous, nor for the continuous, use of these fields to see them as evidence for man's exploitation of the environment on a scale commensurate to that of the medieval period. The organisation and the permanence of function are there to the same extent.

We should consider also the evidence that man had altered the rather bland environment of the Atlantic forests into a mosaic of forest, field and pasture that varied in its proportions and potential from region to region. Environmental variation would permit if not demand some variation in the techniques of exploitation adopted by prehistoric communities, which would give rise to greater differences in terms of economic strategies between the communities of later prehistory than was probably the case with the first farmers. Turning once more to southwest England, we can see indications of this variety in two localities, Dartmoor and the Somerset Levels.

On Dartmoor, slight differences in geology and aspect were probably magnified by human interference with the natural vegetation of the area. Peat growth began in some localities *c.* 5000 b.c. (Wainwright, pers. com.), and after 2000 b.c. there are indications that four separate socio-economic regions had been created, possibly reflecting differences in the environment. There was high moorland, apparently not permanently settled but probably grazed and used for its wild resources. On the north-eastern fringes of the Moor, where soils are today most suitable for agriculture, a fairly dispersed prehistoric settlement pattern is preserved, with huts set among small, squarish fields. The likelihood is that the inhabitants were engaged in mixed agriculture with a bias to crop-raising. The settlement pattern from southern Dartmoor is more nucleated, and the recent surveys and excavations carried out by Fleming and Wainwright (e.g. Fleming 1978) have shown that crops were grown in addition to the animal husbandry traditionally assumed for this area. On the western side of the Moor, the settlement evidence includes large villages straggling up small river valleys, and there is as yet less evidence for crop-raising than from the other two regions (Simmons 1969, Fox 1974). The significance of the environmental and settlement variation within the relatively small region of Dartmoor is that it probably encouraged the parallel development of cultural variations (cf. Southall 1976 for a similar argument in respect of the Nuer and the Dinka), and these would have contributed to the successful inception of a complex society, that incorporated several different sorts of economy and sub-culture which functioned together in the larger organisation.

The evidence from the Somerset Levels takes us slightly further back in time, and to a smaller geographic region. Here, the area under study is only *c*.10,000 ha., and combined archaeological and palaeo-botanical investigations have shown that by the late third millennium b.c. it contained areas of forest, areas of regenerated or regenerating woodland, and areas of coppiced woodland harvested on a regular basis. Amid these were clearings sufficiently extensive to show in the pollen record, and kept open for up to four centuries. Pollen from both pasture and arable weeds shows that the clearings were part grazing-land, part cultivated for crops, and the wooden ard-like implement already noted is additional proof of the latter practice (*Somerset Levels Papers 1-6*). It is not suggested that this one small area saw the same economic and cultural variation likely at a later date on Dartmoor, but rather that its significance lies in the successful manipulation of the environment by farmers whose way of life was far from simple.

The evidence for wheeled transport seems almost like a footnote to the case for advanced agriculture. The same groups of rock-carvings which show animals being used to pull ploughs show two-wheeled carts and four-wheeled waggons, some of which are pulled by horses or oxen (Fig. 76). The Trundholm model vehicle from the Danish Early Bronze Age shows that wheeled vehicles were known there in the early second millennium b.c., and perhaps pulled by horses. And the discovery of a wooden wheel in the Netherlands takes this knowledge back to the Neolithic in northwestern Europe at least. As

Figure 76. Wheeled vehicle, probably a cart, drawn by two animals. Bronze Age rock-carving (recently painted); Backa, Bohuslan (B.J. Orme)

with the ploughs, we cannot say that there was continuous use
throughout all of western Europe from this early stage, but it is clear
that Iron Age chariots, like Iron Age ploughs, had a lengthy local
ancestry.

All these strands of evidence, when brought together, show that
western Europe was exploited from the third millennium b.c. to the
end of the prehistoric period by farmers whose activities were
comparable to those of their Roman and medieval successors in the
same regions. And so we come back to the alternative
interpretations proposed earlier: advanced agriculture and simple
and egalitarian communities? Or advanced agriculture and
relatively complex social organisation?

Because ploughs and waggons are signs of economic
specialisation, and because field-systems depend on organisation
both within and between communities for their development and
maintenance, it is possible to opt for the second interpretation and
to suggest that the farmers of western Europe lived in well-ordered
and relatively large and complex societies. There are other
categories of evidence to support this line of interpretation, which we
shall not investigate now but which include the diversity of
contemporary settlement types within a region, the presence of
specialised occupations that increase in variety with the advent of
metallurgy but are known from long before this, and the complexity
of redistribution patterns which by the later second millennium look
like trade networks rather than ceremonial exchange cycles.

The organisation of societies does not have to have been
hierarchical to have been effective (cf. Chapter 3), and it
undoubtedly varied from one region to another and with time. We
have already noted some of the possible evidence for the means of
organisation in previous chapters, and referred to the relevant work
of Renfrew and of Bender. If anything, our interpretations for later
prehistory have erred on the cautious side, perhaps held back by the
obvious absence of true urban developments, literacy and coinage in
prehistoric western Europe before infiltrations from the classical
world. But here again, comparative studies show that a wide range
of social developments are possible without these features, despite
their common association in the Mediterranean civilisations, and
some of these developments have been discussed in the preceding
chapters. Therefore in some senses we can adopt both alternatives: a
different Europe but also one that was far from static, simple and
egalitarian.

For the present, what matters is not whether one chooses to stress the uniqueness of European prehistory or whether one emphasises instead the complexity and diversity of social organisation. What does matter is the recognition of the anomalies in the present model of interpretation – a recognition based on the study of anthropology. And this is anthropology's greatest potential contribution to the interpretation of archaeological evidence: not the identification of odd artefacts, nor the provision of information about any single aspect of human activity, however valuable these may be, but the provision of a framework for human action that shows us when the past has not been satisfactorily explained. If we are fortunate, the study of anthropology may also prompt new avenues of interpretation.

References

Albrethsen, S.E., and Brinch Petersen, E. 1976. Excavation of a Mesolithic cemetery at Vedbaek, Denmark. *Acta Archaeologica* 47, 1-28.

Alcock, L. 1972, *'By South Cadbury is that Camelot ...' the excavations of Cadbury Castle 1966-1970*. Thames & Hudson, London.

Alexander, J.A. 1972. The beginnings of urban life in Europe, in P.J. Ucko, R. Tringham and G.W. Dimbleby (eds), *Man, Settlement and Urbanism*, 843-850. Duckworth, London.

Alexander, J.A. 1978. Frontier studies and the earliest farmers in Europe, in D. Green, C. Haselgrove and M. Spriggs (eds), *Social Organisation and Settlement*, 13-30. (BAR International Series [Suppl.] 47i) British Archaeological Reports, Oxford.

Allan, W. 1965. *The African Husbandman*. London.

Ammerman, A.J., and Cavalli-Sforza, L.L. 1971. Measuring the spread of early farming in Europe. *Man* NS6, 674-688.

Ammerman, A.J., and Cavalli-Sforza, L.L. 1973. A population model for the diffusion of early farming in Europe, in C. Renfrew (ed.), *The Explanation of Culture Change: Models in Prehistory*, 343-358. Duckworth, London.

ApSimon, A. 1976. Ballynagilly and the beginning and end of the Irish Neolithic, in S.J. de Laet (ed.), *Acculturation and Continuity in Atlantic Europe*, 15-31. (Dissertationes Archaeologicae Gandenses vol. XVI.) De Tempel, Brugge.

Bahn, P.G. 1978. The 'unacceptable face' of the West European Upper Palaeolithic. *Antiquity* 52, 183-192.

Balikci, A. 1970. *The Netsilik Esquimo*. Natural History Press, New York.

Beckett, S.C., and Hibbert, F.A., 1978. The influence of man on the vegation of the Somerset Levels – a summary. *Somerset Levels Papers* 4, 86-89.

Bellwood, P. 1971. Fortifications and economy in prehistoric New Zealand. *Proceedings of the Prehistoric Society* 37 (i), 56-95.

Bender, B. 1978. Gatherer-hunter to farmer: a social perspective. *World Archaeology* 10, 204-222.

Best, E. 1916. *Maori Storehouses and Kindred Structures*. Dominion Museum Bulletin No 5.

Best, E. 1924. *The Maori* (2 vols). Memoirs of the Polynesian Society No. 5. Harry H. Tombs, Wellington.

Best, E. 1925. *Maori Agriculture*. Dominion Museum Bulletin No. 9. Wellington.

Best, E. 1927. *The Pa Maori*. Dominion Museum Bulletin No. 6. Wellington.
Binford, L.R. 1967. Smudge pits and hide smoking: the use of analogy in archaeological reasoning. *American Antiquity* 32, 1-12.
Birmingham, J. 1975. Traditional potters of the Kathmandu Valley: an ethnoarchaeological study. *Man* NS. 10, 370-386.
Bohannan, P. 1967. *Social Anthropology*. Holt, Rinehart and Winston, New York.
Bohannan, P., and Dalton, G. (eds.) 1962. *Markets in Africa*. Northwestern University Press, Evanston.
Bonnichsen, R. 1973. Millie's Camp: an experiment in archaeology. *World Archaeology* 4, 277-291.
Bowen, H.C., and Fowler, P.J. (eds) 1978. *Early Land Allotment*. (BAR 48) British Archaeological Reports, Oxford.
Bradley, R. 1976. Maumbury Rings, Dorchester: the excavations of 1908-1913. *Archaeologia* 105, 1-98.
Bradley, R. 1978. Prehistoric field systems in Britain and north-west Europe – a review of some recent work. *World Archaeology* 9, 265-280.
Brain, R. 1978. Transsexualism in Oman? *Man* NS 13, 322-323.
de Brisay, K.W., and Evans, K.A., (eds) 1975. *Salt: The Study of an Ancient Industry*. Colchester Archaeological Group, Colchester.
Brookfield, H.C., and Hart, D. 1971. *Melanesia: A Geographical Interpretation of an Island World*. London.
Bruce-Mitford, R.L.S. 1968. *The Sutton Hoo Ship Burial*. British Museum, London.
de Bry, T. 1590. *America*, Part 1. Frankfort.
Burch, E.S. 1971. The nonempirical environment of the Arctic Alaskan Esquimo. *South Western Journal of Anthropology* 27, 148-165.
Burnham, P. 1973. The explanatory value of the concept of adaption in studies of culture change, in C. Renfrew (ed), *The Explanation of Culture Change*, 93-102. Duckworth, London.
Burridge, K. 1969. *New Heaven, New Earth*. Blackwell, Oxford.
Burrow, J.W. 1966. *Evolution and Society*. Cambridge University Press, Cambridge.
Caesar, J. 1951. *The Conquest of Gaul*, trans. S.A. Handford. Penguin, Harmondsworth.
Campbell, J.M. 1968. Territoriality among ancient hunters: interpretations from ethnography and nature, in B. Meggers (ed), *Anthropological Archaeology in the Americas*, 1-21. Anthropological Society of Washington, Washington.
Case, H.J. 1969. Neolithic explanations. *Antiquity* 43, 176-186.
Catherall, P.D. 1976. Henge monuments: monument or myth?, in C. Burgess and R. Miket (eds), *Settlement and Economy in the Third and Second Millenia B.C.*, 1-10 (BAR No. 33) British Archaeological Reports, Oxford.
Caulfield, S. 1978. Neolithic fields: the Irish evidence, in H.C. Bowen and P.J. Fowler (eds) *Early Land Allotment*, 137-144. (Bar No. 48) British Archaeology Reports, Oxford.
Chagnon, N.A. 1968a. *Yanomamö: The Fierce People*. Holt, Rinehart and Winston, New York.

Chagnon, N.A. 1968b. The culture-ecology of shifting (pioneering) cultivation among the Yanomamö Indians. *Proceedings of the VIII International Congress of Anthropological and Ethnological Sciences, 1968*, 3, 249-255.

Childe, V.G. 1925. *The Dawn of European Civilisation*. Routledge and Kegan Paul, London.

Clark, J.G.D. 1951. Folk culture and the study of European prehistory, in W.F. Grimes (ed), *Aspects of Archaeology*. Edwards, London.

Clark, J.G.D. 1957. *Archaeology and Society* (3rd ed.). Methuen, London

Clark, J.G.D. 1965. Radiocarbon dating and the expansion of farming culture from the Near East over Europe. *Proceedings of the Prehistoric Society* 31, 58-73.

Clark, J.G.D. 1966. Traffic in stone axe and adze blades. *Economic History Review*, 1-28.

Clark, J.G.D., and Piggott, S. 1965. *Prehistoric Societies*. Hutchinson, London.

Clarke, D.L. 1976. Mesolithic Europe: the economic basis, in G. de G. Sieveking, I.H. Longworth and K.E. Wilson (eds), *Problems in Economic and Social Archaeology*, 449-482. Duckworth, London. (Also published separately.)

Clarke, W.C. 1971. *Place and People: an Ecology of a New Guinean Community*. University of California Press, Berkeley and Los Angeles.

Cohen, Y.A. 1974. *Man in Adaptation: the Cultural Present* (2nd. ed.). Aldine, Chicago.

Coles, J.M. 1973. *Archaeology by Experiment*. Hutchinson, London.

Coles. J.M. 1976. Forest farmers: some archaeological, historical and experimental evidence relating to the prehistory of Europe, in S.J. de Laet (ed), *Acculturation and Continuity in Atlantic Europe*, 59-66. De Tempel, Brugge.

Coles, J.M., Heal, V., and Orme, B.J. 1978. The use and character of wood in prehistoric Britain and Ireland. *Proceedings of the Prehistoric Society* 44, 1-46.

Coles, J.M., and Orme, B.J. 1976. The Sweet Track, Railway Site. *Somerset Levels Papers* 2, 34-65.

Coles, J.M., and Orme, B.J. 1979. The Sweet Track, Drove Site. *Somerset Level Papers* 5, 43-64.

Coles, J.M., Fleming, A.M., and Orme, B.J. 1980. The Baker Site. *Somerset Levels Papers* 6, 6-23.

Coles, J.M., Orme, B.J. Bishop, A.C., and Woolley, A.R. 1974. A jade axe from the Somerset Levels. *Antiquity* 48, 216-220.

Collis, J. 1974. A functionalist approach to pre-Norman coinage, in J. Casey and R. Reece (eds.), *Coins and the Archaeologist*, 1-11. (BAR 4) British Archaeological Reports, Oxford.

Collis, J.R. 1976. Town and market in Iron Age Europe, in B. Cunliffe and T. Rowley (eds), *Oppida in Barbarian Europe*, 3-24 (BAR Supplementary Series II) British Archaeological Reports, Oxford.

Conklin, H. 1957. *Hanunóo Agriculture in the Philippines*. FAO, Rome.

Crawford, O.G.S. 1927. Editorial, *Antiquity* 1, 1-4.

Cunliffe, B. 1974. *Iron Age Communities in Britain*. Routledge and Kegan Paul, London.

288 *Anthropology for Archaeologists*

Cunliffe, B.W. 1976a. Danebury, Hampshire: Second Interim Report on the Excavations, 1971-5. *Antiquaries Journal* 56, 198-216.
Cunliffe, B.W. 1976b. Hillforts and oppida in Britain, in G. de G. Sieveking, I.H. Longworth and K.E. Wilson (eds), *Problems in Economic and Social Archaeology*, 343-358. Duckworth, London.
Daniel, S. 1612. *The First Part of the History of England*. London.
Darwin, C. 1859. *The Origin of Species*. Murray, London.
Daryll Forde, C. 1934. *Habitat, Economy and Society*. Methuen, London.
Dimbleby, G.W. 1967. *Plants and Archaeology*. John Baker, London.
Dixon, P. 1973. *Crickley Hill, Fifth Report*. Glos. College of Art and Design, Cheltenham.
Douglas, M. 1954. The Lele of Kasai, in D. Forde (ed), *African Worlds*, 1-26. Oxford University Press, London.
Douglas, M. 1966. *Purity and Danger: an Analysis of Concepts of Pollution and Taboo*. Routledge and Kegan Paul, London.
Douglas, M. 1970. *Natural Symbols: Explorations in Cosmology*. Cresset Press, London.
Drewett, P. 1976. The excavation of a Neolithic causewayed enclosure on Offham Hill, East Sussex, *Proceedings of the Prehistoric Society* 43, 201-242.
Drewett, P.L. 1978. Field systems and land allotment in Sussex, third millennium B.C. to fourth century A.D., in H.C. Bowen and P.J. Fowler (eds), *Early Land Allotment*, 67-80. (BAR 48) British Archaeological Reports, Oxford.
Drucker, P. 1963. *Indians of the Northwest Coast*. Natural History Press, New York.
Durkheim, E. 1915. *The Elementary Form of the Religious Life* (Eng. trans.). Allen and Unwin, London.
Edelberg, L. 1966-67. Seasonal dwellings of farmers in North-Western Luristan. *Folk* 8-9, 373-401.
Ekvall, R.B. 1968. *Fields on the Hoof: Nexus of Tibetan nomadic pastoralism*. Holt, Rinehart and Winston, New York.
Ellison, A., and Drewett, P. Pits and postholes in the British Early Iron Age. *Proceedings of the Prehistoric Society* 37, 183-194.
Evans, J.G. 1975. *The Environment of Early Man in the British Isles*. Elek, London.
Evans, J.G., Limbrey, S., and Cleere, H. (eds), *The Effect of Man on the Landscape: the Highland Zone*. (CBA Research Report No. 11.) Council for British Archaeology, London.
Evans, P. 1975. The intimate relationship: a hypothesis concerning pre-Neolithic land use, in J.G. Evans, S. Limbrey and H. Cleere (eds), *The effect of Man on the Landscape: the Highland Zone*, 43-48. (CBA Research Report No. 11) Council for British Archaeology, London.
Evans-Pritchard, E.E. 1940a. *The Nuer*. Oxford University Press, London.
Evans-Pritchard, E.E. 1940b. The Nuer of the Southern Sudan, in M. Fortes and E.E. Evans-Pritchard (eds) *African Political Systems*, 272-296. Oxford University Press, London.
Evans-Pritchard, E.E. 1950. *Witchcraft, Oracles and Magic among the Azande*. Oxford University Press, London.
Evans-Pritchard, E.E. 1971. *The Azande: history and political institutions*. Oxford University Press, London.

Faron, L.C. 1967. Symbolic values and the integration of society among the Mapuche of Chile, in J. Middleton (ed) *Myth and Cosmos*, 167-184.

Fenton, A. 1974. The Cas-Chrom. *Tools and Tillage* 2, 131-148.

Firth, R. 1936. *We, The Tikopia.* George Allen and Unwin Ltd.

Firth, R. 1939. *Primitive Polynesian Economy.* Routledge and Kegan Paul, London.

Flannery, K.V. 1972. The origins of the village as a settlement type in Mesoamerica and the Near East: a comparative study, in P.J. Ucko, R. Tringham and G.W. Dimbleby (eds), *Man, Settlements and Urbanism*, 23-54. Duckworth, London.

Fleming, A. 1971. Territorial patterns in Bronze Age Wessex. *Proceedings of the Prehistoric Society* 37 (i), 138-166.

Fleming, A. 1978. The prehistoric landscape of Dartmoor. *Proceedings of the Prehistoric Society* 44, 97-124.

Forge, A. 1972. Normative factors in the settlement size of Neolithic cultivators (New Guinea), in P.J. Ucko, R. Tringham and G.W. Dimbleby (eds, *Man, Settlement and Urbanism*, 363-376. Duckworth, London.

Fowler, P.J. 1971. Early prehistoric agriculture in Western Europe: some archaeological evidence, in D.D.A. Simpson (ed), *Economy, and Settlement in Neolithic and Early Bronze Age Britain and Europe*, 153-182.

Fox, A. 1973. *South-West England B.C. 3500-600 A.D.* (2nd ed.). David and Charles, Newton Abbot.

Fox, A. 1976. *Prehistoric Maori Fortifications* (Monograph No. 6 of the New Zealand Archaeological Association). Longman Paul, Auckland.

Fox, A. 1978. *Tiromoana pa, Te Awanga, Hawke's Bay, Excavations 1974-5.* (Vol. II University of Otago studies in prehistoric anthropology. Monograph 8 of the New Zealand Archaeological Association.) University of Otago.

Frazer, J.G. 1907-1936. *The Golden Bough* (11 vols.) Macmillan, London.

Freeman, D. 1970. (1st edition 1955) *Report on the Iban.* Athlone Press, London.

Freeman, L. 1968. A theoretical framework for interpreting archaeological materials, in R.B. Lee and I. DeVore (eds), *Man the Hunter*, 262-267.

von Fürer-Haimendorf, C. 1975. *Himalayan Traders: life in highland Nepal.* Murray, London.

Gardner, R., and Heider, K.G. 1968. *Gardens of War: Life and Death in the New Guinea Stone Age.* Penguin (1974), Harmondsworth.

Gibbs, J.L. (Ed.) 1965. *Peoples of Africa.* Holt, Rinehart and Winston, New York.

Gluckman, M. 1940. The Kingdom of the Zulu of South Africa, in M. Fortes, and E.E. Evans-Pritchard (eds), *African Political Systems*, 25-55. (1970 edition). Oxford University Press, London.

Goodale, J. 1971. *Tiwi Wives.* University of Washington Press, Seattle and London.

Goody, J. 1976. *Production and Reproduction: a Comparative Study of the Domestic Domain.* Cambridge University Press, Cambridge.

Green, D., Haselgrove, C., and Spriggs, M. (eds) 1978. *Social Organisation and Settlement.* (BAR International Series [Supplementary] 47) British Archaeological Reports, Oxford.

Griaule, M. and Dieterlen, G. 1954. The Dogon of the French Sudan, in D.

Forde (ed), *African Worlds*, 83-110. Oxford University Press, London.

Groube, L.M. 1977. The hazards of anthropology, in M. Spriggs (ed) *Archaeology and Anthropology*, 69-90. (BAR Supplementary Series 19) British Archaeological Reports, Oxford.

Gulliver, P.H. 1965. The Jie of Uganda, in J.L. Gibbs (ed), *Peoples of Africa*, 157-196. Holt, Rinehart and Winston, New York.

Hansen, H.O. 1969. Experimental ploughing with a Dostrup ard replica. *Tools and Tillage* 1, 67-92.

Harriot, T. 1588. *A Brief and True Report of the new found land of Virginia*. (1951 Facsimile Edition). History Book Club, New York.

Hart, C.W.M., and Pilling, A.R. 1960. *The Tiwi of North Australia*. Holt, Rinehart and Winston, New York.

Heider, K. 1970. *The Dugum Dani*. (Viking Fund publications in Anthropology 49.) Aldine, Chicago.

Henriksen, G. 1973. *Hunters in the Barrens: The Naskapi on the Edge of the White Man's World*. Newfoundland Social and Economic Studies No. 12, Memorial University of Newfoundland. University of Toronto Press, Toronto.

Henshall, A.S. 1950. Textiles and weaving appliances in Prehistoric Britain. *Proceedings of the Prehistoric Society* 16, 130-162.

Hertz, R. 1907 and 1909. *Death and The Right Hand*. trans. Needham 1960. Cohen and West.

Higgs, E.S. (ed) 1975. *Palaeoeconomy*. Cambridge University Press, Cambridge.

Higham, C. 1967. Stock rearing as a cultural factor in prehistoric Europe. *Proceedings of the Prehistoric Society* 33, 84-106.

Hill, J.N. 1971. A prehistoric community in Eastern Arizona, in J. Deetz (ed), *Man's Imprint from the Past*, 323-343. (First published in 1966.)

Hodder, I. 1977. A study of ethnoarchaeology in Western Kenya, in M. Spriggs (ed), *Archaeology and Anthropology*, 117-142. (BAR Supplementary Series 19) British Archaeology Reports, Oxford.

Hodder, I. 1978. The maintenance of group identities in the Baringo district, Western Kenya, in D. Green, C. Haselgrove and M. Spriggs (eds), *Social Organisation and Settlement*, 47-74. (BAR International Series [Supplementary] 47i) British Archaeological Reports, Oxford.

Hoebel, E.A. 1960. *The Cheyennes: Indians of the Great Plains*. Holt, Rinehart and Winston, New York.

Hutton, J.H. 1951. Less familiar aspects of primitive trade. *Proc. Prehistoric Society* 17, 171-176.

Jarman, M. 1971. Culture and economy in the north Italian Neolithic. *World Archaeology* 2(3), 255-265.

Jarman, M.R. 1972. European deer economies and the advent of the Neolithic, in E.S. Higgs (ed), *Papers in Economic Prehistory*, 125-148. Cambridge University Press, Cambridge.

Jochim, M.A. 1976. *Hunter Gatherer Subsistence and Settlement: a Predictive model*. Academic Press, New York.

Kehoe, A., and Renfrew, C. 1974. Saints of Wessex? *Antiquity* 48, 232-234.

Kimmig, W. 1975. Early Celts on the Upper Danube ... The Heuneberg, in Bruce-Mitford (ed), *Recent Archaeological Excavations in Europe*.

Klindt-Jensen, O. 1976. Influence of ethnography on Scandinavian archaeology, in J.V.S. Megaw (ed), *To Illustrate the Monuments*, 44-48. Thames and Hudson, London.

Kuper, H. 1963. *The Swazi: a South African Kingdom*. Holt, Rinehart and Winston, New York.

de Laet, S.J. (ed) 1976. *Acculturation and Continuity in Atlantic Europe*. (Papers presented at the IV Atlantic Colloquium, Ghent 1975: Dissertationes Archaeologicae Gandenses Vol. XVI.) De Tempel, Brugge.

Lauer, P.K. 1970. Amphlett Islands' pottery trade and the Kula. *Mankind* 7, (3), 165-176.

Leach, E. 1969. *Genesis as Myth*. Jonathan Cape, London.

Leach, E. 1977. A View from the Bridge, in M. Spriggs (ed), *Archaeology and Anthropology*, 161-176. (BAR Supplementary Series 19) British Archaeological Reports, Oxford.

Lee, R.B., 1968. What hunters do for a living, in Lee and DeVore (eds), *Man the Hunter*, 30-48. Aldine, Chicago.

Lee, R.B. 1969. !Kung Bushman subsistence: an input-output analysis, in A.P. Vayda (ed), *Environment and Cultural Behaviour*, 47-79. Natural History Press, New York.

Lee, R.B. 1972. Work effort, group structure and land use in contemporary hunter-gatherers, in P.J. Ucko, R. Tringham and G.W. Dimbleby (eds), *Man, Settlement and Urbanism*, 177-185. Duckworth, London.

Lee, R.B., and DeVore, I. (eds) 1968. *Man the Hunter*. Aldine, Chicago.

Leeds, A. 1965. Reindeer herding and Chukchi social institutions, in A. Leeds and A.P. Vayda (eds), *Man, Culture and Animals*. A.A.A.S., Washington DC.

Leeds, A., and Vayda, A.P. (eds) 1965. *Man, Culture and Animals*. Publication No. 78 of the American Association for the Advancement of Science. Washington, D.C.

Leroi-Gourhan. 1964. *Les religions de la Prehistoire*. Paris.

Levi-Strauss, C. 1964. *Mythologiques I: Le Cru et le Cuit*. Plon, Paris.

Levi-Strauss, C. 1967. The social and psychological aspects of chieftanship in a primitive tribe: the Nambikuara of northwestern Mato Grosso, in R. Cohen and J. Middleton (eds), *Comparative Political Systems*, 45-62. (First published 1944.) Natural History Press, New York.

Lewis, I.M. 1961. *A Pastoral Democracy: A Study of Pastoralism and Politics among the Northern Somali of the Horn of Africa*. Oxford University Press, London.

Lewis, I.M. 1965. The northern pastoral Somali of the Horn, in J.L. Gibbs (ed) *Peoples of Africa*, 319-360. Holt, Rinehart and Winston, New York.

Lhuyd, E. 1713. Letters in *Philosophical Transactions of the Royal Society*, Vol. XXVIII. (In Abridged Series, VI, 1809, 19-22.)

Lloyd, P.C. 1965. The Yoruba of Nigeria, in J.L. Gibbs (ed), *Peoples of Africa*, 547-582. Holt, Rinehart and Winston, New York.

Lubbock, J. 1865. *Prehistoric Times*, Williams and Norgate, London.

McCarthy. F.D., and McArthur, M. 1960. The food quest and the time factor in aboriginal economic life, in Mountford (ed), *Records of the American-Australian scientific expedition to Arnhem Land, Vol. 2: Anthropology and Nutrition*. Melbourne University Press, Melbourne.

McFadyen Clark, A. 1974. *The Athapaskans: Strangers of the North*. National Museum of Man, Ottawa.

Mair, L. 1962. *Primitive Government*. Penguin, Harmondsworth.

Malinowski, B. 1922. *Argonauts of the Western Pacific*, Routledge, London.

Manuel, F.E. 1959. *The Eighteenth Century Confronts the Gods*. Harvard University Press, Harvard.

Megaw, J.V.S. 1970. *Art of the European Iron Age*. Adams and Dart, Bath.

Mellaart, J. 1965. *Earliest Civilisations of the Near East*. Thames and Hudson, London.

Mellars, P.A. 1976. Fire ecology, animal populations and man: a study of some ecological relationships in prehistory. *Proceedings of the Prehistoric Society* 42, 15-46.

Mercer, R.J. 1970. The excavation of a Bronze Age hut-circle settlement, Stannon Down, Cornwall. *Cornish Archaeology* 9, 17-46.

Middleton, J. (ed) 1967. *Gods and Rituals*. Natural History Press, New York.

Middleton, J. (ed) 1967. *Myth and Cosmos*. Natural History Press, New York.

Morgan, S. 1968. Iban aggressive expansion: some background factors. *Sarawak Museum Journal* 16, 32/3, 141-85.

Nadel, S.F. 1940. The Kede: a riverain state in Northern Nigeria, in M. Fortes and E.E. Evans-Pritchard (eds), *African Political Systems*. 165-196. Oxford University Press, London.

Nilsson, S. 1868. *The Primitive Inhabitants of the Scandinavian North: an essay on the comparative ethnography and a contribution to the history of the development of mankind*. (3rd ed., English translation; 1st ed. 1843.) London.

Orme, B.J. 1972. *The Development and Use of Ethnographic Parallels in the Study of Prehistoric Archaeology*. (Unpublished M.Phil. thesis, University of London.)

Orme, B.J. 1974. Governor Pownall. *Antiquity* 48, 116-125.

Orme, B.J. 1974. Twentieth century prehistorians and the idea of ethnographic parallels. *Man* NS 9, 199-212.

Orme, B.J. 1977. The advantages of agriculture, in J.V.S. Megaw (ed), *Hunters, Gatherers and First Farmers beyond Europe*, 41-50. Leicester University Press, Leicester.

Ottaway, B., and Strahm, C. 1975. Swiss Neolithic copper beads: currency, ornament or prestige items? *World Archaeology* 6, 307-321.

Palmer, R. 1976. Interrupted ditch enclosures in Britain: the use of aerial photography for comparative studies. *Proceedings of the Prehistoric Society* 42, 161-186.

Peacock, D.P.S. 1969. Neolithic pottery production in Cornwall. *Antiquity* 43, 145-149.

Pennington, W. 1974. *The History of British Vegetation* (2nd ed.). English Universities Press, London.

Piddocke, S. 1965. The potlatch system of the southern Kwakiutl: a new perspective. *Southwestern Journal of Anthropology* 21, 244-264.

Piggott, S. 1965. *Ancient Europe*. Edinburgh University Press, Edinburgh.

Piggott, S. 1968. *The Druids*. Thames and Hudson, London.

Plot, R. 1686. *The Natural History of Staffordshire*. Oxford.

Pollard, S. 1974. A Late Iron Age settlement and a Romano-British villa at Holcombe, near Uplyme, Devon. *Proceedings of the Devon Archaeological Society* 32, 59-162.

Pospisil, L. 1972. *Kapauku Papuan Economy*. Yale University Publications in Anthropology No. 67. (1st ed. 1963). Human Relations Area Files Press, New Haven.

Pownall, T. 1795. *An Antiquarian Romance*. London.

Quarcoo, A.K., and Johnson, M. 1968. Shai Pots. *Baessler-Archiv., Neue Folge, Band* 16, 47-74.

Radcliffe-Brown, A.R. 1922. *The Andaman Islanders.*

Rappaport, R.A. 1968. *Pigs for the Ancestors*. Yale University Press, New Haven and London.

Renfrew, C. 1969. Trade and culture process in European Prehistory. *Current Anthropology*, 10, 151-169.

Renfrew, C. 1973a. *Before Civilisation*. Jonathan Cape, London.

Renfrew, C. (ed) 1973b. *The Explanation of the Culture Change: Models in Prehistory*. Duckworth, London.

Renfrew, C. 1973c. Monuments, mobilisation and social organisation in Neolithic Wessex, in C. Renfrew (ed) *The Explanation of Culture Change: Models in Prehistory*, 539-558. Duckworth, London.

Renfrew, C. 1973d. *Social Archaeology*. (Inaugural Lecture, University of Southampton.) University of Southampton, Southampton.

Renfrew, C. 1976. Megaliths, Territories and Populations, in S.J. de Laet (ed), *Acculturation and Continuity in Atlantic Europe*, 198-220.

Renfrew, C. 1978. Varna and the social context of early metallurgy. *Antiquity* 52, 199-203.

Reynolds, P.J. 1974. Experimental Iron Age storage pits: an interim report. *Proceedings of the Prehistoric Society* 40, 118-131.

Reynolds, P.J. 1976. *Farming in the Iron Age*. Cambridge University Press, Cambridge.

Reynolds, V. 1972. Ethology of urban life, in P.J. Ucko, R. Tringham and G.W. Dimbleby (eds), *Man, Settlement and Urbanism*, 401-408. Duckworth, London.

Rogers, E.S. 1970a. *Algonkians of the Eastern Woodlands*. Royal Ontario Museum, Toronto.

Rogers, E.S. 1970b. *Iroquoians of the Eastern Woodlands*. Royal Ontario Museum, Toronto.

Rowlands, M.J. 1971. The archaeological interpretation of prehistoric metalworking. *World Archaeology* 3, 210-224.

Rowlands, M.J. 1972. Defence: a factor in the organisation of settlements, in P.J. Ucko, R. Tringham and G.W. Dimbleby (eds), *Man, Settlement and Urbanism*, 447-462. Duckworth, London.

Rowlands, M.J., and Gledhill, J. 1977. The relation between archaeology and anthropology, in M. Spriggs (ed), *Archaeology and Anthropology*, 143-160. (BAR Supplementary Series 19) British Archaeological Reports, Oxford.

Sahlins, M. 1968. Notes on the original affluent society, in R.B. Lee and I. De Vore (eds). *Man the Hunter*, 85-89. Aldine, Chicago.

Sahlins, M. 1974. *Stone Age Economics*. (1st ed. 1972 USA.) Tavistock, London.

Sanderson, M. n.d. *The development of the boat*. National Maritime Museum, Greenwich.

Severin, T. 1973. *Vanishing Primitive World*. Thames and Hudson, London.

Shennan, S. 1975. The social organisation at Branč. *Antiquity* 49, 279-288.

Sherratt, A. 1976. Resources, technology and trade: an essay in early European metallurgy, in G. de G. Sieveking, I.H. Longworth and K.E. Wilson (eds), *Problems in Economic and Social Archaeology*, 557-581. Duckworth, London.

Sieveking, G. de G., Longworth, I.H., and Wilson, K.E. (eds) 1976. *Problems in Economic and Social Archaeology*. Duckworth, London.

Simmons, I.G. 1969. Environment and early man on Dartmoor, Devon, England. *Proceedings of the Prehistoric Society* 35, 203-219.

Simmons, I.G. 1975. The ecological setting of Mesolithic man in the Highland Zone, in J.G. Evans, S. Limbrey and H. Cleere (eds), *The Effect of Man on the Landscape: The Highland Zone*, 57-63. Council for British Archaeology, London.

Simonsen, P. 1972. The transition from food-gathering to pastoralism in north Scandinavia and its impact on settlement patterns, in P.J. Ucko, R. Tringham and G.W. Dimbleby (eds), *Man, Settlement and Urbanism*, 187-192. Duckworth, London.

Slavin, K. and Slavin, J. 1973. *The Tuareg*. Gentry Books, London.

Smith, B. 1960. *European Vision and the South Pacific, 1768-1850*. Oxford University Press, Oxford.

Smith, I. 1971. Causewayed enclosures, in D.D.A. Simpson (ed), *Economy and Settlement in Neolithic and Early Bronze Age Britain and Europe*, 89-112. Leicester University Press, Leicester.

Smith, I. 1974. The Neolithic, in C. Renfrew (ed), *British Prehistory*, 100-136. Duckworth, London.

Smith, M.A. 1955. The limitations of interference in archaeology. *Archaeological Newsletter* 6, 3-7.

Smith, M.G. 1965. The Hausa of Northern Nigeria, in J.L. Gibbs (ed), *Peoples of Africa*, 119-156. Holt, Rinehart and Winston, New York.

Sollas, W.J. 1911. *Ancient Hunters and their Modern Representatives*. Macmillan, London.

Southall, A. 1976. Nuer and Dinka are people: ecology, ethnicity and logical possibility. *Man* NS 11 (4), 463-491.

Speed, J. 1611. *The History of Great Britaine*. London.

Spencer and Gillen. 1968. *The Native Tribes of Central Australia*. (1st ed. 1899). Dover, New York.

Spriggs, M. (ed) 1977. *Archaeology and Anthropology*. (BAR Supplementary Series 19.) British Archaeological Reports, Oxford.

Starr, F. 1904. *The Ainu Group*. Open Court Publishing Company, Chicago.

Steensberg, A. 1973. A 6,000-year-old ploughing implement from Satrup Moor. *Tools and Tillage* 2, 105-118.

Steiner, F. 1956. *Taboo*. (1967 Pelican edition). Cohen and West, London.

Stennings, D.J. 1965. The pastoral Fulani of Northern Nigeria, in J.L. Gibbs (ed), *Peoples of Africa*, 361-402. Holt, Rinehart and Winston, New York.

Stiles, D. 1977. Ethnoarchaeology: a discussion of methods and applications. *Man* NS 12, 87-103.

Suttles, W. 1968. Coping with abundance: subsistence on the Northwest

Coast, in R.B. Lee, and I. De Vore (eds), *Man the Hunter*, 56-68. Aldine, Chicago.

Thomson, D.F. 1939. The seasonal factor in human culture, illustrated from the life of a contemporary Nomadic Group. *Proceedings of the Prehistoric Society* 5, 209-221.

Thomson, D.F. 1949. *Economic Structure and the Ceremonial Exchange Cycle in Arnhem Land*. Macmillan, Melbourne.

Trigger, B. 1969. *The Huron: Farmers of the North*. Holt, Rinehart and Winston, New York.

Tringham, R. 1971. *Hunters, Fishers and Farmers of Eastern Europe, 6000-3000 B.C.* Hutchinson, London.

Turnbull, C.M. 1961. *The Forest People*. Jonathan Cape, London.

Turnbull, C. 1965. *Wayward servants: the Two Worlds of the African Pygmies*. Natural History Press, New York.

Turner, J. 1975. The evidence for land use by prehistoric farming communities: the use of three-dimensional pollen diagrams, in J.G. Evans, S. Limbrey and H. Cleere (eds), *The Effect of Man on the Landscape: The Highland Zone*. Council for British Archaeology, London.

Tylor, E.B. 1865. *Researches into the Early History of Mankind*. London.

Tylor, E.B. 1871. *Primitive Culture*. Murray, London.

Ucko, P.J. 1969. Ethnography and archaeological interpretation of funerary remains. *World Archaeology* 1(2), 262-277.

Ucko, P.J., and Rosenfeld, A. 1967. *Palaeolithic Cave Art*. Weidenfeld and Nicolson, London.

Ucko, P.J., and Dimbleby, G.W. (eds) 1969. *The Domestication and Exploitation of Plants and Animals*. Duckworth, London.

Ucko, P.J., Tringham, R., and Dimbleby, G.W. (eds) 1972. *Man, Settlement and Urbanism*. Duckworth, London.

Van-Stone, J.W. 1974. *Athapaskan Adaptations: Hunters and Fishermen of the Subarctic Forests*. Aldine, Chicago.

Wainwright, G.J. 1975. Religion and settlement in Wessex, 3000-1700 B.C., in P.J. Fowler (ed), *Recent Work in Rural Archaeology*, 57-71. Moonraker Press, Bradford-on-Avon.

Wainwright, G.J. 1977. A Celtic farmstead in southern Britain. *Scientific American* 237 (6), 156-169.

Wainwright, G.J., and Longworth, I.H. 1971. *Durrington Walls: Excavations 1966-68*. (Reports of the Research Committee of the Society of Antiquaries of London No 29.) Society of Antiquaries, London.

Watanabe, H. 1968. Subsistence and ecology of northern food gatherers with special reference to the Ainu, in R.B. Lee and I. De Vore (eds), *Man the Hunter*, 69-77. Aldine, Chicago.

Weir, S. 1976. *The Bedouin*. (British Museum Department of Ethnography.) World of Islam Festival Publishing Co. Ltd., London.

Whittle, A. 1977. Earlier Neolithic enclosures in north-west Europe. *Proceedings of the Prehistoric Society* 43, 329-348.

Wilson, D. 1851. *Archaeology and Prehistoric Annals of Scotland*. Sutherland and Knox, Edinburgh.

Wilson, D. 1862. *Prehistoric Man: Researches into the Origin of Civilisation in the*

Old and New Worlds. Edinburgh University Press, Edinburgh.

Wilson, D. *Archaeology and Prehistoric Annals of Scotland*. (2nd ed. 2 volumes, revised and enlarged.) Edinburgh University Press, Edinburgh.

Wilson, D.R. 1975. 'Causewayed camps' and 'interrupted ditch systems'. *Antiquity* 49, 178-186.

Wood, W.R. 1973. Contrastive features of native North American trade systems. *Anthropological Papers* 4, 153-169. University of Oregon.

Wood, W.R. 1974. Northern Plains Village Cultures: Internal Stability and External Relationships. *Journal of Anthropological Research* 30(1), 1-16.

Woodburn, J. 1968. An introduction to Hadza ecology, in R.B. Lee and I. De Vore (eds), *Man the Hunter*, 49-55. Aldine, Chicago.

Woodman, P.C. 1976. The Irish Mesolithic/Neolithic transition, in S.J. de Laet (ed), *Acculturation and Continuity in Atlantic Europe*, 296-308. De Tempel, Brugge.

Worsley, P. 1957. *The Trumpet Shall Sound*. MacGibbon and Kee, London.

Yarnell, R.A. 1964. *Aboriginal Relationships between Culture and Plant Life in the Upper Great Lakes Region*. Museum of Anthropology, University of Michigan *Anthropological Papers* 23.

Yellen, J.E. 1977. *Archaeological Approaches to the Present: Models for Reconstructing the Past*. Academic Press, New York.

Index